INVESTING IN MAPS

Frontispiece of Mortier's *Neptune Francois*,
published in 1700. Usually in black and
white, but coloured copies are particularly
attractive.
Size: 19½ by 14 in., 50 by 36 cm.

INVESTING IN MAPS

Roger Baynton-Williams

Barrie & Rockliff
The Cresset Press

Produced by Design Yearbook Limited, 21 Ivor Place, London N.W.1.
Published by Barrie and Rockliff, The Cresset Press, 2 Clement's Inn, Strand, London, W.C.2.
Text filmset by Yendall & Company Limited, Riscatype House, 22–25 Red Lion Court, London E.C.4.
Jackets and colour pages printed by L. van Leer & Company N.V. of Amsterdam.
Printed and bound by Jarrold & Sons Limited, Cowgate, Norwich.
© Design Yearbook Limited 1969.
Art Director: Ian Cameron.
Designer: Tom Carter.
First published 1969.
Printed in England.

SBN 214.65066.9

All the illustrations have been provided from maps which have at sometime been in the possession of the Baynton-Williams Gallery, 70 Old Brompton Road, London, S.W.7.

The following colour illustrations have been taken from maps now in private collections and have been kindly lent for reproduction purposes.

Saxton's Frontispiece	Mr D. Kingsley
Jorden's map of Denmark	Mr and Mrs C. Hagerup
Plot's map of Staffordshire	Mr E. A. Wright
Cellarius' chart of the Heavens	Mr and Mrs C. Hagerup
Bailleul Mappe monde	Mr Christopher Rainbow

CONTENTS

Introduction 6

Map-making 12

The First Printed Maps 20

Early British County Maps 40

18th & 19th Century British Maps 64

French & German Map-making 84

Sea Charts 90

Large Scale Maps 96

County Histories 106

Town Plans 110

Oddities 120

The Continents 126

Frontispieces 146

Prices 150

Bibliography 152

Index of Map-makers and their Work 153

INTRODUCTION

The atlas by Britain's John Speed, published in 1627 and titled *The Theatre of Great Britain and the Prospect of the Most Famous Parts of the World*, sold originally for £2. Up to the First World War the value of the atlas was still about the same; by the Second World War it had risen to about £40. In 1965, twenty years after the war, the price had risen to around £700-£800, about $2,000, and by 1969 it had passed £2,000, $4,800. This example is not unique; it typifies the general trend in the prices of antiques caused by an unprecedented demand by the public. Of all the reasons for the increase, one of the most important is investment.

In the context of this book it should be understood that the word 'investing' means buying old maps wisely, that the purchaser should have some fundamental knowledge of map collecting which will assist him to make a decision and to ensure that any capital outlay is money well spent. The collector is not looking for a quick profit but it is reassuring for him to know that, in the event of realisation of capital being necessary, he should recoup a large proportion of his capital. If it should happen that in the interim the value of the investment has risen to such an extent that he actually makes a profit on the re-sale, then this is fortunate.

It is difficult to imagine that prices will continue to rise at the same rate as they have done over the last few years. Hardly an auction sale goes by with-

John Speed: Map of the World published by Bassett and Chiswell in 1676. One of the most decorative maps of the world. The first edition of this map appeared in the *Prospect of the most Famous Parts of the World* in 1627, the first edition of Speed to cover countries other than Great Britain. From the illustration it can be seen that the impression is still black and clear even though this is one of the later editions. The title claims that the map is 'Drawne according to ye truest Descriptions latest Discoveries & best Observations yt have beene made by English

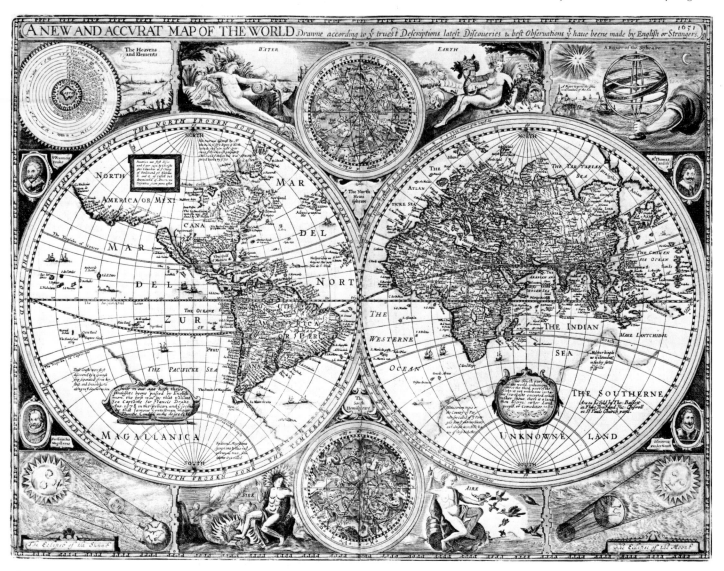

6

out a record price being reached; everyone thinks that the peak must have been reached—only to find how wrong he was when the next sale comes along. It is equally difficult to imagine that there will be a levelling out of prices, for the simple reason that there are not enough fine, or even good, antiques in circulation to meet the demand.

There is some similarity between investing in antiques and investing in the Stock Exchange. Some knowledge of the market is desirable and the aid of a dealer or broker is almost essential for the beginner, particularly when there are large sums of money involved. In the field of antiques there is the advantage that the buyer can enjoy owning a purchase even if it does not rise in value to the extent that he had originally hoped. Perhaps this can be classed as a speculation. Antiques will not provide a financial dividend, as will stocks and shares, but the dividend is the reward obtained from the pleasure of owning a work of art, a pleasure which is impossible to value.

The field of antiques covers a vast extent and no one person can expect to command a sufficiently wide knowledge to be able to invest in a range of different subjects without the assistance of a dealer, whose rôle should not be underestimated. Whatever his speciality he has built his reputation on his knowledge of his subject and he relies on his goodwill to a large extent to bring him new customers. He cannot afford to misguide a buyer. Nor can he afford to overcharge, though there can hardly be two dealers who will mark an article at the same price. He is always ready to give advice and to hand on his knowledge and experience, invaluable to the beginner. Dealers are the most important source, and usually they will undertake special searches for particular desiderata and will operate part exchanges. The auction sale rooms are also an important source but they are more suitable for dealers and experienced collectors—the temptation seems to be for the inexperienced bidder to pay too much in his enthusiasm for an article.

There is also a temptation for the private collector to try to deal. Occasionally he can be lucky but more often his efforts can be disastrous. He should remember that he is working in strict competition with the trade, and should

or Strangers'. The Far East is shown with more accuracy than preceding maps but this is one of the earliest to make the mistake of showing California as an island. The engraving was most probably carried out by Jocodus Hondius and it is interesting to compare this map with that of Henry Hondius engraved a few years later in 1630. The Henry Hondius version is undoubtedly the more accomplished piece of engraving, but as with all Speed's maps he has squeezed in as much extra detail as he can. Notice the similarity of the title tableaux and the borders. The later map shows some improvement in the detail of the Far East. Both are equally difficult to obtain.

7

only enter into this field when he has enough experience to be certain that an article is perfectly 'right' and to know that he can re-sell the article to a dealer, who must be able to take a fair margin of profit. No one can expect to obtain this knowledge simply by reading books.

The beginner is well advised to look round the stocks of as many specialist dealers as possible to help him become accustomed to the extent of the market, the prices and the quality which he must expect. This book is written as a guide to the maps which are likely to be found on the market, to describe how they were made and as far as possible to give an idea of their values, in order that the prospective purchaser should invest his money wisely.

ABOUT MAPS

Of all the various categories of antiques, old maps must have the most general and the widest appeal. No particular knowledge is required to appreciate and enjoy them, either for their geographical interest or for their aesthetic value. They conjure a picture of people's lives and habits when the maps were made and illustrate the changing face of the earth.

The history of maps is as ancient as the history of man. There has always been a need for diagrams to illustrate a route, or a good hunting area, or some dangerous terrain. The earliest maps were not printed, of course, but were manuscripts, drawn on parchment—some of the very earliest were made on clay or stone. Though these are not the subject of the book, they do help to illustrate the derivation of later maps. Undoubtedly the greatest influence on mapping was Claudius Ptolemy, who as early as the 2nd century A.D. produced a set of twenty-seven maps of the known world, that is Europe and Asia, and these were the basis of all maps for the following fourteen hundred years.

It was in the second half of the 15th century that maps began to be printed. There are maps in circulation which were made at this period, but they are few and far between. It was about one hundred years later, when printing methods improved and when detailed maps of other countries were required for trading purposes, that maps were made in any quantity.

These maps were comparatively expensive when they were made, particularly those in bound volumes. Purchasers were wealthy people and maps were kept in dry houses and libraries, essential for their preservation, and were properly cared for. Unfortunately many have not survived to this time, but have been accidently destroyed, house fires being far more common than they are today. During the 19th century they were not considered to have any value and many were destroyed. Some must simply have been lost. There are references in Pepys' Diaries to great consternation in the household because his copy of Speed's atlas was lost during a move of house.

Undoubtedly the two main factors for the survival of so many examples are their initial expense and the careful maintenance by generations of people who have been fascinated by them, whether they realised their value or not. Another factor is that many maps were preserved in volume form, and, stored in libraries, were protected from fading and being torn. Exposure to light and air tends to discolour the paper and make it brittle.

Much is said today about breaking up these volumes, and there are arguments both for and against. In the first place many of the earliest atlases are worth more in book form. Sometimes it is worthwhile making up any deficiency in an atlas to make it complete, and a fine volume of any period is worth more complete than as individual pages. A dealer will not split up an atlas unless it comes into the category of being a 'breaker', that is that the contents are not complete, and are not worth completing, or the binding has been ruined. Generally speaking the maps are worth more in this situation if they are sold individually but this is not always the case. If a dealer breaks an atlas he has to find a buyer for each map, not an easy process and usually a lengthy one. On the other hand if the maps are sold individually, each one goes to a buyer who will appreciate that particular map and is familiar with the territory covered, whereas it is unlikely that one is familiar with all the

territory contained in an atlas. The price of a single map is well within the average pocket, while the price of an atlas is obviously high. Bound volumes are not easy to look at and one runs some risk of damaging them when one is looking through them, but a framed map can safely be admired by everyone.

The question of financing these atlases was always a problem for their publishers. Although labour was cheap by today's standards, the capital outlay involved in publishing an atlas, providing the copper-plates, buying the paper and all the other necessary materials, was very high. Fortunately there were wealthy people prepared to sponsor map publishers. Both Britain's Christopher Saxton and John Speed were supported in their work by wealthy men, Thomas Seckford and Sir Fulke Greville, who bore the full cost of the work carried out by their respective protegés. It was more usual for an individual to subscribe to one particular map in a series, and in return the map would bear his arms and be dedicated to him. Richard Blome is noted for this practice. Many of his maps are seen with a dedication printed on the map, as they were first published, and a further dedication stuck on over the top of the existing one, probably caused by the first withdrawing his patronage. Some of the English maps published in the 18th century have a profusion of coats of arms of the subscribers, particularly the large map of Warwickshire by Henry Beighton. Each subscriber paid a sum of ten shillings for the privilege of having his arms and his name on this map. This case is perhaps unusual in that the subscriber could if he wished have only his name on the map, a lower rate being charged.

Surveying was an expensive business, and therefore many of the map-makers copied extensively from other sources. The county of Wiltshire offers an example of the sort of plagiarism that was rife. The first map of the county by Christopher Saxton marked a town without giving it a name. Later Speed used Saxton's information for the basis of his maps: he noticed the error and marked 'Quare' against the town, obviously intending that he should check the name of the town before the maps went to the engraver. This was neglected, Quare was engraved onto the plate and subsequently printed. This error was copied by the later map-makers, Blaeu, Jansson and Blome (even by Morden, who was generally considered to have taken great care to achieve accuracy with his maps), and was repeated on into the 18th century, finally to be restored to its correct title of North Burcombe by Bowen in the series published in 1755, one hundred and forty-five years after the mistake was perpetrated.

Good examples of maps need not be expensive. Many very acceptable maps can be bought for less than £10, $25, though apart from the intervention of pure luck, the best investments are the more expensive items. Some of the early 19th century atlases can be bought for less than £50, $120, but there is, of course, no ceiling. Probably the first thing to strike an intending purchaser is the wide range of prices asked by dealers for apparently similar articles. Two uniform maps, published at the same date and by the same man, can vary enormously in price. This is caused purely by supply and demand. Generally speaking the demand is created by the size of the population of the area covered by the map, the demand being greater for the heavily populated areas. There is a big demand for the maps covering all the big cities and thus they tend to be more expensive than those for the less populated areas. Most map-makers made series of maps, for example, John Speed, one of the most important English map-makers, made maps of all the English counties and these maps can vary from about £10 up to as much as £50, $25-120. His map of the whole world is most attractive and the demand for it comes from all over the world, the price being about £100, $250. This price difference applies to maps of all parts of the world, but the British Colonies and the most recently discovered countries are usually priced relatively highly because there are not enough maps to satisfy the present demand. There are few maps of Australia on the market made prior to 1800, and any maps made at this period will be expensive, whereas a similar map of a European country would be far cheaper. With a little practice a collector will soon understand how the dealer arrives at his prices.

Politics can play an important part in the pricing of maps. After the Second World War maps of Germany were very difficult to sell in England, but nowadays the situation is somewhat changed and the demand for them is

as great as any other European country. Maps of Russia are currently cheap, but seldom bought by the Russians, interest in them stemming mainly from the Westerners who have visited the country. There has always been a great demand for maps of the West Indies, especially the holiday islands, but currently there is little demand for maps of Cuba.

Dealers are always looking for more stock, but they will only buy when they can see that they have a reasonable chance of making a profit. There are certain kinds of stock which the dealer is constantly seeking, and the reasons are varied. He may have a collector customer who will buy anything on a certain subject, other subjects may be constantly popular for his regular customers, and he always needs to have rarities. He may avoid buying for the opposite reasons, that he has no buyer nor is likely to have one, or that he already has a stock of a particular subject. This can be the case with old maps possibly more than with any other kind of antiques, for a map-maker made equal numbers of maps of each place, and if a dealer buys a set of maps, there are some he can sell at once and some which will be left on his hands.

There are many different ways of making a collection. The most usual is to commence by buying maps of the county or country with which one is familiar. Some collectors prefer a particular period, or a subject which may coincide with another hobby, for example, railways or canals, or a particular period of history. Others will collect any maps by one particular maker or engraver. There is a limit to the number of pictures that one can hang on one's walls. Should a collection ever exceed this number, unframed prints can easily be stored in portfolio. Some collectors have all their maps mounted to a uniform size so that they can be stored firmly in solander cases. It is possible to have frames made to the same size with special backs so that the maps are interchangeable.

There are no special rules for the framing of maps, the style of frame is entirely up to the purchaser. It is usually recommended that a black and gold moulding is the most suitable, called Hogarth. This moulding will be in keeping with any surroundings—the black of the moulding picks up the black of the print, the gold helps to set off the colouring. Some maps have a text on the reverse, and in these cases it is customary to frame them with glass on the back of the frame as well, not a difficult operation. This procedure is also recommended for framing where the map is to hang in humid climates.

The only care that need be taken once a map is framed is to ensure that it does not hang in direct sunlight, or the colouring will soon fade. Normal daylight will not harm it.

The golden rule for purchasers is to look for good examples. The question of colouring is a matter of personal opinion, but the price of the map is arranged according to its overall condition. The most common damage is found on the centre folds of maps but, provided it is carefully mended, this will not detract from the value of a map. It is preferable to obtain maps without marginal tears, but again the value is not seriously affected unless the tear extends into the printed surface of the map. The buyer will not always have a choice so when the chance does arise he should take the copy which is in the best condition even though it may be a little more expensive. If possible make sure that the margins are good and that the paper is strong and clean. Above all one should buy the maps one likes, a choice which may not always coincide with the established names in cartography.

MAP-MAKING

SURVEYING

The purpose of making a survey is to make an exact reduction of the earth's surface. The first maps were made to illustrate routes and were made purely diagramatically, some of these are easier to follow than the maps which were intended to be accurate. They are parallel to maps which are now made for underground and subway railways, which are not drawn to scale and would be very confusing if they were. There is no object in marking in any other detail than the route and the stations. There are old maps which were made for other purposes, for instance, geological maps and those of canals and railways, and in these cases all the other detail is sketchily marked.

Some of the earliest maps made long before the discovery of printing were crude affairs surveyed from charting by the stars, their cycles and annual positions having been established. It is believed that as long ago as 1600 B.C. the Chinese were using some kind of compass. The earliest known compass was constructed with a magnetised needle in a cork which floated in a bowl of water.

It was not until mediaeval times that the Arabs made use of the astrolabe, and surveying began in earnest. An astrolabe is an instrument used to measure the altitude of the sun or the stars in order to plot a position and to tell the time. It is an evenly balanced disc with an inner rotating wheel with a rule attached, turning in a complete circle of 360°, by which the altitude of the sun could be ascertained, and from this reading one's position could be deduced. The maps of Ptolemy were made in this way. The astronomer Hipparchus, two centuries before Ptolemy, was the first to suggest that the inhabited world could only be accurately mapped by taking observations of latitude and longitude from all the principal parts of the world. Ptolemy worked on these theories, using the notes and itineraries of Marinus of Tyre, the most accurate then available. Unfortunately most of Ptolemy's mistakes occur because there were not enough observations taken. His Mediterranean Sea measured 62°, in fact about 20° too long. Mercator reduced the discrepancy to about 10°. Having plotted the main positions on the map, it was then possible to fill in the detail between the lines of latitude and longitude from the written itineraries.

By the end of the 16th century maps were being printed and a need arose for a more accurate system of surveying. Gemma of Friesland, who was a friend of Mercator, began a survey of the area between Michlen and Antwerp in about 1550, working on the system of triangulation. The method was to select three prominent positions, for example, hills, churches, towers or any high landmark. The distance was then measured between two of the landmarks and this formed the base line. The angles between the three points were calculated using a plane table, or circumferentor, and the position of each landmark is plotted on the map. It was then a simple matter to fill in the detail within the triangle. It was necessary to use a compass only at the beginning of the survey to establish the north point. The distance between the two landmarks forming the base line could be measured with a chain for a short distance, or a way-wiser for a longer distance. A way-wiser is a wheel which records the distance covered on a dial near the handle, one revolution of the wheel being half a pole, or $8\frac{1}{4}$ feet. One is shown in the Ogilby frontispiece which is illustrated. Similar wheels to these are used today where accurate measurements are essential, sophisticated affairs with pneumatic wheels like bicycle wheels, instead of the cumbersome wooden ones used by the early surveyors. Christopher Saxton carried out his survey in this way and, in the circumstances, achieved a remarkable degree of accuracy. Many of the towns would have been named by asking the locals of each place he visited. Thus many place names appear with phonetic spelling and in some cases bear little resemblance to modern names. These spellings cannot be relied upon to give old names accurately.

Paper

If a piece of old paper is held up to the light it is possible to see pale lines in parallel across the sheet, about an inch apart in one direction, those at right angles being very much closer. These lines are caused by the fine wires in the bottom of the tray used in paper making.

First of all a pulp is made out of rags, linen being the most suitable for the finer papers, coarser rags making coarser paper. The pulp is liquid in texture and when it has been thoroughly mixed in a large deep vat with an oar-shaped wooden stick the wired tray is dipped into the vat and enough pulp is lifted out to cover the tray to the required thickness. The water drips through the wires, leaving the paper. As soon as possible the sheet is raised from the tray and placed between two pieces of felt. The sheets are piled up with felt in between and then pressed to remove the surplus water, before being finally hung up to dry. Watermarks are made by fixing a wire design to the bottom of the tray, the lighter effect being caused by the impression of the design on the paper. The lines are apparent in some modern hand made papers. In old paper they cause some discolouring. Though the lines themselves are still white, the paper on each side is slightly yellower. Looking from one line across to the next, the line appears white, then the paper looks quite brownish and fades to a pale yellow in the centre and then turns brown again before the next line.

All paper used for maps was made in this way until the second half of the 18th century when the wires were replaced by a piece of silk, thus eliminating the watermark lines. Manufacturers continued to use wire to watermark the paper with their names or trade marks. Probably the most famous paper manufacturer of all was Whatman who flourished in the early 19th century, but his paper was used mainly for other types of prints. The Italians were the first to print maps, a craft which moved away to the Low Countries, but they retained their ability to make paper and supplied the paper for the monumental Dutch series of maps, including that of Blaeu, who considered that only the finest was good enough. All the early paper was carefully made and it is usually very strong, even to this day, provided that it has been kept dry. The slightest dampness softens the fibre and it becomes soft and flabby. It is possible for a restorer to renovate such paper and it is well worth while in order to reduce the risk of damage. It is possible for an expert to date a piece of paper accurately just by the feel of it, but it is not possible to explain how this is done and it takes years of experience. It will not take long for a collector to accumulate sufficient knowledge of the subject to know instinctively that the paper of a particular map is as old as it should be, and will find that he can date various issues of one map-maker's work by the differences in the papers used.

The size of the sheet of paper was almost standard, about 28 inches by 24 inches (70 by 60 cms). This was a convenient size of tray for a man to handle. There was also a limitation on the size of printing presses, so in fact a larger sheet would not have served a useful purpose. When a map-maker wanted to make a map larger than the normal sheet size, he had to use more than one sheet of paper and more than one plate, the pieces subsequently being joined. If a map is described as being, for example, 'four sheet' it means that it is printed on four separate sheets and is capable of being joined together.

Not all paper has a manufacturer's watermark and the value of a map is not altered by its presence or absence. The only indication given is to the age of the paper, but sometimes there were several years between the date that the paper was made and the date that it was used for printing. It was once suggested that all the first edition Saxton maps have a watermark of a bunch of grapes, and thus could be easily detected, but in fact virtually all

the paper made at this period has the same watermark. This is therefore no guide at all. There was only one watermark in each sheet of paper, so that if a sheet was cut into four pieces for the purpose of printing small maps, there would only be one watermark, on average, on every fourth map.

At the present time there is hardly any faking of maps. There is an increasing number of reproductions appearing from different sources, but far from undermining the value of the original, they make it still more sought after. Reproductions are usually made of the rarer maps and are therefore useful for reference purposes, and where an original is not available, for completing a collection. Some of them are beautifully produced in limited editions and it is possible that they could become collector's pieces in their own right. So far, however, few have been made with the intention of deceiving the purchaser. Some less scrupulous dealers will blandly say that they do not know whether a reproduction is old or not, a hazard likely to be encountered by patronising such people. Some years ago the British Museum made some excellent reproductions in good colour of some of the rare maps in the museum, which sold for a matter of shillings. Beneath the map is printed the title and maker of the map and the original date of manufacture. Now that they have had some time to 'age', and the paper has yellowed a little, and when they are cut close and framed, the uninitiated could well be forgiven for taking them for originals. Perhaps later on when some of todays reproductions are deliberately discoloured and 'distressed' even the expert will be misled. Some makers have had the foresight to make their prints slightly smaller than the original so that no one will ever be misled, an example which should be followed. There is no doubt that as prices continue to rise there will gradually be more scope for the forger. At the moment the biggest problem in forgery is copying the paper, though modern techniques will no doubt discover a method of making an 'antique' paper, complete with watermarks and discoloured lines, when it becomes worthwhile.

Because of the standard size of a sheet of paper, book sizes fall into groups and are named accordingly. A book made up of pages where the sheets have been folded once is called 'folio', a larger unfolded sheet is still called folio, sometimes large folio. If the sheet is folded twice, making four pages, the book is then called 'quarto', abbreviated to 4to. If folded once more, making eight pages, it is called 'octavo', abbreviated to 8vo or oct. Duodecimo (12mo) is a twelfth part of a sheet, and sextodecimo (16mo) is a sixteenth part. The last two sizes are very small, and for the most part atlases were not made so small, but there are a number of charming octavo atlases, particularly those published early in the 17th century.

Maps were usually bound in folded sheets, in which case a map measuring 28 by 24 inches in a folio atlas would be described as 'double page'. Generally maps were bound from the middle by folding the map in half and glueing a piece of paper, known as the guard, along the whole length. The guard could then be sewn into the binding without damaging the map thus ensuring that the whole of the map could easily be seen in the volume. The guard allows the map to be removed from the volume without damage, and it is because the maps were so easily removed that many atlases had maps taken out, destroying their value as atlases. It is advisable to have the guard removed prior to framing, to help keep the map flat inside the frame.

The quality and condition of the bindings are important factors in the value of an atlas. Unlike some books, atlases were given functional and robust bindings, usually of a plain nature: calf, morocco and vellum were the leathers most commonly used, with tooling and titles picked out in gilt. Binding was probably done to the customer's specification in many cases, so there are no hard and fast rules applicable. Some volumes have the owner's arms on the covers, some are decorated with motifs. Atlas holding the World on his shoulders is a common decoration on 18th century specimens. The later atlases had less elaborate bindings, and more of them were bound in half leather with cloth or marbled paper panels, being cheaper materials. Marbled paper did not stand up to heavy wear and is usually marked and scuffed. Leather bindings have to be carefully maintained. If they are allowed to become too dry they will soon crack at the sides of the spine. Occasional application of a good quality leather oil will keep them in good order.

PRINTING TECHNIQUES

There were two methods of printing maps. The first, and generally the earliest, was printing in 'relief' using wood blocks. The other method was known as 'intaglio', employing metal plates, usually copper. As the systems are described it will be seen how they vary and how copper was much more suitable for the purpose.

Printing in 'relief' was so called because the parts of the wood block which are inked and which transfer the ink onto the paper, are those parts of the block which are left untouched by the engraver and are left standing in relief on the block. The woods used were relatively soft with close grain, pear, apple, box, or sycamore were the most common, cut 'in plank', or along the length with a knife. (In the 19th century wood-cuts were revived for illustrative purposes, but not for maps, and the wood was sometimes cut across the grain.) The design is drawn on the block and all the areas which are to remain white are cut away leaving the design standing up on the block. The surface is then inked with a roller and the paper laid over the block and put into the press.

Copper plate engraving was printed in exactly the reverse method, that is to say that a groove on the copper would print on the paper. When the engraver had completed the work, the whole plate is inked and the surface wiped clean, leaving the ink in the grooves. At about 1820 steel plates began to supercede copper, and though the same method was used the harder metal had the advantage that it gave finer definition and did not wear as did copper.

Wood blocks were not well suited to the purpose of printing maps, and had several disadvantages over the intaglio method. Although it was possible to make alterations and corrections to the blocks, it was a complicated procedure, entailing cutting out the part of the block which required altering and replacing it with a fresh piece of wood which was then re-engraved. Additions to an intaglio plate were simple, amounting only to a question of engraving the detail onto the untouched surface. Alterations could be made by gently tapping the back of the plate where the alteration was to be made, levelling off and re-engraving, easier with copper than with steel. Later it will be seen how some publishers made alterations to their plates to keep them up to date, particularly in the case of John Speed's work, which continued to be published over a period of some one hundred and sixty years, each publisher putting his own name to the plate. The maps by Christopher Saxton were made barely recognisable by re-engraving.

It was very difficult to engrave lettering on wood, an essential part of the map. This was overcome by the use of ordinary metal type let into the block: the printing process was a single one, and the lettering was not over-printed onto an existing print.

By the time that the first printed maps were being produced, presses had come into operation. The earliest printing was done by rubbing the paper from the back, it being very difficult to obtain a good even impression all over the surface. The first presses were like linen presses, operated on the screw principle, and made of wood. These were a great improvement, and though an even impression was still not guaranteed, it was a step towards better things, and iron presses were soon in operation. The inked plate was laid on the bed of the press, covered with paper slightly dampened to assist the absorbence of the ink, over this were laid several thicknesses of fabric, and, finally, the press was screwed down. The paper was forced into the grooves, causing ridges known as 'bite'. The press was unscrewed, the print hung up to dry and the plate re-inked ready for the next print to be taken. The most obvious place to look for the ridge caused by the pressure of the plate is the outer extremity of the plate, known as the 'plate mark'. From the depth of this mark can be judged the immense pressure to which the plate has been subjected. Both wood and steel withstood this pressure without much sign of heavy use, but copper was comparatively soft and soon began

to deteriorate, especially around the shallowest grooves, where the fine detail lost its clarity and definition. The number of impressions that could be made from one copper plate would depend on the depth of engraving and the amount of fine work on the plate. In the case of the ornamental maps of the early 17th century about 800 to 1,000 copies could be taken before the signs of wear detracted from the print, but some atlases were re-issued many times, probably up to 3,000, by which time the plates were very worn unless they were re-engraved.

The basic tool of the engraver is called a 'burin'. It has a small steel blade about four inches long with a fine cutting point, shaped according to the requirements of the engraver. The wooden handle is shaped like a mushroom and is held in the palm of the hand with the stalk housing the blade protruding between the fingers, which are curled round inside the mushroom. The blade is put into the copper and is pressed away from the engraver, always in the same direction to ensure an even pressure, and when he needs to change the direction of a line he turns the plate accordingly. With a tool that is correctly sharpened, a fine strip of metal is cut away from the plate. The depth of the groove will determine the eventual blackness of the print, the deeper groove will contain more ink and will therefore print a blacker line on the paper. The finest detail is hardly discernible on the plate, even though it will print clearly on the paper, and it is this detail which is the first to show signs of wear. The plates were, of course, engraved in reverse in order to obtain a right-reading impression on the paper.

COLOURING

All early maps are printed in black and white. It was not until the latter part of the 19th century that coloured lithography was used, and this falls outside the period covered by this book. The British Ordnance Survey maps were not printed in colour until as late as the 20th century. The difficulty was to obtain the correct register, that is the exact placing of each individual colour, to avoid either overlapping or a gap between two adjoining colours. In either case the result is most unsatisfactory. In the middle of the 19th century George Baxter perfected a colour printing process using a series of blocks, one for each colour, with the correct register. His method was a closely guarded secret, and he obtained a very high standard of work, probably by destroying any print which was not entirely to his satisfaction. His prints were Victorian sentimental subjects and he was not concerned with maps, but his techniques were handed down, and it was through his inspiration that colour printing began.

Many of the maps published in black and white were subsequently coloured by hand and rather more original colouring was carried out than is generally supposed. (It is sometimes thought that such maps have all been coloured in recent years.) In many cases it is very difficult, even for an expert, to establish whether or not the colouring of a particular map is old. In the main it is most desirable to acquire maps which are in original colour, but some old colouring is very poor, is crudely applied, inappropriate, and garish, carried out with insufficient attention to detail. Conversely some is really magnificent, with a quality and richness which has not been dulled by the passage of time. All the colour illustrations in the book are taken from examples in original colour, and it is surprising that they should have existed so well for so long. As a rule it is best for the buyer to use his own discretion: the main thing is that he should like the colouring himself. The dealer cannot assist over this, nor can he always state categorically the period at which the colouring was applied.

In most cases the colour enhances the map and makes it easier to read, one of the reasons why they were coloured in the first place. Though the colourist had a free hand to colour the map as he wished, there was a kind of formula which was normally followed by the professional. Each colourist mixed his own colours and had his own techniques for their application. Various materials were used as size to prevent the paper absorbing the colour

too rapidly or unevenly, white of egg being the most common. Judging from books on the subject, some colourists went to great lengths to obtain the correct colour, the constituents coming from all over the world and taking several days to prepare. These colours are generally remarkably good, retaining their brilliance and showing little sign of fading since they were applied. The greens can cause some trouble: they were made from verdigris which in time rots through the paper to the extent of disintegration. This occurred mainly with the maps which were coloured before 1700, and if there is any doubt about the strength of the paper which has been coloured in this way, it is advisable to have the paper strengthened from the back, not a difficult operation and one which may save the paper from cracking.

The standard procedure was to begin by colouring in the boundary lines, a different colour being applied on either side of the line. Sometimes each division is coloured in a pale wash. Estates, parks and woods are coloured green, seas and rivers in blue, hills in brown or occasionally in green, and the cities and towns in red. The extra decoration is coloured as naturally as possible, animals, humans, shipping and all the things that appear in the cartouches. Sea monsters are usually green, their large mouths coloured in red, but this was entirely left to the imagination of the colourist. Mistakes can easily occur. One particular map of the County of Cheshire, famous for its cheeses, shows whole cheeses in the cartouche looking like huge millstones, coloured in unappetising magenta and blue.

The armorial shields, of course, had to be coloured correctly, and this was done by following two simple codes, either by a guiding letter or by a system of engraving the background of the shield. The traditional names for each colour are derived from mediaeval French. Gules (red) was marked G, or the engraved lines were vertical. Bleu (blue) was indicated by B, and had the lines engraved horizontally. Sable (black) marked by S, or by lines engraved both horizontally and vertically. Vert (green) was lettered V, or the lines were engraved diagonally from top left to bottom right.

Key to the colouring code internationally used in heraldry. This is an enlargement of a section of a page of flags which is printed at the front of a sea atlas by Bellin.
Size of this section: 2⅛ by 1¾ in., 5.5 by 4.5 cm.

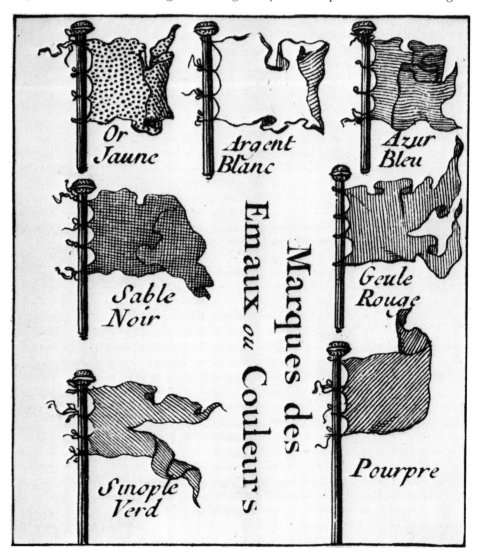

Purpure (purple), an unusual colour in heraldry, was lettered P, or had engraved lines crossing from top right to bottom left. Or (gold) is lettered O and the engraving is geometrically dotted. Argent (silver) lettered A, is left plain and is not usually coloured on old maps. The system worked very well, an easy guide for the professional colourist who knew the code, but not all colourists were professionals and sometimes the armorials are incorrectly coloured. The Dutchmen unfortunately reversed red and blue, the two most important colours in heraldry. This would not have mattered had all Dutch maps been coloured there but many of them have been coloured elsewhere, according to the usual code.

Colouring is still being added to maps today, generally speaking with great care and consideration by experienced colourists who know the right colouring for each map-maker and often their work is preferable to that of the early colourists. Whether this practice is aesthetically right or wrong has been the subject of many long discussions. There are some maps which were not intended to be coloured. The Italians thought that colouring obscured the detail and the quality of their engraved work and this is true to a certain extent. There are other maps which lend themselves to colour, particularly the plainer maps of the 18th century and those which are crowded with detail. The very early wood-cuts are spoiled by the addition of colour.

A section of the page of 188 flags, illustrating the method of systematic engraving as a guide to the colourist.
Overall size of page: 23 by 34 in., 60 by 87 cm.

THE FIRST
PRINTED
MAPS

In 1477 at Bologna in Italy, an atlas was published containing twenty-seven maps by Claudius Ptolemy, and these are the earliest printed maps. The work was the publication of a Greek manual on the construction of maps compiled in manuscript by Ptolemy, a famous astonomer and scientist from Alexandria, as long before as A.D. 120 and titled *Geographia*. The discovery that maps could be printed, coupled with the revival of Ptolemy's maps, brought about the renaissance of map-making. Almost at once further editions were published, not only in Italy but in Germany as well. The maps covered the known world and were therefore confined to Europe and Asia, with the north part of Africa along the Mediterranean coast. Their information remained virtually unchallenged by any other maps until the supremacy of map-making moved to the Low Countries in the latter part of the 16th century. These early editions are occasionally available, usually in volume form, rather than single sheet, but the versions by Sebastian Munster in the mid-16th century are the most commonly found, pleasing wood-cuts with primitive decoration on them. Such was the importance of Ptolemy that his maps continued to be published into the 17th century, usually as parts of the modern atlases and described as 'antient maps'.

Although Sebastian Munster was born and educated in Germany, he published his maps in Basle in Switzerland. His first map is a rarity, a map of Europe published in 1525. His first edition of Ptolemy was published in 1540 and included twelve new maps. The *Cosmographia* which was published in 1550, contained some revision of his previous maps and fifty-two further maps were added. Considering their antiquity these maps are not expensive as Munster was fairly prolific. The map of America is of course one of the earliest that is available and is therefore the most difficult to obtain. Coupled with this, the inclusion of the map in the series made up the four continents in an atlas for the first time, most succeeding atlases following the example of Munster. He also published some views of Cities and Towns, mainly of

Sebastian Munster: The World. Taken mostly from Ptolemy and published in 1540. One of the earliest maps of the world that can be bought. Wood-cut.

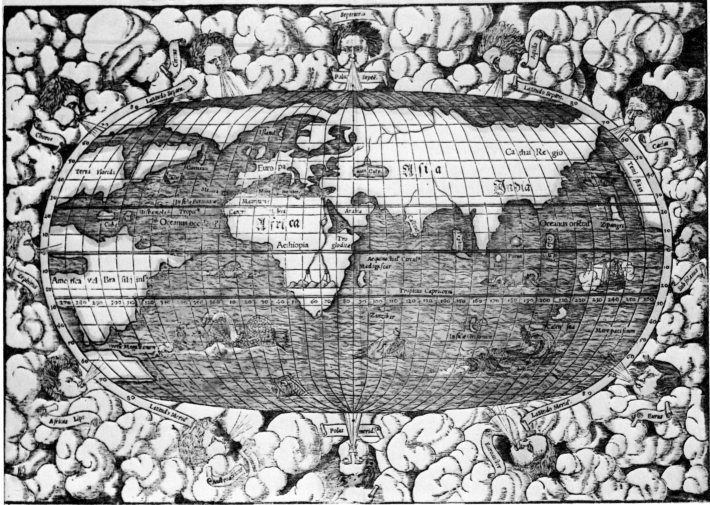

20

Germany and central Europe, drawn as a bird's eye view and largely diagramatic, similar to the prints by Braun and Hogenberg.

The Italians continued to be the world's most important map-makers for about one hundred years, and, though their maps are rare, the following names are some which may be encountered. Giacomo Gastaldi, who worked in Venice, published maps from about 1540 to 1570, including thirty-four new maps for the later editions of Ptolemy. Antonio Lafreri, who was born in France and moved to Rome in 1544, had his own publishing business where he printed a large number of fine maps. His atlas sold at auction in London in 1967 for £13,000, $36,000. Later in the century Tomaso Porcacchi published an atlas of the world in Venice. Vincenzo Valgrisi was a publisher who also worked on the editions of Ptolemy.

It was the Low Countries that emerged to lead the way in map publishing. The Flemish and then the Dutch were to reign for over one hundred years, producing some of the finest maps that were ever made, developing new techniques of map-making and perpetually improving their existing maps. The greatest inspiration was Gerard Mercator, but it was in 1570 that Abraham Ortelius produced the first edition of his *Theatrum Orbis Terrarum*, and one can judge the immediate success of the work by the fact that fourteen different editions appeared before the end of 1575. They continued to be successful up until the last edition, the forty-second, was published in 1612.

Abraham Ortelius was born in Antwerp in 1527 and died there in 1598. He began trading as a map colourist, buying black and white maps which he found he could colour and re-sell for a large profit. Some of these would have been obtained from the Italians and the Germans, some would have been the work of Mercator, but being single sheet maps they are now extreme rarities because their mortality rate was so high. He also used to

Sebastian Munster: America. Published in Basle about 1550. A delightfully inaccurate map of the 'New World'.
Size: 10 by 13½ in., 25 by 34 cm.

Sebastian Munster: wood-cut map of Great Britain, published about 1550.
Size: 12½ by 14 in., 32 by 36 cm.

purchase small quantities of books for re-sale from the greatest printer of the period, Christopher Plantin, who later was to become a good friend, and eventually took over publication of the *Theatrum*. The first map that Ortelius made was a large eight sheet map of the world, of which only one copy is now known to exist, followed by a map of Egypt and one of Asia. The dates of these are between 1564 and 1570.

The *Theatrum* was the first volume of uniform sized maps to cover all known parts of the world, made from the most up-to-date knowledge available and assembled to provide useful and practical information. Ortelius deserved all the success that he achieved, not only were the maps masterly works of art, but no one had attempted such a momentous task before, and an atlas of this kind was much needed. The first edition contained seventy maps but this number was gradually increased as more knowledge and accuracy of geographical detail was acquired. The total was eventually in excess of one hundred and sixty maps. Ortelius drew his information from every possible source. The map of Portugal, for example, is taken from a map by Secco, whose name is credited on the map. The map of Wales is taken from a map by Humphrey Lhuyd, a friend of Ortelius. Lhuyd also provided the general map of England and Wales in the early editions but it was superseded by the very spectacular map by Vrints in the later editions, a great improvement and typical of the way Ortelius used the best possible maps. Thus it happens that some of the Ortelius maps are quite rare because

Ptolemy: Scandinavia. Published in 1551.
Wood-cut.
Size: 11½ by 15 in., 29 by 38 cm.

they appear in only a few editions and consequently this is reflected in the price. Unlike most atlases, the later editions of the complete work tend to be more expensive than the early ones because of the increase in the number of maps. The early editions of the single maps are, of course, the most sought after and, most especially the ones which are slightly altered, for example, the first map of the American continent showing the tip of South America quite square, a fault which was soon rectified.

The first edition of Ortelius was not published by Plantin, for some reason, though from Plantin's records it appears that he provided Ortelius with a large quantity of paper at the end of 1569, probably for the atlas. Instead the atlas was published by the Antwerp printer Gilles Coppens van Diest. In 1579 Plantin printed the atlas, but still at the expense of Ortelius, and in 1588 he took over the entire production himself and continued to print the work until the last edition. To increase the sales of the atlas the text on the reverse of each map, describing the history and the features of the map depicted on the face, was published in several languages. Latin was the common language of the period, but the others were Dutch, French, German, Spanish and, rather surprisingly, there was only one English edition, which is quite uncommon, published in 1606.

In 1575 Ortelius published a miniature atlas, a pocket edition measuring only about four inches by seven inches (10 by 18 cms). It contained over one hundred charming little maps of all parts of the world and it continued to be printed until the middle of the 17th century, long after the folio atlas had been discontinued. Copies are not usually found in original colour and because they are so small, the decoration on them is restricted. The titles are mainly contained in ruled rectangles but some of them are in pleasing rococo cartouches. Like the folio atlas, the maps have a text on the reverse but in each case it refers to and faces the following map.

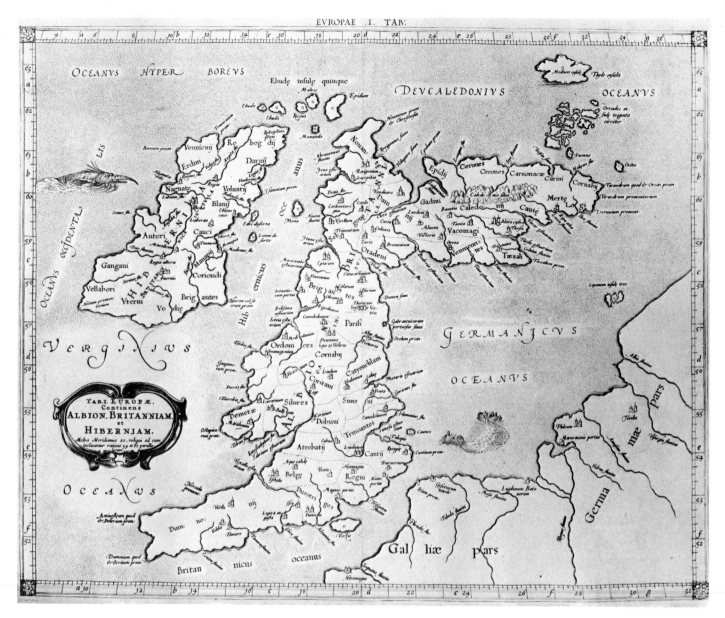

TAB.I.EVROPÆ,
Continens
ALBION, BRITANNIAM,
et
HIBERNIAM.

Gerard Mercator was born in Rupelmonde in Flanders in 1512. Though he had been publishing single maps long before Ortelius was in operation, he published his atlas some fifteen years after that of Ortelius, in 1585. This atlas, together with the fact that he is famous for Mercator's Projection, a system of projecting a map with the lines of latitude and longitude set at right angles, made him the greatest influence on map-making since Ptolemy. His large single sheet maps are as rare as those of Ortelius: the two different maps of Europe were printed on fifteen sheets and a fine map of the world, in 1569, was printed on eighteen sheets. In 1578 Mercator published an edition of Ptolemy's *Geographia* which appears to have been very popular and it was re-issued seven times. The maps are beautifully engraved, and this edition is the most attractive of all the editions of Ptolemy. It is surprising that Mercator should have published an atlas of maps by a man with whom he technically disagreed, and the problem of shaking off the deep impression made on the whole world by Ptolemy must consequently have been made even more difficult.

Apart from his career of producing maps, Mercator was also involved in the geographical work of the University of Duisberg, where he died in 1594, and he founded his own geographical school at Louvain in 1534, and he had to flee from that town to save an inquiry into his religious beliefs. Later he was arrested and charged with heresy and was lucky to escape serious consequences.

It has been suggested that Mercator withheld publication of his atlas to allow his friend Ortelius a free field, but this is extremely unlikely in view of the expense involved and also the fact that only part of the atlas was ready for publication in 1585. In 1590 the second part of the atlas was published,

Mercator: Great Britain. Published for Mercator's edition of Ptolemy's *Geographia* from 1578. This example is the re-issue of 1619. Although the orientation of Scotland is wrong by 90 degrees, the outline shape of the country is recognisable. Size: 13 by 15½ in., 33 by 40 cm.

Colour illustrations on following pages:
Christopher Saxton: Frontispiece. 1579.
Christopher Saxton: Cornwall. 1579.
Mark Jorden: Denmark. 1585.

Clemens et Regni moderatrix iusta Britāni
Hac forma insigni conspicienda nitet.

Tristia dum gentes circùm omnes bella fatigant,
Cæciq̃ errores toto grassantur in orbe.
An. Dñi { pace beas longa, Vera et pietate Britannos: 1579
Iusticia moderans miti sapienter habenas.
Chara domi, celebrisq̃ foris, longæuaq̃ regnū
Hic teneas, regno tandem fruitura perenni.

HONI · SOIT · QVI · MAL · Y · PENCE

DIEV·ET·MON·DROYT

PROMONTORIVM HOC
IN MARE PROIECTVM
CORNVBIA DICITVR

OCCIDENS

The mar rock

Moruah

Bref an Jnfull

Whifand bay

Sennan

The Landes end
Treuille
Bofaftow
Rockeftall

Longfhips rock

Sct Iees
Sct Iees baye

Sct Sener
Tewidnak
Halamouth

Masdarway
HV

Luggan

PENWITH
Sct Maddarn
Sancrete
PESANCE
Kneage
Guliuall
Newlyn
Sct Burien
Sct Pauls
Moufhole
Moufhole Insull

Efcoles

Vuy lalant
Lydgeuan
Mercalue
Sct Hilarye
Sct Michaels
mount

Mountar baye

Cuddan
poynte

Guethan in
conerton
Phelnek

Cambron

Sct Woer
Redreuth

Killigren
Sct Alyn
Trewirgan

Sct Earth

Gwynyer

Sct Kennuer
Sct Erne

Pelewith

Gwynyer

TRVRO

Sct Peran
Vehns

Goodalhin

Goodalhyn in
Cohor flu
Wendron

Crowan

Clowance

Garmon
Breake

Synnyie

Sct Gwenap

Sct Sothians

Kirklewe
Reftrow awes

Sct Perananwothill

Sct feoke
Sct Feke
Taluart

Sct clemens

Sct Merther

Fentangolon

PERYN

Myler

Miler
poole

KERIAR

Methley

Lys flu

HV

HELSTON

Weke

Conftan
tyne

Mohe

Budoc

Armenah

PERYN

Trefofen
poynt

Arduenora

Phifre

Sct Tuft

Sct Veryon

Pengwenyon poynte

Carmyno

Maugan

Trelawarren

Podenans caft

Arwenak

y paeradge
Manackey

Mauan

Helford hauen

Y rock

Sct Maries
cofe

Sct Tuft

Sct Gre
rence
Sct Anthonye

Predannok poynte

Melyan

Curye
Sct merter

Sct Anthony

Faulmouth hauen

Sct Anthons poynt

Wrynyrin

MENEGE

Ruan mag

Sct Keuern

The Manacles poynt

Gurn'at la

Ruan pua
Sct Grade

O   C.

E

Lefard poynte

A

Scala   M. iliarum

1 2 3 4 5 6 7 8 9 01 LL 12

Christophorus Saxton defcripfit

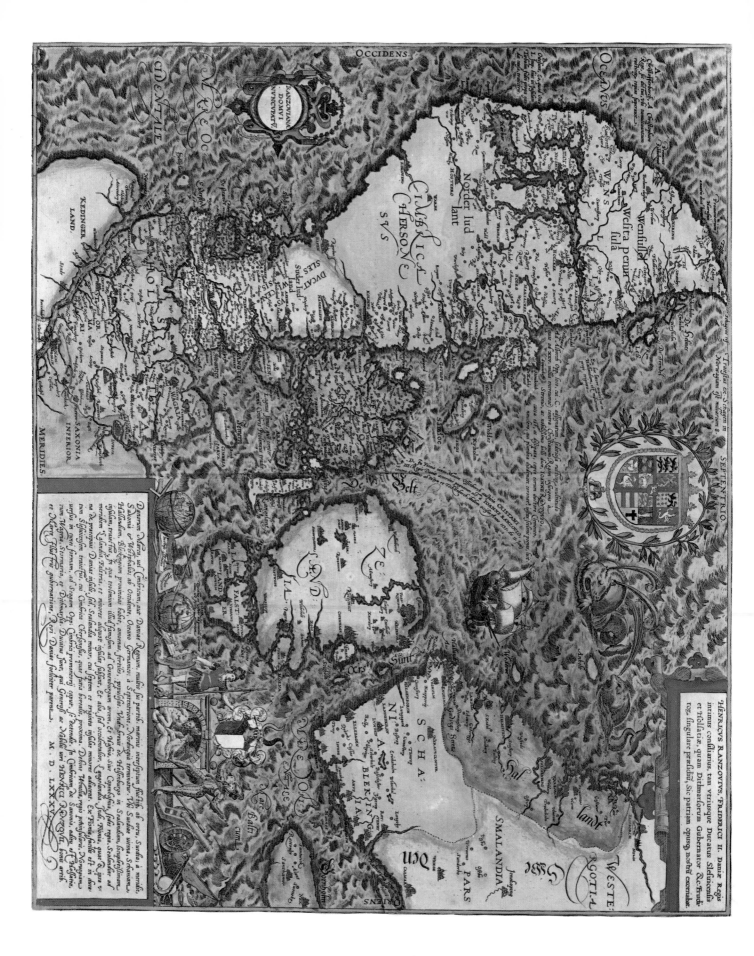

An unusual map from the series of Islands by Thomas Porcacchi, a 16th century Italian map-maker, published in Venice in 1576. The text continues on the reverse of the page.

Page size: 10½ by 7½ in., 28 by 19 cm.

DESCRITTIONE
DELL'ISOLA
D'ISLANDA,
DI THOMASO PORCACCHI.

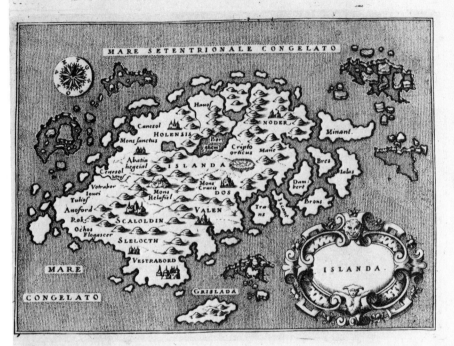

L'ISOLA d'Islanda giace sotto il Polo Artico fra l'Auftro, e'l Borea, vicina al mar Glaciale, ò agghiacciato : la qual cosa fece credere à tutti gli auttori antichi, ch'essa fosse l'ultima Thile, tanto da essi celebrata, & chiamata Terra Glaciale : & però è detta Islanda, che vuol dir Terra di ghiaccio; ma i nostri Scrittori alcune volte l'hanno chiamata anchora Isola perduta, per la gran lontananza, così del paese, come della cognition nostra. Et certo se Strabone Geografo antichissimo, & molto accurato disse nel quarto della sua Geografia, che dell'Isola Thile era oscura l'historia, per esser riposta ne gli ultimi luoghi della terra, che douerò io dir di questa, scrittor trascurato rispetto a lui, la quale è tanto piu oltre posta, che Thile? Distendesi l'Islanda, come dissi, fra

La sua parte Settentrionale è in altezza di gradi 69.m. 15. & nella parte più occidenta le è in longhezza di gradi 353. m. 45. L'Anama la pone in altezza di gradi 73.

A

followed by the last part in 1595, the year after his death. Mercator had two sons, Rumold, who collaborated on the third part of the atlas with his father and was eventually responsible for its publication, and Arnold, who was the elder, born in 1537. Arnold had three sons, Gerard, John and Michael, but though they each remained in the world of cartography, none of them attained a fraction of the success of their exalted patriarch.

There is some similarity between the maps of Mercator and Ortelius. The Mercator maps are more heavily engraved, the dark cross hatching on the seas tending to detract from the decorative cartouches. The Ortelius maps were mostly engraved by Franciscus Hogenberg (brother of Remigius, who worked on some of the maps for Saxton's atlas of England and Wales), before he joined Braun in the publication of their magnificent set of town plans, titled *Civitates Orbis Terrarum*. The decoration on the Mercator maps is not as elegant as that on the Ortelius. Like Ortelius, the Mercator atlas was published in several languages, mainly Latin and French, with

TERRA SANCTA.

Persei Specula

Cynos

Tanis

Pelusium

Onuphis

ÆGY P TVS.

Delta

Vicus Iudeorum

Nilus flu.

Rameses

Paludes

Strabonis lacus

Gerra

Ostracina

Casius mons

Rinocorura

Anthedon

Gaza

RE

MAGNVM

Heroum ciuitas

Sur de

Gosen.

sertum.

A RABIA

Casius mons

Berfoba

Ascalon

Azotus

Ioppe

Emaus

Caesarea

Dora

Ptolemais

Tyrus

Berytus

MARIS

PE

Cades

IVDEA

Hebron

Hierusalem

GALILÆA

Sidon

RVBRI SINVS

TREA

Petra

Moabitæ.

Mare mortuum

Iorda nis flu.

Genezaret lacus

Samachonitis lacus

Antilibanus mons

Damascus

Mons Sinai

Leucæ.	5	10	15	20	25	30
Mil. Germ.		5.		10.		15.
Stadia.	80	160	240	320	400	480
Mil. Ital.		40		80		120

ARABIÆ DESERTÆ PARS.

COELE: SYRIA.

Ortelius: miniature map of Palestine. Published in 1601. The first edition of the miniature atlas appeared in 1570, and the work was gradually enlarged and re-issued until it contained over 120 maps. This map shows the route taken by Moses and the Children of Israel on the flight from Egypt. Size: 3½ by 4⅝ in., 9 by 12 cm.

Below left

A map by Johan Baptist Vrints of 1605. Published by Ortelius and shown here in the atlas. It is unusual and appeared only in the last few editions of Ortelius, in place of the Lhuyd map of England and Wales, the Vrints being more accurate and much more decorative. It is finely engraved, and, when in rich colour, is a spectacular map. The 'tree' at the right depicts the Kings and Queens of England from William the Conqueror. A difficult map to value; the atlas would fetch up to £3,000, $7,200, in good condition, and the single sheet about £80-100, $190-240.

Below

P. Coronelli: Malta. Published in Venice and dated 1689. Like most Italian maps this is generally found in black and white, but occasionally copies are found with later colouring, and these can be very decorative. Approximate size: 20 by 25 in., 50 by 65 cm.

Dutch, Flemish, German and English added after 1633. Again there is only one English edition, which was published in 1636, and although this is a comparatively late edition the quality of the impressions is still good and is often preferred in the English speaking countries.

In 1606 the business was taken over by Jocodus Hondius, an engraver with a fine reputation but until then not a publisher. Like Mercator, he had to flee from religious problems and he took refuge in England, where he worked on subjects varying from portraits to maps. The experience he acquired put him in good stead and he began to add his own maps to the Mercator atlas, gradually extending the number of maps from one hundred and seven, the number in the three volumes published together in 1595, to a total of around three hundred. However, Mercator's name was always retained for the atlas and the work is known by that name, though sometimes hyphenated with Hondius in order to differentiate between the editions. There were even more editions of Mercator's atlas than that of Ortelius, being a total of fifty up to the last in 1642.

Jocodus Hondius had a son, Henry, who followed him into the business. Henry was an engraver of equal merit, and the influence that the two made on the atlas was soon apparent. Their engraving is finer and more delicate than the previous Mercator engravers, perhaps their maps were calculated to attract attention by the rich decor, a practice which would probably have been frowned on by Mercator. Jocodus died in 1611, the same year as the first edition of the English maps by John Speed, a work which had been engraved by him; probably the two had met during the period that Hondius was in refuge in England. Henry continued to publish the atlas and he was joined by Jan Jansson in 1633. Jansson became the brother-in-law of Hondius, and he eventually acquired the business when Hondius died. From 1642 Jansson started publishing his own maps. While they are fine quality engravings, they lack the originality of the Ortelius and Mercator

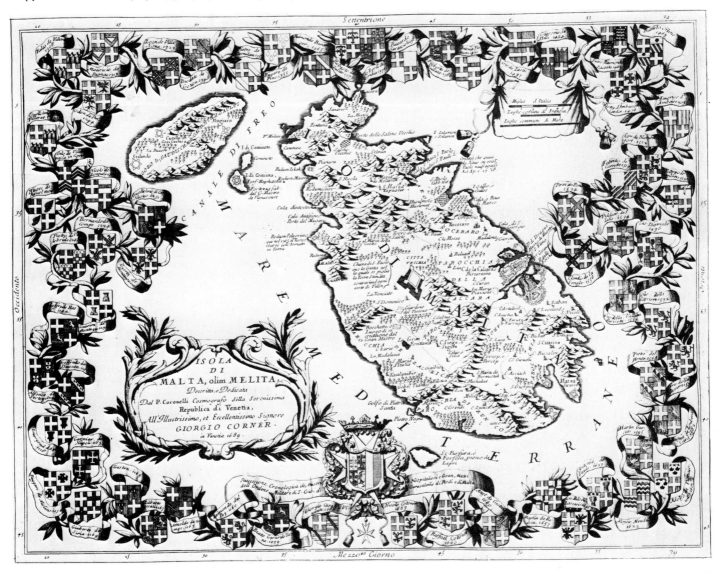

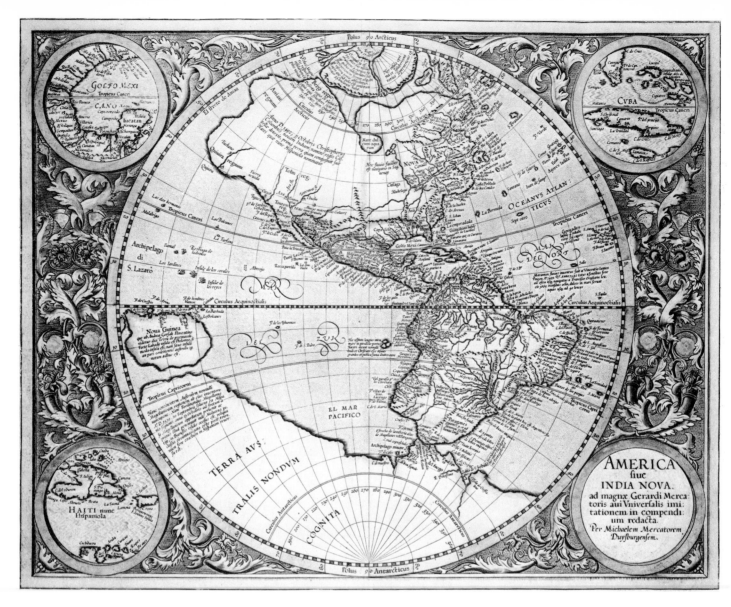

maps, Jansson being a publisher first and foremost. He collected the information for his maps without giving credit to his sources, there being no form of copyright at this period. Jansson's most important work was his *Atlas Novus* which was gradually extended until in 1661 there were eleven volumes published, a veritable monument of map production, equalled only by his contemporary and rival, Blaeu. It is particularly apparent that Jansson copied much of Blaeu's work, by comparison of the maps of the English counties, some of them being difficult to tell apart.

The finest Dutch map publishers were the Blaeu family, and they hold the title of map-makers supreme for any period of cartographical history. There are several different pronunciations of Blaeu, but it is generally accepted that it rhymes with cow. There were three members of the family in the business; William Janszoon, born in 1571, and his sons, Johann and Cornelius. Some of the early work of William has caused some confusion because he signed himself in a variety of ways, Guilielmus Janssonius and Willems Jans Zoon being especially puzzling, but there was no link with his rival. The majority of his work is signed G. or Guilielmus Blaeu and there were not four members of the family as is sometimes supposed.

William Blaeu's earliest work was centred round terrestrial and celestial globes and the first atlas was a sea atlas, probably inspired by the fine maps of his fellow countryman Waghenaer, published a few years earlier. Previously Blaeu had published a few single sheet maps, mainly of the continents and one of particular merit, a magnificent map of the world on twenty sheets, but all of these are great rarities and should any of them come onto the market they would command very high prices. The atlases which we know today began to be published in 1630, and, like his predecessors, Blaeu added more maps to the work until the *Atlas Major* published in 1662 comprised eleven

Mercator: America. 1606. Mercator kept his atlas well up to date and the later editions by Hondius replaced this map with another which has more detail and some improvements to the shape of South America. This example illustrates the elaborately engraved borders often used by Mercator.
Size: 14½ by 18 in., 37 by 50 cm.

32

Humphrey Lhuyd: the first map of Wales by itself, published by Ortelius from 1573. The map was reprinted nearly fifty times by various publishers, who retained the body of the map but altered the decor.
Size: $14\frac{1}{2}$ by $19\frac{1}{2}$ in., 37 by 50 cm.

Baptista Boazio: Ireland. An Italian living in London, Boazio is renowned for his map of Ireland published in 1599, which is a rarity. This example was engraved by Vrints and included in the Ortelius atlas of 1608.
Size: 17 by 22 in., 44 by 57 cm.

volumes. This was a pinnacle in map-making history, everything about the work was superlative, beautifully engraved and printed, the paper being the finest available, and most of them were coloured in the Blaeu establishment and have a rich quality which was unrivalled.

The maps covered all the known world, with particular emphasis on Europe, though one volume is devoted to America and another to China.

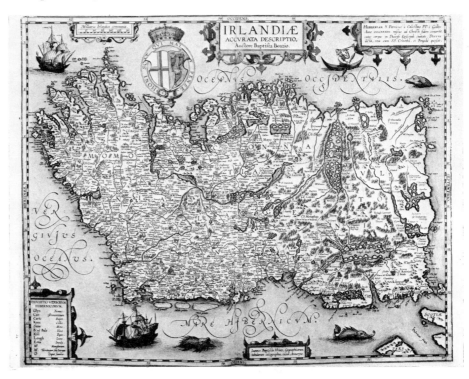

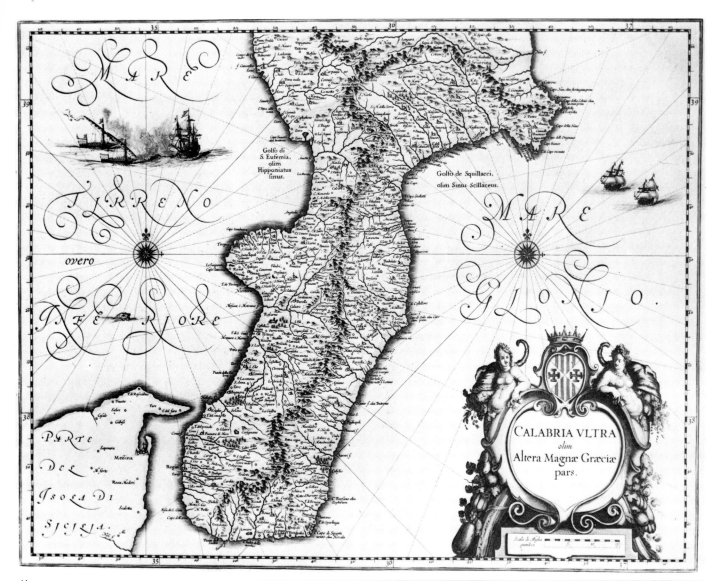

Above

Blaeu: Calabria, the 'toe' of Italy, published in 1648. A fine map with a decorative cartouche. The demand for maps of this part of Italy is not as high as the industrial north, an example like this is therefore comparatively cheap, despite the quality.
Size: 15 by 19½ in., 38 by 50 cm.

Above left

Secco map of Portugal published by Ortelius in the *Theatrum Orbis Terrarum*, one of several instances where Ortelius drew on other cartographers' work to keep his atlas as up to date as possible. We have become accustomed to looking at maps with the North point at the top but many early examples were turned round in order to make the best use of the paper without altering the format of the completed atlas. It can cause some confusion, but every map carries a compass rose or cardinals, as in this case.

Below left

One of the most decorative maps of Iceland, published by Blaeu in about 1650. As well as Blaeu, Mercator and Ortelius made exceedingly fine maps of the island.

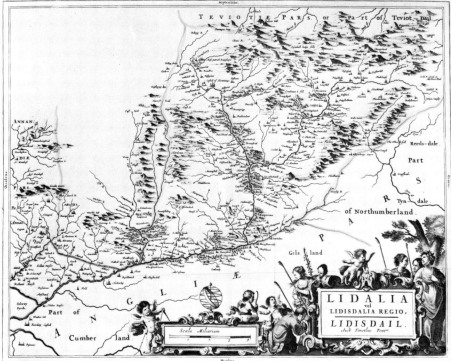

Timothy Pont: Lidisdale, part of the Scottish border country. The first and by far the most important series of maps of parts of Scotland were made by Pont as early as 1610 but were not printed until 1654 when Blaeu published them as Volume V of his great work. This is one of the most decorative maps in the series; the cartouche is most spectacular in full colour. Like all Blaeu's engraving the lettering is unsurpassed.

Size: 16¼ by 21½ in., 41 by 55 cm.

The volumes were available separately—the cost of the complete work must
have been beyond the pockets of most people. Great Britain was covered by
two volumes, number four for England and Wales, and number five for
Scotland and Ireland. The maps of England, Wales and Ireland were

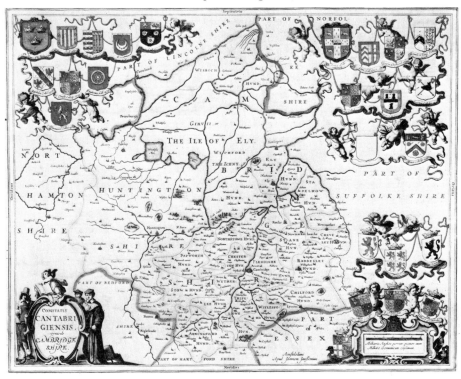

J. Jansson: Cambridgeshire, published in
1646. The style of Jansson is very similar
to that of Blaeu, both of them taking their
detail from Speed. The armorials at the top
corners are those of the University Colleges,
with the dates of their foundation, and those
in the lower corner are the Earls of the county.
Size: 16½ by 20½ in., 42 by 52 cm.

Nicholas Visscher: Europe. Published about
1680. An example of the fine engraving and
craftsmanship which made the Dutch famous.
Even though the map is crowded with place
names, every one is perfectly legible.
Size: 17 by 21¼ in., 43 by 54 cm.

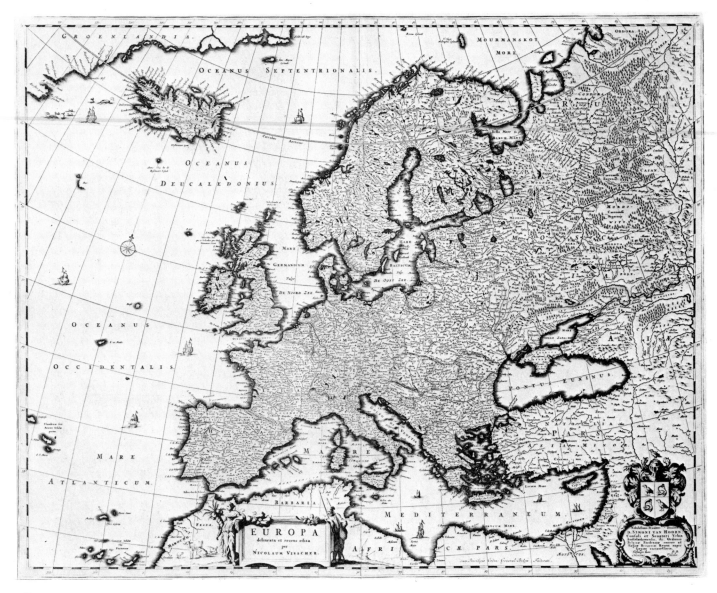

taken from the maps by John Speed in geographical content, and Blaeu copied the armorials, but there the similarity ends. The town plans which were a feature of the Speed maps are omitted by Blaeu and the decor is completely altered: Blaeu introduced cherubim and rural scenes. The maps are therefore in a totally different style. One has the impression that Speed was doing his best to fill the page with as much engraving as he possibly could, while the Blaeu maps are much more spacious and are laid out with artistry.

The maps of Scotland are of great importance because they were the first maps of the counties to be made, and they have an interesting history. Timothy Pont was a Scottish minister, who made a series of thirty-six maps in his spare time, but was unable to find a publisher. When he died in 1610, his widow carefully stored the precious manuscripts until she found a buyer in Robert Gordon of Stroloch, himself a surveyor. Gordon continued the work adding some of his own maps and making additions and corrections to Pont's maps. Even though Gordon greatly improved the maps he was not able to find a publisher in Britain and they were eventually printed and published by Blaeu in Amsterdam in 1654. They are similar in style to the English maps without the armorials, but some have the armorials of the person to whom the map is dedicated, and they are richly embellished with fine cartouches. It is difficult to say whether or not the venture was successful from Blaeu's point of view. Certainly his intention was that people would be tempted to buy the Scottish volume in order to complete the set. One would think that Blaeu would have published the maps with an English text, but this was never done, even though he had an eye on a wide market and published the atlas in Dutch, Flemish, Latin, French and Spanish.

Frederick de Wit: Sicily. Published in Amsterdam at about 1680. A well engraved map in the Dutch tradition, though this is one of the most decorative and one of the few to have inset plans.
Size: 19½ by 23¼ in., 50 by 59 cm.

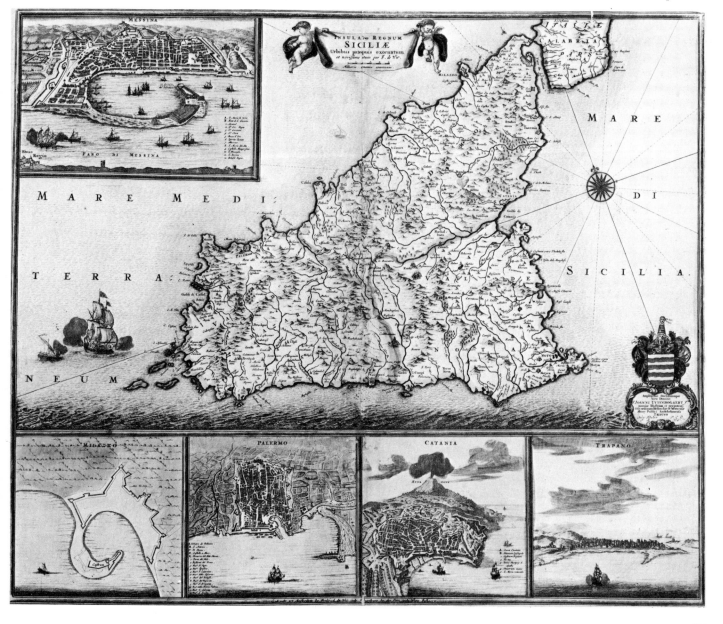

37

Possibly Blaeu thought that the English market had been satiated by the maps of Speed.

It is interesting to note that Blaeu developed his own printing press, one of the greatest advances in printing since presses were first used. He introduced a press with a sliding bed, enabling the printer to set up the plate, ink it, lay the paper and cover with layers of fabric outside the press itself, making it easier for him to see what he was doing and ensuring that the paper was perfectly flat. Blaeu was meticulous in obtaining perfect prints, he employed the finest labour and was obviously a very successful and shrewd businessman. His printing works contained no less than nine letter-press machines, and six copper-plate presses. After William's death Johann and Cornelius carried on the business with equal success. Cornelius died in 1642, only four years after his father, and Johann was left to continue on his own. Finally a disaster overtook him, the plant was severely burned in 1672, the majority of the irreplaceable plates were ruined. What little that was left was sold to Schenk and Valk, who also bought Jansson's business. The heyday of Dutch mapping was over but there were still many fine maps to be published, the makers who flourished were numerous and include the Allards, Van der Aa, de Wit, Covens and Mortier, Visscher, Ottens and Danckerts.

EARLY
BRITISH
COUNTY MAPS

While the Flemish and the Dutch were enjoying their successes, across the Channel the English had also begun a thriving map industry. They were inclined to keep their attentions within their own nation but, from the first surveys of small estates, some fine maps of the country were constructed. The two important early maps of the country which are on show are Matthew Paris's map of Great Britain, made at about 1250 and now housed in the British Museum, and Richard Gough's map of about 1335, now in the Bodleian Library in Oxford. The latter is surprisingly well detailed considering the basic surveying equipment available. The Paris map is drawn as if to illustrate, rather than to be accurate. Shortly after Ortelius had begun to publish his atlases, the monumental task of surveying the whole country was begun—the first national survey.

Christopher Saxton was one of the most influential map-makers in Britain. He has been described as the father of English map-making, but his importance was international because he was the first man to produce an atlas consisting of detailed maps of parts of the country: an example which was later followed in other parts of the world. Unfortunately, little is known of his private life. There is some doubt, about not only the date of his birth but also the place. He was probably born at Dunningley, near Wakefield in Yorkshire, in about 1542, and he died about 1610. For all that we know of his working life he was a surveyor, but he was fortunate in meeting Thomas Seckford, a Master of the Requests to Queen Elizabeth, during his education at Cambridge. It was Seckford's financing that allowed Saxton to make his series of maps.

Saxton's surveying began in 1573 and was completed in 1579 when the thirty-seven maps of the counties and a general map called 'Anglia' were published in atlas form. The maps bear dates from 1574 to 1579 and were issued as separate sheets as the plates were completed in order to recoup some

Christopher Saxton: Warwickshire and Leicestershire. 1579. One of the most attractive of Saxton's inland maps. It is dated in the right cartouche '1576', the date at which the engraving was completed. Seckford's coat of arms in the lower left corner bears both his mottoes.
Size: 15 by 19½ in., 38 by 50 cm.

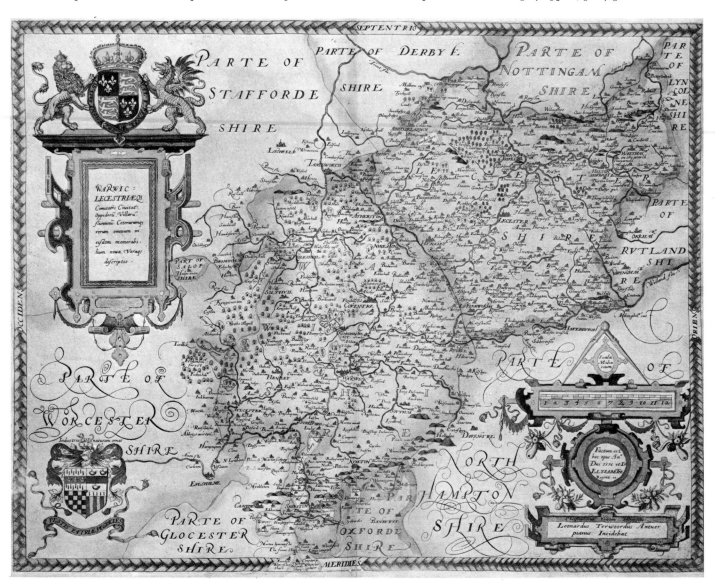

capital, though the price of four pence a sheet does seem trivial. The work had the blessing of Queen Elizabeth and Saxton was granted permission to travel anywhere he needed in order to survey the country, and to commandeer any help that he needed from the locals.

With the exception of Yorkshire, which was printed on two joined sheets of paper, all the maps are double page. In nine cases more than one county appears on the plate, grouped as follows:

Northamptonshire, Bedfordshire, Cambridgeshire, Huntingdonshire and Rutland:
Kent, Surrey, Sussex and Middlesex:
Warwickshire and Leicestershire:
Oxfordshire, Buckinghamshire and Berkshire:
Lincolnshire and Nottinghamshire:
Radnorshire, Breconshire, Cardiganshire, and Carmarthenshire:
Merionethshire and Montgomeryshire:
Denbighshire and Flintshire:
Anglesey and Caernarvonshire.

From the point of view of the collector this grouping is very unfortunate because the demand is greatly increased, particularly for the 'Home Counties' map, making it very difficult to obtain and very expensive. Each map is decorated with the arms of Queen Elizabeth I and of Saxton's sponsor, Thomas Seckford, whose motto *Pestis Patriae Pigrities* appears on all the maps dated up to 1576, and thereafter the motto changed to *Industria Naturam Ornat*. All the maps are dated except for that of Northumberland, which is probably 1577, the date which coincides with that of the sourrounding counties. Each map is signed 'Christopher Saxton descripsit'.

Six engravers' names appear on the set, eleven are anonymous, but it is reasonable to suppose that these were engraved by the same six. Two of

Detail of the cartouche in the lower right hand corner of the Webb edition of Saxton's map of Warwickshire and Leicestershire, the only distinguishing feature being the addition of the date. All the maps in the Webb edition are dated 1642 but they were published in 1646.

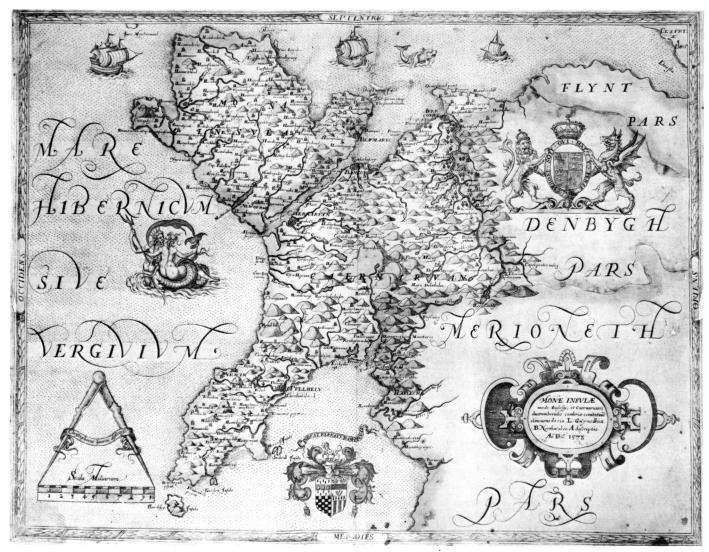

Christopher Saxton: Anglesey and Caernarvonshire. First edition of 1579.
Size: 14 by 19 in., 36 by 48 cm.

the most important were Remigius Hogenberg and Augustine Ryther. Hogenberg, the brother of Franciscus, who is renowned for the monumental series of bird's eye views entitled *Civitates Orbis Terrarum*, engraved nine maps and Ryther engraved five maps including the England and Wales. It has been suggested that Ryther engraved the rare twenty sheet map of England and Wales but this is pure supposition and there is no real proof at all. It has also been suggested that Saxton himself engraved some of the unsigned maps but this is unlikely because the quality of the engraving throughout the series is of a standard too high to be achieved by anyone but a professional. Ryther was born in Leeds and as he and Saxton lived in the same area they may well have known each other before they worked together on the series. Saxton could have picked up some fundamentals of engraving from Ryther: if this is so then it is possible that Saxton engraved the large map himself, the quality of the engraving not being as good as the maps in the atlas.

The remaining engravers were Cornelius de Hooghe, Nicholas Reynolds, Francis Scatter, and Nicholas Terwoort. With such a formidable list one would expect a high standard of engraving in the series, and for the most part this is indeed the case. For sheer spectacle it is difficult to imagine a more decorative map than the one of Cornwall, delicately engraved by Nicholas Terwoort and decorated, not only with ships and galleons, but with elaborate cartouches to display the title and armorials. The illustration is taken from a fine specimen in original state and in magnificent colour, typical of the style of the period, and shows how well the colours can be preserved. In comparison some of the inland maps are overcrowded with detail and have very little decoration on them, especially where the counties have been grouped together.

See colour illustration on pages 26 and 27.

The frontispiece, believed to have been engraved by Hogenberg, appears in two states, the second state is illustrated. Various alterations were made to the Queen's robes so that though the skirt is simpler, it folds more

See colour illustration on page 25.

42

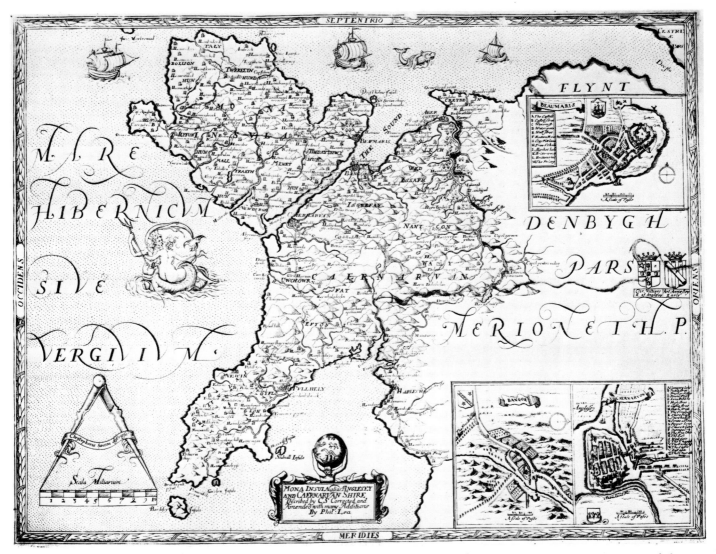

Christopher Saxton: Anglesey and Caernarvonshire. Philip Lea edition published in 1690. Various alterations have been made to the plates of the earlier edition which are referred to in detail in the text.

naturally over her knees. In the earlier state the Queen wears more elaborate jewellery which adds richness to the print, but the folds of the dress are so badly engraved that the Queen appears to be standing up instead of seated and is therefore out of proportion. The first state is rare, probably the Queen disliked the picture and ordered the alterations.

There was considerable demand for an atlas of this kind and it is therefore surprising that there were not more of the maps printed, particularly when one sees how popular and successful was John Speed's atlas, only a few years later. The early editions of Saxton are now very difficult to find and are consequently expensive. The 'Anglia' map, the 'Home Counties' and Cornwall will be priced in the region of £200, $480, for a good example, and even the map of Merionethshire and Montgomeryshire will cost about £60, $145.

In 1645 the atlas was re-issued by William Webb. Some alterations were made to the plates making it easy to pick out the edition. All the maps are dated 1642 except that of Oxfordshire, Buckinghamshire and Berkshire which is dated 1634. The arms of Queen Elizabeth I are changed to the arms of Charles I, and town plans (taken from the maps of John Speed) are added to the maps of Northumberland and Yorkshire. Webb's name appears only on the title page. The edition is as uncommon as the original and the prices are therefore high, being approximately one third less than for the first edition. Philip Lea published another edition in 1690. This time numerous alterations were made to the plates. The Royal Arms and some of the decoration are replaced by town plans, again from the maps of Speed. Some slight geographical alterations were made, but most important was the inclusion of roads, taken from John Ogilby's *Britannia*, published a few years earlier. The Lea edition was out of date even before it was published, but the roads were a feature of the maps and would have assisted the sales. There were still more editions. In 1720 the maps were re-printed and published by George Willdey, adding in some cases different maps by other

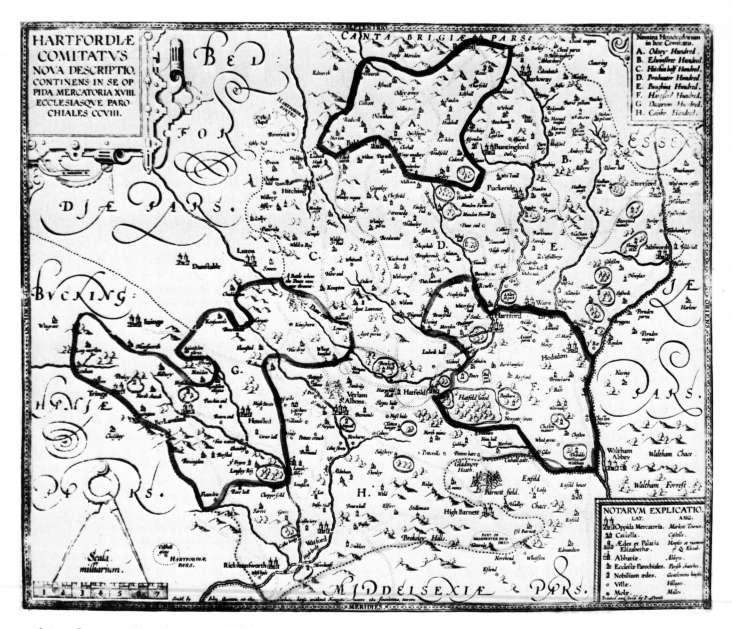

makers. In 1749 the atlas was published by Jefferys and finally by Dicey and Co. in 1770. Of all the editions the one by Lea is the most common.

The two illustrations of the Anglesey and Caernarvonshire map show how Lea erased the arms from the earlier plates and substituted plans of the cities and towns, and make an interesting comparison. The blacker appearance of the first edition is caused by the richer colouring, whereas the later map is coloured only in outline, but they were both printed from the same copper plate. Notice how the arms of Queen Elizabeth I and of Thomas Seckford have been removed and replaced by a new title and a plan of Beaumaris. The tails of the scroll of Seckford's motto are still just visible on the Lea plate. The plans probably served a more useful purpose than the decorative armorials and cartouches, but a lot of the charm has been lost, the new title being a poor substitute for the original. The additions to the map itself are the roads, after John Ogilby, and the markings of the hundreds. The plate has not worn very much, and there is little difference in the impressions of the two editions, a sign that few maps were printed.

John Norden was a contemporary of Saxton's, but he was unlucky never to have gained the exalted position of Saxton and was perpetually short of money. His county maps were confined to the south-east of England: Essex, Hampshire, Hertfordshire, Kent, Middlesex, Surrey and Sussex. The original maps are virtually unobtainable and should any more of them come to light, their rightful place would be in one of the museum collections. The reason for mentioning Norden here is that later editions are to be found, printed about one hundred years later by Peter Stent and later still by John Overton. These maps are superior to those of Saxton, more place names being marked and with slightly better accuracy. Norden's

The Anonymous map of Hertfordshire. Originally engraved in 1602-3, being extremely rare. Peter Stent owned the plates and published the maps from 1643-1660. Subsequently John Overton took over the plates and this edition was published about 1680. Detail taken from the map by John Norden. The first map of Hertfordshire to show roads.
Size: 15¼ by 19 in., 39 by 48 cm.

Colour illustrations on following pages:
Ortelius: America. 1587.
Gaspar Bailleul: The World. 1750.
Vrints: North Italy, published by Ortelius. 1608.

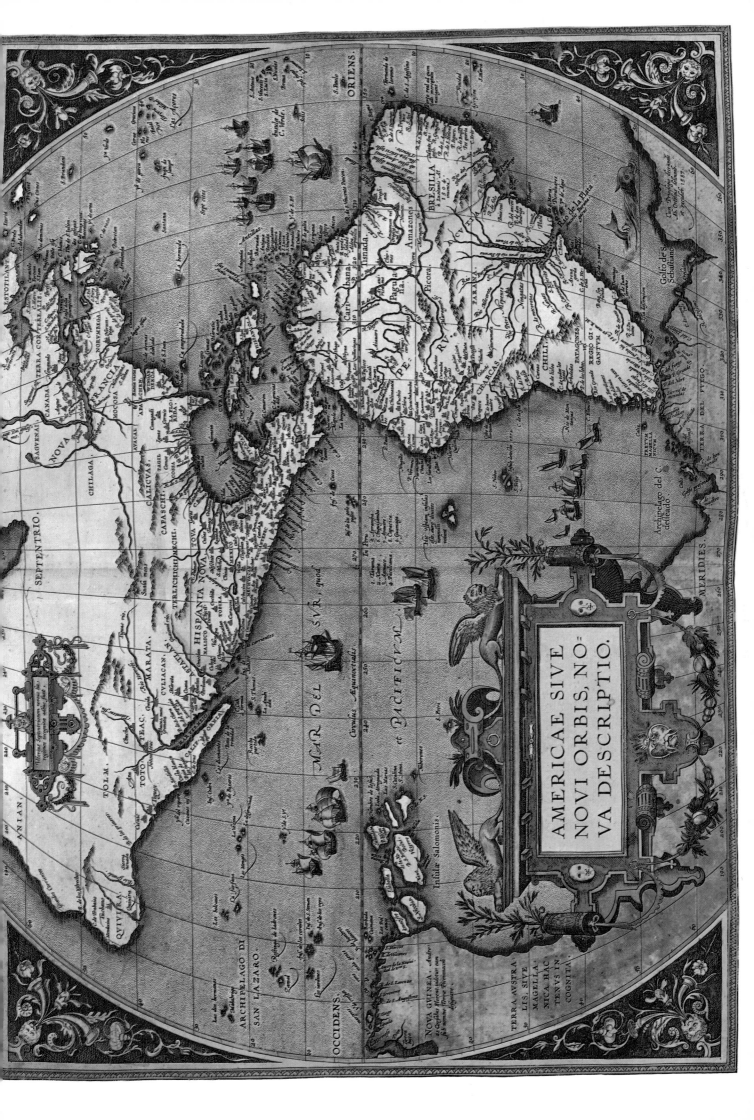

AMERICAE SIVE NOVI ORBIS, NO= VA DESCRIPTIO.

NOUVELLE
avec la representation des deux Emispheres Celestes, les Disques des Planetes. Dédiée à Messire BERTRAND RENÉ PALLU, Intendant de la
Disque du Soleil.
l'Hemisphere de la Terre eclairée par le Soleil au Solstice d'Eté
Sisteme de Copernique
Sisteme de Tico-brahe
Eclipse de Soleil.
le Soleil
la Lune
la Terre
Zone Froide Septentrional
POLE ARCTIQUE
TERRES ARCTIQUES
Cercle Polaire
Tropique du Cancer
MER DU NORD
MER DU SUD ou MER PACIFIQUE
EQUATEUR ou LIGNE
ISLES DE SALOMON
AMERIQUE SEPTENTRIONALE
AMERIQUE MERIDIONALE
PAYS DES AMAZONES
PARAGUAY
BRESIL
Tropique du Capricorne
NOUVELLE ZELANDE
Cercle Polaire
ANTARCTIQUE POLE Midy
Zone Froide Meridional
Zone Temperée
EUROPE
ASIE
HEMISPHERE
EMISPHERE

Delamonce Inv. et del. Avec Privilege du Roy

A LYON Chez I

MAPPE-MONDE
du Soleil, et de la Lune, et les diferents sentiments sur le mouvem.
Ville et Generalité de Lyon, par son trés humble et obeiss.º serviteur BAILLEUL

Disque de la Lune.

l'Hemisphere de la Terre éclairé par l'œil du Soleil.

Sisteme de Ptolomée

Sisteme de Descartes.

Eclipse de Lune.

BOREALE

AUSTRALE

TERRES AUSTRALES INCONNUES

Cercle Polaire

POLE ARCTIQUE

ANTARCTIQUE POLE

NOUVELLE HOLLANDE

MER DU SUD

MER DES INDES

AFRIQUE

AMERIQUE

de rue Merciere

John Norden: Hampshire. Published by
John Overton *c.* 1670. Illustrated is the
third state with Overton's imprint in the
lower right corner. The first edition was
published in 1580, the second by Peter
Stent *c.* 1660.

Size: 15½ by 16¾ in., 39 by 43 cm.

maps were preferred to Saxton's by William Camden for the *Britannia*, published in 1607, which will be discussed later on. Lack of finance prevented
Norden from publishing some of the work that he had completed. He had
grandiose plans for a series of county hand-books with descriptions and maps,
but he only published two, dealing with Middlesex in 1593 and Hertfordshire
in 1598. The detail included valuable information omitted by Saxton, main
roads being of particular interest and the key to symbols used was an innovation. He devised a system of numbering adjacent margins, marked off to
correspond with the scale of miles so that distances could easily be deter-
mined, and introduced a gazeteer section to simplify looking for specific
places. Norden was also responsible for the institution of the triangular
distance table, giving the distance between two given places. Both of these
systems are still being used today, and are most helpful aids to travelling.

The influence of Saxton and Norden was widespread. Every new set of
maps which appeared in Britain for the following hundred years and more
was based on their work, and the example set by Saxton of a national survey
was soon followed in other countries.

William Camden, the historian, was born in London in 1551. Although
he was not a map-maker, the edition of his *Britannia* published in 1607 contained a set of maps of the English and Welsh counties, and this is the first
series of individual maps of each county, since some of the Saxton maps were

made in groups. Since too, Saxton's maps are rare and extremely difficult to obtain, this series is the earliest which is generally available.

Camden was educated at Christ's Hospital and St Paul's School and in 1566 went to Magdalen College, Oxford, probably as Servitor or Chorister. He returned to London in 1571 and devoted himself to antiquarian studies. In 1575 he became the second master at Westminster School and Headmaster in 1593. During the school vacations he was able to travel about England, collecting material for the *Britannia*, which was first published in 1586 without the maps. It was immediately successful and the enlarged edition with the maps published in 1607 was guaranteed to be an even greater best seller. The maps are taken mainly from Saxton, whose name

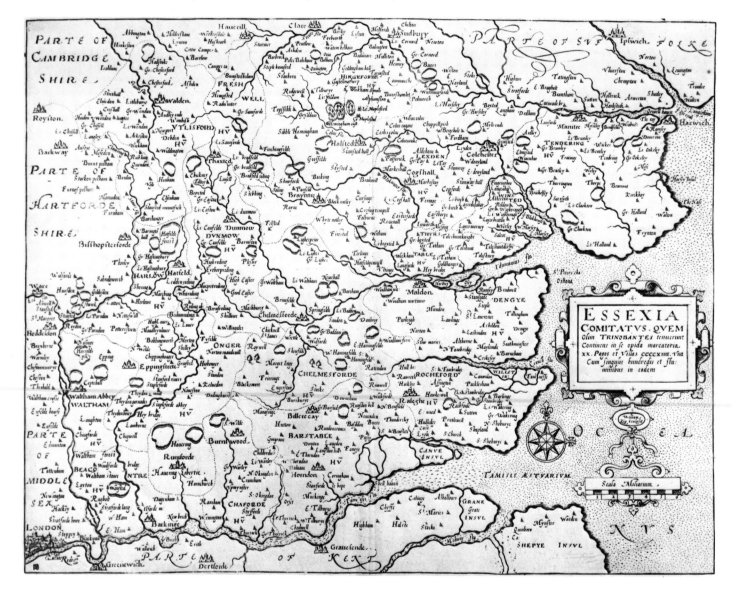

appears on most of them, but Camden preferred the maps of Norden wherever possible, that is to say, the maps of Hampshire, Hertfordshire, Middlesex, Kent, Surrey and Sussex. Pembrokeshire was taken from a map by George Owen, and the general maps, England/Wales, Scotland, and Ireland from Mercator. The average size of the maps was reduced to about ten inches by fourteen inches (25.5 by 35 cm) and were engraved by two well known workers, William Kip, who made 34 of the maps, and William Hole, who made 21. They are not as decorative as the first Saxton maps, but they are clearly engraved and most of them have attractive cartouches. The maps of the coastal counties are decorated with ships and serpents; particularly pleasing are those of Sussex, Dorset and Somerset.

There were three editions of Camden's *Britannia* with these maps. The first was printed with a text in Latin on the reverse and this sometimes shows through the thin paper, obscuring the printing on the face of the maps, a point which should be carefully watched. Although the first edition is usually the most desirable, the second edition was printed in 1610 without

Christopher Saxton: Essex. Engraved by William Kip and published in 1637, the third edition. Although the date is not actually printed on the face of the maps in this series, it is one of the easiest to date. The first edition has a Latin text on the reverse of each map, sometimes showing through the thin paper and obscuring the face of the print; the second is without the text; and the third has the small number inserted in the lower left hand corner. This series should not be confused with the earlier Saxton maps which are larger and very much rarer. William Kip and William Hole engraved this series from the detail of Saxton and Norden and William Camden published the maps in the first illustrated edition of his *Britannia*.
Size: 11 by 14 in., 28 by 36 cm.

50

Robert Morden: Staffordshire. Published in 1695. Morden made maps of all the counties in a similar style, though most of them are horizontal rather than vertical in shape. The map of Northamptonshire is horizontal and has the north point on the right of the map instead of the top. The three scales of miles were all in use at this period, hence the origin of the term 'a long mile'. This map is engraved by Sutton Nicholls and is one of the few in the series to be signed.
Size: 16¾ by 14½ in., 43 by 37 cm.

the text and the impressions are often very much sharper because the paper is not made grey by the text on the reverse. The third and last edition with these maps was published in 1637. They again had plain backs and most of them had small numbers inserted in the lower left-hand corner. Twelve of them, mostly of Wales, are without the number. The loose maps are therefore quite easy to date.

It is not known in what quantities the *Britannia* was published, but there seems to have been a greater number printed for each edition, the first edition being the most difficult to find. They are fairly common and therefore not as highly priced as one might expect for a map of this age. The single maps range from as little as £4 or £5 up to about £20, $10-50. In 1969 the com-

plete atlas could be bought for under £500, $1,200.

In 1695, after a long gap, a new edition of the *Britannia* was published. The English translation of the history was by Bishop Edmund Gibson. The whole format of the work was changed and contained a new set of maps by Robert Morden. It continued to be popular, probably even more so than the earlier volumes, and Morden's maps are numerous. Their prices are just half those of the Saxton edition. Artistically they are less appealing than the earlier maps and for the first time, the decoration has given way to more functional details. The cartouches are usually highly coloured, but, in comparison to the Dutch maps, they are crudely engraved. When the boundaries of the hundreds and the borders of the maps are coloured they are very pleasing.

Geographical detail has improved as, although Morden did not carry out a survey himself, he made every possible use of whatever reliable material he could find and he sent his manuscripts to people in various parts who he considered would be able to make additions and corrections. This was quite successful, save for a few careless mistakes, like Quare on the Wiltshire map. Ogilby's *Britannia* again was used to provide the necessary information for the roads and this was the first county atlas to include them, shown either by a single or a double engraved line on the map. There had not been a new survey conducted since the publication of Speed and these maps were therefore a great improvement on any of those by Morden's predecessors. Gibson refers to Morden in his preface: 'Upon the whole, we need not scruple to affirm, that they are by much the fairest and most correct that have yet appear'd'.

Most of the maps are of a uniform size, about 14 inches by 16 inches (35 by 40·5 cm). The maps of Kent and Norfolk are folding, measuring half as long again as the other sheets. Several of the maps were just wide enough to be trimmed by the binder, and when looking at complete volumes, special attention should be made to the maps of Devonshire, Hertfordshire and Scotland. The work was published by Abel Swale, Awnsham and John Churchill, who were leading booksellers, and their names appear on the maps. The engravers Sutton Nichols and John Sturt put their names to a few of the maps, though they probably engraved the complete set between them, there being a marked similarity of style all through the series. The first edition consisted of fifty maps of the English counties, one of Scotland, one of Ireland, two of Wales divided north and south, and three general maps.

A second edition was published in 1722 with some minor changes. The map of the whole of Scotland is replaced by two maps, one of the south part and one of the north. One would think that this arrangement would be preferable, being on a larger scale, but unfortunately the best use was not made of the paper, the maps were made to overlap and too much territory is covered by both maps. These were not by Morden but by Andrew Johnston. They lack the charm of Morden's maps, the titles being enclosed in rectangular ruled lines instead of a cartouche. The map of North Wales is replaced by an anonymous map and suffered the same fate as the Scottish maps. There were subsequent re-issues in 1753 and in 1772, following the same format as the 1722 edition, though these are comparatively unusual, because during the 18th century there were some magnificent surveys undertaken, with much improved detail, superceding the outline maps. When the maps are loose they are difficult to date and a rough guide is useful. The majority of the first editions were printed on a thin, crisp paper, generally with narrow margins. There were some which were printed on a very fine quality thick paper of a large size, probably special copies. The later editions were also printed on a thick paper but of a much coarser texture. The impressions are always clear, despite the fact that large numbers were printed. As necessary the plates were re-engraved to keep the prints sharp.

John Speed has already been mentioned several times. He produced the best known, the most appealing and most popular of all the early maps. He was born in Cheshire in 1552, and like his father he became a tailor, and was admitted to the Freedom of the Merchant Taylor's Company in 1580. He prospered and in his leisure took a keen interest in antiquities and historical research. Between the years 1598 and 1600 he presented various

maps to the Queen and to the Merchant Taylors' Company. The latter acknowledged his 'Very rare and ingenious capacitee in drawing and setting forth mappes and genealogies and other very excellent inventions'. His work came to the notice of the wealthy Sir Fulke Greville, who agreed to make him an allowance in order that he should be free to study, with the object of writing a history of Great Britain. This was published in 1611 in conjunction with *The Theatre of the Empire of Great Britain*, which contained the now famous maps. Whilst the work was published separately the pagination was continuous and *The Theatre* was intended purely as a prologue to illustrate the history, but the latter has now been virtually forgotten and the current price for a well bound copy is in the region of a mere £15, $36.

The maps contained in *The Theatre* had been commenced in the early part of the century, and many were issued before 1611 as separate sheets. They may have been in the nature of proofs in some instances but a number found their way into the hands of the public. These are without text on the reverse and as the mortality rate for these loose maps was undoubtedly high the surviving few are greatly prized.

The complete set consists of general maps of England, Wales, Scotland, and Ireland, individual maps of the English and Welsh counties and of the four Irish provinces. Nearly all the county maps are based on the surveys of Saxton and Norden, those of Ireland and Scotland being from Mercator's maps of 1595. Speed, however, made great improvements and additions. He has been criticised for being a plagiarist, he admits that 'I have put my sickle into other mens corne', but he acknowledges his sources where possible, as in the cartouches of the maps, some of which read for example: 'Described by J. Norden and augmented by J. Speed'. His information was obtained from every other available source, from notes made by local antiquaries, from regional manuscript maps and from his own personal observations made on his travels. He introduced entirely new features into the maps. Plans of the principal towns and views of the important buildings

John Speed's map of Dorset, published in 1611. This is one of the most decorative of the Speed maps, and is a good example for illustration purposes. Nearly all of the series show maps of the principal towns and contain armorials. The map was engraved by Jodocus Hondius, whose name appears at the centre of the bottom. The sea is usually 'hatched' in the same manner and the ships and serpents are typical of the work of Hondius. The map is dated 1610 at the top right hand corner. This was the date of engraving and cannot be relied upon as an accurate date of the printing of the map. The later editions were printed from the same plates and bore the same date until it was altered for the edition published by Bassett and Chiswell in 1676, when the second '1' was simply changed into a '6', to read '1660'.

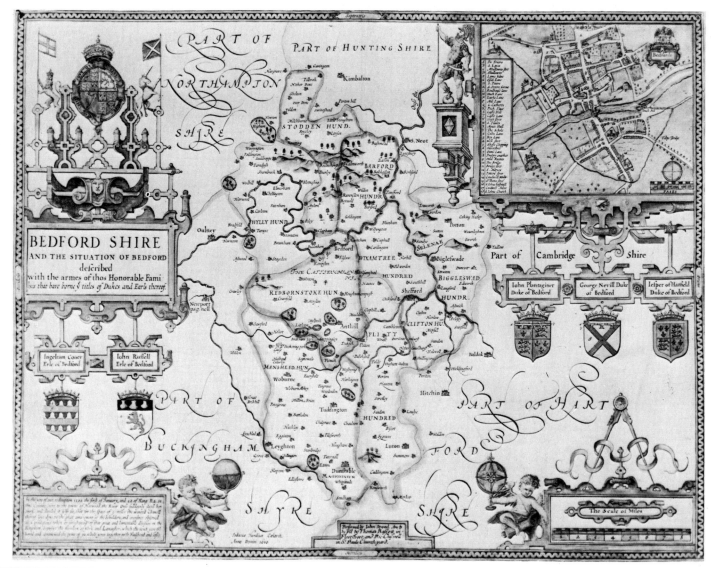

were inserted in the corners of each map, coats of arms of the families who had borne the county title, college arms in the cases of Cambridgeshire and Oxfordshire, and illustrations of the inhabitants in contemporary costumes in the borders of the general maps of the Kingdoms. The counties are divided into hundreds and many place names are added. The sites of battles are marked with a tent, or are shown as clashing ranks of soldiers. On the reverse of each sheet he printed an historical description of the area covered by each map, and included notes regarding the length and circumference of each county, the principal palaces, castles, religious houses, the 'Ayre' and 'Soyle', the ancient inhabitants and important battles. All the places marked on the face of the map are listed on the back, followed by the name of the hundred in which the place is contained, serving as a guide.

The maps were sent to Amsterdam to be engraved and printed. The majority were engraved by Jocodus Hondius, whose name appears on thirty-three of the maps. Although most of them bear the date 1610, the work was commenced in 1605, the year after Hondius had returned to Amsterdam from London, where he had been living in exile since 1583. No doubt he had worked with Speed during his stay in England and as an engraver he surpassed any Englishman of the time. Hondius acquired the presses and plates from Mercator's establishment in 1604—the presses for such a large work as these folio-sized maps were not available in England until a later date.

In 1611 the labour of many years was offered to the public by the publishers John Sudbury and George Humble. The volume must have represented a very large capital investment, unfortunately there is no accurate record of the price of the first edition, but the later edition of 1627, possibly cheaper than the first edition, sold for £2, at that time a very large sum of money. The venture was successful—the maps sold more readily than those of Saxton, and almost as well as the Camden edition which was priced more

John Speed's map of Bedfordshire, published in 1676. The imprint at the bottom reads 'Performed by John Speed. Are to be sold by Thomas Bassett in Fleetstreet, and Ric. Chiswell in St. Pauls Churchyard'. Each publisher engraved his own name in the space and this is one way of determining the date of publication.

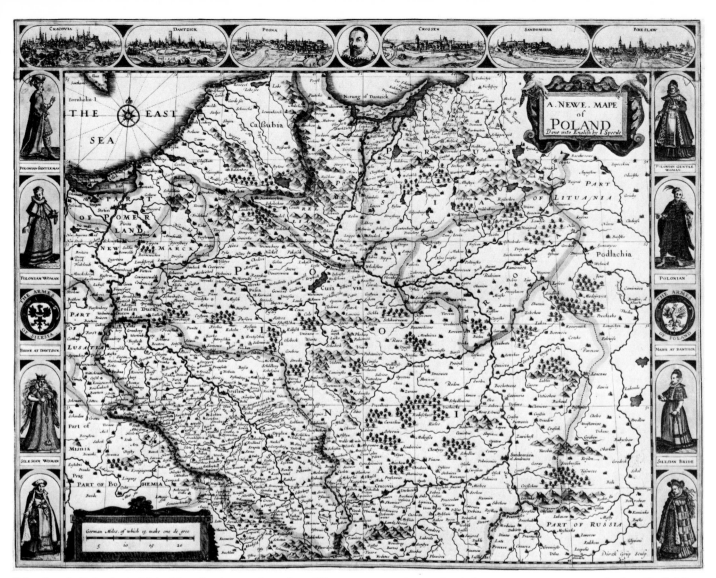

John Speed: Poland. Published in 1627 in the *Prospect of the most Famous Parts of the World*. This is typical of the style of the maps in the *Prospect*, with the costumes of the inhabitants down the sides and the views of the cities across the top. Like the English county maps there is a descriptive text on the reverse.

Size: 16 by 20 in., 41 by 51 cm.

cheaply. The maps were required for many purposes and the Civil Wars gave further impetus to their sale. Pepys, when he was Lord of the Admiralty and in search of timber for ship building, writes in 1622 that he 'turned to the Forest of Deane in Speede's mappes and there showed me how it lies'. In spite of the competition from the fine maps of the English counties imported from Amsterdan by Blaeu and Jansson from 1645 to 1670, Speed's maps continued to be best sellers. The maps were re-issued many times, the last recorded edition being in 1770, one hundred and sixty years after the first. By that time the plates were extremely worn and also the maps had been superseded. Consequently very few of them were sold and now they have a value as collector's pieces, worth almost as much as the first editions. This last edition was published by Dicey, who also published the last edition of Saxton, in the same year.

The editions were as follows:

1611 and 1614   The imprint bears the names of Sudbury and Humble, or Humble alone. The paper is not usually as white as some maps of the period, but a mellow off-white. The impressions are always good, the fine detail in the engraving being clear and black. Unless the origin of a loose map is known, they can be difficult to date. This can be done by comparison of the text with a known edition. The text was type-set and was therefore not retained from one edition to another. Although the wording is the same, the layout is always slightly different, even the initial illuminated letter is changed.

1616   One of the easiest to date as the text on the reverse is in Latin. This is the only edition which is not in English. Otherwise the face of the maps is not changed.

1627   The maps still bear the same imprint though Sudbury had died by

this time, and Humble published on his own. The paper is whiter, thinner and crisper. This was the first edition to include the maps of other parts of the world.

1646 The imprint is changed to 'William Humble'—an uncommon edition. The plates show signs of wear by this time, but the impressions are good.

1662 The imprints read 'Roger Rea'. Many of the dates of 1610 are altered to 1666. Some editions are without text on the reverse.

1676 The most common edition, published by Bassett and Chiswell. By this time the plates of the British maps begin to show serious signs of wear. The maps of the other parts of the world are still good impressions. This is the first edition of the maps of parts of America.

1713 The imprint is changed yet again to John Overton. Though the roads were added to the maps for the first time, it did not appear to have any great effect on the sales and there were not many of the maps printed.

1770 The edition published by Dicey. Poor, very pale impressions, not recommended except as interest pieces for collectors.

The maps contained in the extention of the atlas published in 1627, and titled *The Prospect of the Most Famous Parts of the World*, were very similar in style to the British maps. Round the borders of most of them are views of the principal towns and cities, and show the inhabitants in their national costume. Shipping, sea-monsters and wild animals decorate the maps. There is also a text on the reverse, covering the whole sheet, but the index of place names is omitted. This was the first attempt of an Englishman to enter into the market of maps of other parts of the world. Speed was competing with the Dutch, who at the time had no other opposition. The venture was probably successful, judging by the fact that the later publishers continued to print the maps.

Speed's maps were used for many subsequent series. The Dutchmen Blaeu and Jansson and the Englishman Richard Blome published complete sets of the counties without altering Speed's detail. Blaeu and Jansson did not always copy Speed's spelling exactly. Blome freely admitted that he published a volume of maps 'which are the epitome of John Speed'.

In 1627 George Humble published another atlas which erroneously became known as 'miniature Speed'. In fact he had nothing to do with the venture, and the detail of the maps was not his. They were published by Peter Keere, known also as Petrus Kaerius, several of the maps being signed by that name, or Pieter van den Keere. The collection of forty-four maps of the British Isles appears to have been published in Amsterdam between 1605 and 1610. The first edition is extremely rare and is not likely to be found on the market, the second edition of 1617 is not so rare but still unusual, the third edition was the one of 1627. The pocket edition, measuring only about 7 inches by 4 inches (18 by 10 cm), was titled: *England, Wales, Scotland and Ireland Described and Abridged with ye Historic Relation of things worthy of memory from a farr larger Vouloume Done by John Speed*. Humble was a businessman, he used Speed's name because that was the known name of the period. His intention was to provide an atlas for those who could not afford the costly folio-sized maps. There were some differences between the Humble edition and the Keere, mainly that Keere followed the format of Saxton, grouping the same counties together as Saxton had done. In the Humble edition there is one map for each county. Scotland was covered in six maps, taken in detail from Mercator, the mainland divided into four maps and the islands into two. The 1627 edition included maps of other parts of the world. There were several later editions up until 1676, published to coincide with the dates of the folio edition. Though the prints are plainly engraved and are without any extra decor, they are not without a certain charm and an example is worth inclusion in any collection. They can be bought for £3 to £10, $7-25.

Keere also engraved other maps, the most important of which was his map of the world on Mercator's Projection. He worked on Norden's map of Middlesex for *Speculam Britanniae* and his series of county maps during his sojourn in England, where he probably met Hondius. Later Keere set

Peter Keere: Devonshire. Published in 1627.
The atlas was known as 'Miniature Speed',
because Speed was the known name of the
period, but in fact there was no connection
except that some of the later editions were
issued by the same publishers.
Size: 3½ by 4½ in., 9 by 12 cm.

up a business in Amsterdam as print maker and seller and collaborated with Hondius on some of his maps. He also engraved a number of portraits.

Richard Blome has the reputation of being the plagiarist par excellence, but although none of his work was his own, he published some very decorative maps, engraved in an unusual free style, while the lettering is not as clear as the work expected of this period. His most important work was a small folio volume of county maps under the title of *Britannia*, which has been described as 'an entire piece of theft', and Blome freely admitted that they were the 'epitome of John Speed'. The maps have attractive cartouches and arms of the subscribers who paid Blome the sum of £4 for the privilege of having the map dedicated to them. Blome was never short of subscribers, and many of the dedications change from one edition to the next. Each edition bears the date of 1673 on the title page and it is therefore difficult to tell how many different editions were actually published. Sometimes copies are seen with the arms pasted over the top of existing arms. In 1681 Blome published a smaller volume of county maps which he titled *Speed's maps Epitomised*, a cheaper edition but otherwise of no added importance. This was re-issued in 1685 and 1691 by Blome, and in 1715 by Thomas Taylor in his volume *England Exactly Described*. In 1670 a general atlas was published, titled *The Geographical Description of the Most Famous Parts of the World*, with maps after Sanson, and no less attractive than the county maps.

John Ogilby was a colourful personality and a man of great charm, energy, wisdom, courage and organising ability. His life was adventurous, and the several calamities which overtook him seem only to have increased his determination. He was a man of many parts, and his various vocations included that of dancing instructor, tutor, theatre owner, scholar, translator, poet, playwright, printer, historian and map-maker. He did not embark on the last profession until he was over sixty years of age, but it was in that capacity that he achieved lasting fame and we shall see how his work in-

fluenced the progress of map-making to such an extent that his ideas are still adopted today.

Ogilby was born in Edinburgh in 1600, and his early life must have been hard. His father was imprisoned for debt, but the illustrious son worked and saved, and what he saved he risked in lottery tickets in connection with the Virginian Plantations. He was fortunate, his winnings not only secured his father's release but allowed him an apprenticeship to a dancing master. His success with his fashionable clientele was proved by the fact that he soon was able to set up as a teacher on his own account. A leg injury cut short these activities but he had met many influential people and he was soon employed as the tutor to the children of the Earl of Stafford, Lord Deputy of Ireland. His next venture was a theatre in Dublin which appears to have been successful until the Civil War in 1641. He lost his theatre and his money, narrowly escaped with his life and returned to London quite destitute. He moved to Cambridge and was befriended by several scholarly gentlemen and we find him translating Virgil and composing poetry.

When Charles II came to the throne, Ogilby was soon in favour, and was appointed to organise part of the Coronation ceremonies. In 1662 he returned to Dublin, having been appointed Master of the Revels in Ireland, no doubt a sinecure. He built another theatre only to have it closed when he was involved in an unfortunate incident regarding the employment of players from the Royal Company. Back in London again he set up as a printer in Whitefriars and produced a number of fine illustrated books. The King issued a proclamation forbidding anyone to copy them within a period of fifteen years. In order to encourage sales Ogilby organised a lottery under Royal patronage, the prizes being his own books.

A national calamity once more overtook Ogilby. His house, presses and entire stock were destroyed in the Great Fire of 1666. Opportunist as he was he accepted an appointment by the City of London as one of the four 'sworn viewers' to survey the burnt out area, a project which had become necessary in order to determine ownership of disputed property. This resulted in a

Richard Blome: Somerset. 1673. Blome was a plagiarist and he confesses to the fact that his maps were the epitome of John Speed. The quality of the engraving is not up to the standard of Speed but the maps have a charm of their own, and are engraved in a pleasant free style. The armorials change almost from map to map; often maps of the same editions appear with another set of arms pasted over the original.
Size: 9½ by 13 in., 24 by 33 cm.

Right
John Ogilby: The Roads from York to Whitby and Scarborough. 1675-98. The last of the 100 road maps, numbered in the lower right hand corner, and one of the best examples of the maps. The map is read from the lower left hand corner, following the road up to the top of the strip and then on to the bottom of the next strip, and so on. The miles are marked along the route, at a scale of 1 inch to 1 mile. The dots in the centre of the road are furlongs, two dots mark the mile; the dotted line at the edge of the road indicates an unfenced road, the solid line being fenced, the same convention as is used by the Ordnance Survey today. The hills are shown in a novel fashion, the apex being the top of the hill, thus, moving North-East from Pickering the traveller

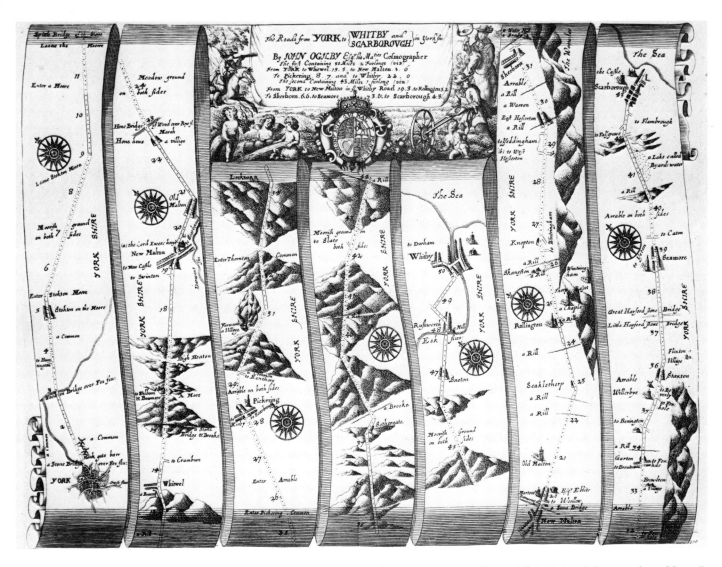

The Roads from YORK to WHITBY and SCARBOROUGH in Yorkshire

By JOHN OGILBY Esq. His Majesties Cosmographer

complete survey which was eventually published by Morgan in 1667. It is a magnificent plan measuring 9 feet by 7 feet (315 by 245 cm), on a scale of about twenty-five inches to the mile.

Meanwhile Ogilby had rebuilt his house and he had been granted the title of King's Cosmographer and Geographic Printer. Soon after the fire he commenced his great work which appeared after years of study and labour in 1675, under the title of *Britannia Volume the First, or an illustration of the Kingdom of England and the Dominion of Wales: By a Geographical and Historical Description of the roads thereof. Actually Admeasured and Delineated in a Century of whole-sheet Copper-Sculps. Accomadated with the Ichnography of Several Cities and Capital Towns; and compleated by Accurate Account of the more Remarkable Passages of Antiquity together with a novel discourse of the present State by John Ogilby Esq., His Majesty's Cosmographer and Master of Majesty's Revels in the Kingdom of Ireland.* This title covered the three volumes that it was intended should be published: the first contained the road maps, the second was to be 'the Ichnography of the Several Cities', and the third 'the more Remarkable Passages of Antiquity'. Ogilby died in 1675, the year that the first volume was printed, and the work was never completed. The first volume of maps, however, was sufficient to establish his name for all time as a map-maker.

In spite of the importance of the roads no series of county maps made up to this time had given any indication of the distances between towns or shown the routes from one to another. Some of the main roads had been included in the Anonymous maps, but not in any detail. It was this obvious need which impelled Ogilby to commence his task which was undertaken by the express desire of King Charles II, whose arms are incorporated in the cartouches of the maps. He underestimated the demand that would be made for this information, and it was necessary to publish two further editions in the same year and another in 1698. Before long they were copied in various forms by other map-makers, abridged, altered in form and made into pocket size, but all based on Ogilby's *Britannia*.

covers about a mile along the flat before encountering a long hill, another mile, before a mile of flat and then a shorter uphill stretch and followed by a long downhill stretch, very easy to understand and can be read at a glance. The type of terrain is indicated, for example 'Moorish on both sides'. Each strip has its own compass rose, on this particular map they all point more or less in the same direction, but on some of the maps the road may swing round and by varying the compass roses the strips are kept in parallel. The cartouche is attractive, with a dedication to Charles II who supported the work, and whose arms are shown below the title of most of the maps. Only four of them illustrate the surveying instruments.
Size: 13 by 17 in., 33 by 45 cm.

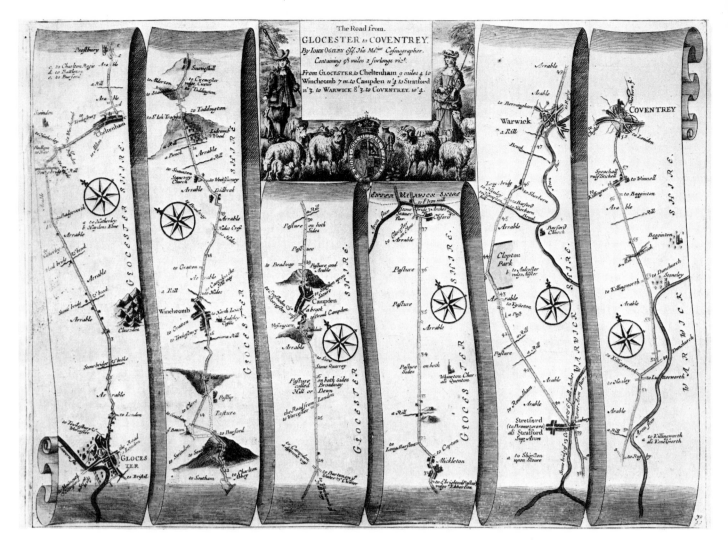

The compilation of the four separate issues differed, but the maps are unaltered except that on the re-issues numbers were added to the plates on the bottom right hand corner, numbered 1 to 100, a most useful addition. The first two editions have an engraved title by Wenceslaus Hollar, of some merit because it illustrates some of the instruments used in map-making.

Ogilby was primarily concerned with the post roads, and the routes he surveyed were those which radiate from London and those which connect the most important cities and provincial towns. Each of the one hundred maps covers a distance of about seventy miles and the longer routes are divided into four or five sheets. It may appear that some of them begin in small and unimportant places, the reason being that the first part of the route has already been covered on another map. They are engraved on representations of parchment scrolls, of which there are six or seven on each map. The route is followed upwards from the left hand strip to recommence at the bottom of the next.

At this time the mile was not of a universal length throughout the British Isles, and whilst London and Westminster had adopted the statute mile of 1,760 yards, the old British mile of 2,428 yards was still in use in other parts of the country. It is interesting to note that the three scales of miles appear on most of Robert Morden's maps published at about this time. Ogilby realised the stupidity of the continuance of such varying miles and used the statute mile throughout the series. It was through his influence that most maps of Great Britain made subsequently were based on the statute mile. The scale is one inch to one mile, the miles not only being marked but numbered, each mile is divided into furlongs indicated by dots in the centre of the road. Each strip is provided with a compass rose, the north point varying in order that, though a road may alter course, the strips would remain in parallel. The road is marked by a double line if fenced and by a pricked line if unfenced, the convention retained and used by the Ordnance Survey today. Turnings off the main road are shown and in many cases the destination is named. Towns, villages, mansions, castles, churches, mills, beacons,

John Ogilby: The Road from Gloucester to Coventry. 1675-98. Another, and a more typical map, from the *Britannia*. Size: 13 by 17 in., 33 by 44 cm.

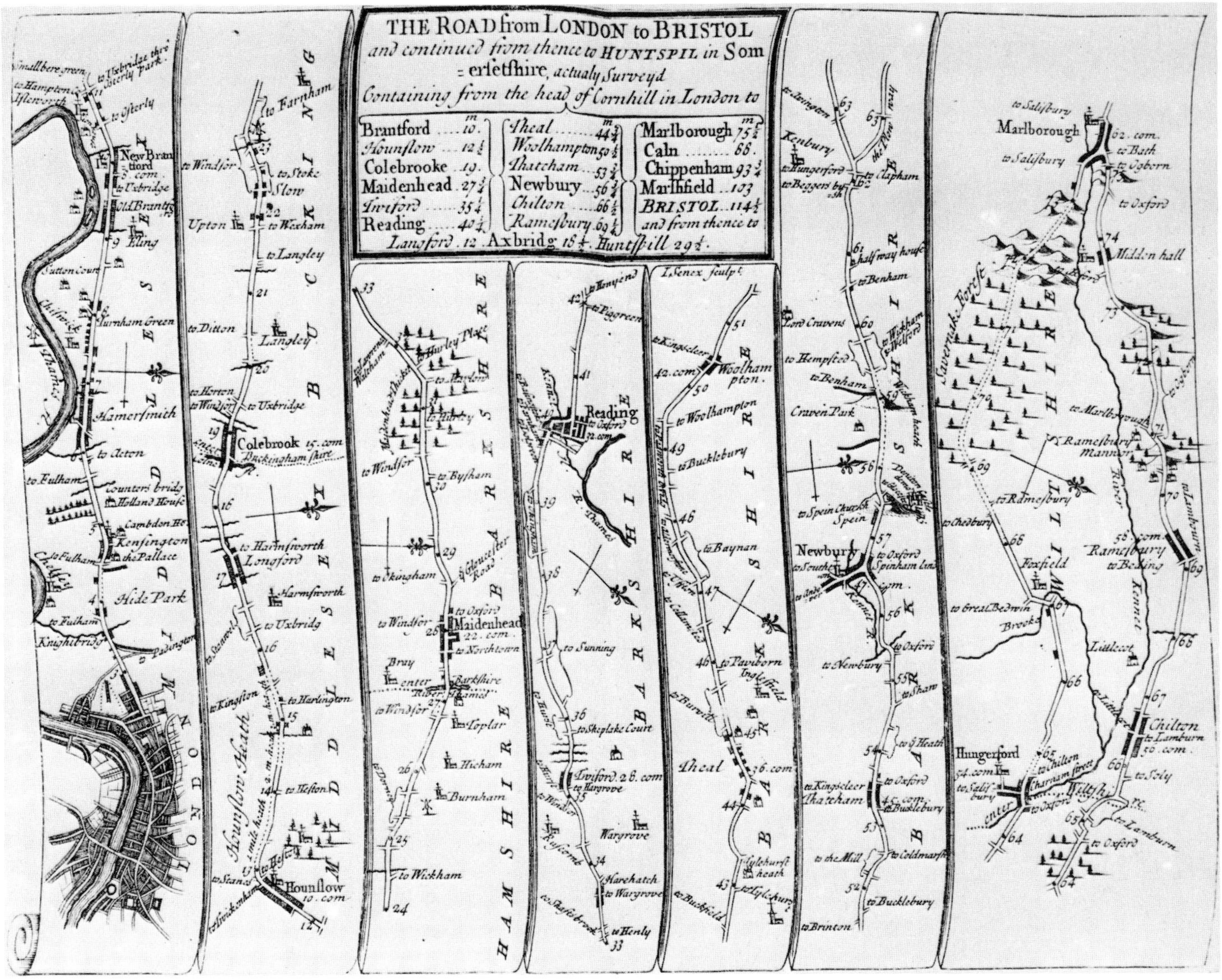
THE ROAD from LONDON to BRISTOL
and continued from thence to HUNTSPIL in Som
=erfetshire, actualy Surveyd
Containing from the head of Cornhill in London to
Brantford ..... 10.
Hounflow 12½
Colebrooke .. 19.
Maidenhead . 27½
Twiford 35¼
Reading 40¾
Theal 44¾
Woolhampton 50½
Thatcham 53¾
Newbury 56¾
Chilton 66½
Ramesbury 69½
Marlborough 75½
Caln .... 88.
Chippenham 93¾
Marshfield .. 103
BRISTOL .. 114½
and from thence to
Langford . 12 . Axbridg 18½ . Huntspill 29½.
I. Senex sculp.
Hounslow
Colebrook
Maidenhead
Reading
Newbury
Hungerford
Marlborough

Senex road map showing part of the route from London to Bristol, the remainder of the route appears on the following sheet in the volume. There is only a single cartouche for each route and therefore some of the pages are plainer than this example.
Sheet size: 6 by 8 in., 15 by 21 cm.

gallows, and woods are indicated, usually pictorially. Bridges are noted with an arched line and the size of the rivers can be guessed by the engraved wavy lines, one to three according to the size of the river. Hills are shown diagramatically, the apex signifying the direction of the incline, and the size of the triangle indicating the size of the hill, thus the traveller could tell at a glance the type of terrain which lay in front of him, an important factor when travelling with horses. At the top centre of each map is an ornamental cartouche containing the names of the places covered on that particular sheet. Four of the maps have a cartouche like the one illustrated, showing some mapping instruments. The wheel is a measuring wheel which records the number of revolutions on a dial at the top, one revolution being half a pole, or $8\frac{1}{4}$ feet. Above the wheel is a man with a quadrant, and the cherubic boy is holding a section of a surveyor's chain. One feels that the rider on the left must have had a specific task. He was probably an out-rider, marking and naming the landmarks seen from the road which were all important in helping the traveller to find his way.

These intriguing maps do not have the decorative appeal of some other maps, but they make up for it in interest and should be included in any collection. The importance they played on the future of mapping cannot be over-emphasised: not only were they the first of all road maps in Britain, but such publications had not been contemplated in any other country. As with all other maps the prices vary from map to map, those covering the heavily populated areas are the most expensive, and those with the measuring wheel are particularly in demand. In 1969 the value of the complete work reached £650, $1,550, the single maps being from £3 to £12, $7-30, a good investment. Anyone buying an Ogilby for the sake of owning one is advised to choose an example which includes all the features which he devised.

The Road from
PRESTAIN to CARMARTHEN.
Containing 46 comp. & 61 measd Miles.

From Prestain	com	mea		com	mea
New Radnor...	4	5'4	Llanimdofry...	26	34'6
Bealth...	12	15'6	Abermarles...	31	41
Ludlowvaugh	21	27'6	Rue Raddor....	37	49
Carmathen 46:61.					

A MAP of RADNOR SHIRE

The Hundreds
1 Knighton
2 Rayadergony
3 Kevenllice
4 Radnor
5 Collovini
6 Paincastle

Map of Radnorshire engraved by Emanuel Bowen and published in *Britannia Depicta, or Ogilby Improved*, by Owen. On the reverse is the road map, and unfortunately only a few of them refer to the same county as appears on the face.
Overall size: 7½ by 4¾ in., 19 by 12 cm.

While Ogilby was working on the *Britannia* he published two other works, an atlas of America and another of Africa, both published in 1670. The small folio maps are attractively decorated, in a style close to that of Blaeu.

Following the publication of the *Britannia* a number of further road books were soon printed, based on the work of Ogilby. In 1719 John Senex produced a replica on a smaller scale and without the decorative cartouches. A more attractive work is the *Britannia Depicta*, published in 1720. It contains a series of county maps as well as the road maps, engraved by Bowen and published by Owen and Bowen. The work is referred to in detail in the section on Bowen.

18th & 19th Century British Maps

Herman Moll was born in Holland and he arrived in London in 1690 where he spent all his life engraving and publishing maps. He worked as an engraver for various publishers before he began publishing his own maps. His most important work was *The World Described; or a New and Compleat Atlas*, a series of twenty-seven large folding two sheet maps, each measuring about 22 inches by 38 inches (56 by 96 cm). They are generally folded in the centre and each side folded into the middle, to make a tall narrow volume. Often the condition is poor because the three folds do not withstand heavy use, and sometimes copies are seen which have been laid on canvas, a help to preserving them. The atlas is one of the most important to be printed in England in the 18th century, the maps are well engraved, have good clear lettering and attractive cartouches. Moll claimed that the information was unsurpassed: several of the maps have interesting advertisements printed on them, for example, on the world map: 'This is very carefully laid down from ye newest observations and unquestionable authorities; most, if not all, of which have been approved by ye Royal Society here in London, the Royal Academy of Paris, and many curious gentlemen of other nations . . .'. He goes on to say that Sanson's maps are 'Notoriously false'. Apart from the fact that he showed California as an island, like his contemporaries, he did use the best information that was available to him. The American maps are particularly important and will be discussed in the chapter on America. On the map of South America is printed another advertisement: 'The World is nothing more scandalously imposed upon than by maps put out by ignorant pretenders, who most falsely and impudently assume the titles of ye Queen's Geographers, more particularly they have published two several copies, each on two sheets, of a falsely projected French map of South America done in Paris in 1703, and to deceive mankind have dedicated both to Dr. Halley, Savilian Professor of Geometry at Oxford, and they pretend in ye dedication that it is corrected by his own discoveries. These copies place C. Horn in Lat. 56 and make ye Long. between C. Horn and C. St. Augustin 27 deg. whereas ye Doctor lays C. Horn in Lat. 57.30 and makes ye long between C. Horn and C. St. Augustin 45. so that these false maps differ from Dr. Halley's and all other late observations, in ye Lat. of C. Horn 1½ and in ye Long. between ye said Capes 18 deg. and consequently make our sailing to ye South Sea less by above a Thousand Miles than it really is, every body may judge easily what a dangerous consequence these maps may produce

Herman Moll: North America. Published about 1720. The scene on the left shows the cod fishing industry in Newfoundland; the fish flaked out to dry in the sun is seen in the foreground. Notice that California is marked as an island and the North Eastern part of the country is labelled 'Parts unknown'. Size: 23 by 38 in., 59 by 97 cm.

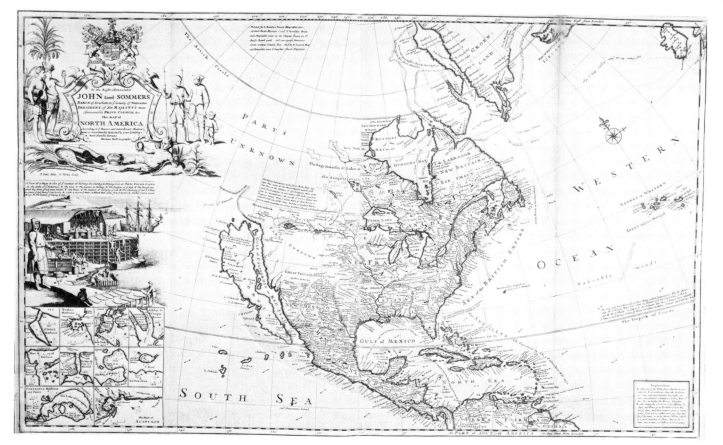

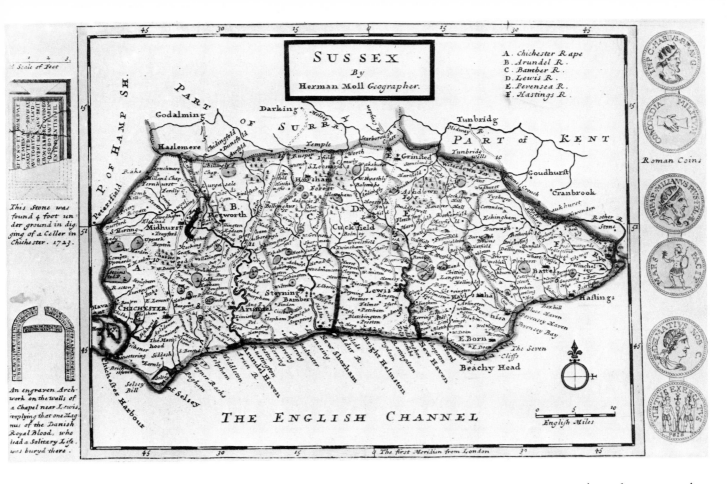

Herman Moll: Sussex. Published in 1724. There is a later edition without the antiquities down each side. The stone on the top left was discovered at Chichester in the year before the map was printed, rather less noteworthy than the recent Roman finds at Fishbourne, close by.
Size: 7½ by 12½ in., 19 by 32 cm.

if ever they should be used at Sea, and ye wrong notions they must give others at land are no less apparent.'

The large maps are decorated with town plans and views, and illustrate the industries and habits of the inhabitants. Particularly interesting is the Scandinavia map which is illustrated with scenes of Laplanders. The South Africa map has an attractive view of Cape Town and the Scotland map has several views of the main towns at each side.

In 1724 Moll published an interesting set of maps of the English and Welsh counties. Though they added nothing of geographical importance, they are pleasantly attractive, and are decorated with antiquities found in each county. The work was re-issued again in 1740 without the antiquities and much of their appeal is lost. In 1725 Moll published the second series of Scottish county maps, the Blaeu series being the first, and in 1728, a set of twenty maps of Ireland, his rarest work. These three were all matching oblong quarto, but the Scotland and Ireland maps are without the antiquities. In 1729 he published the *Atlas Minor*, again in quarto size, and covered all parts of the world.

The value of Moll's maps vary enormously. The English county maps can be obtained for a few pounds. The large maps of America are very difficult to obtain, not because they are rare but because they have such a large demand, and one should expect to pay up to £100, $250, for good examples.

John Senex produced a similar series of maps to Moll's *World Described* which he published in 1721. The maps are derived from the same sources as the Moll maps, but they are less well engraved and lack the views and plans which Moll had included. Senex engraved several maps which were included in other publisher's work, but he is best known for his *New General Atlas*, a folio edition of maps taken mainly from the work of Sanson, and his octavo reduction of Ogilby's road maps, published in 1719.

The early English map-makers were not very successful in their attempts to map other parts of the world. The maps of Speed included in his atlas of 1627 had been taken from maps already published, with Speed adding his own decorations. These were the first 'foreign' maps to be published by an Englishman. Later on, in 1673, the maps published by Richard Blome were nothing more than copies of the work of Nicolas Sanson, the Frenchman. The first real attempt to make a systematic set of atlases of other parts of the

world was made by Moses Pitt, a publisher in Oxford. His large folio volume titled *The English Atlas* was published in 1681, and this included maps from Jansson and Visscher and others mainly of Dutch origin. He had intended to make a set of atlases to cover the whole world, eventually consisting of twelve volumes on the same lines as Blaeu. The venture was doomed to failure because Pitt's maps were not an improvement on the previous Dutch maps. They are not as well printed as the Dutch atlases but they are attractive maps, engraved with similar titles and decoration. Pitt used good materials, the paper is large and usually retains its whiteness, and the bindings are fine. However, Pitt found himself deeply in debt and was imprisoned, after only four volumes of his work had been published. The majority of the maps published were those of western Europe. There were two maps of the world which are particularly attractive.

Another atlas printed in Oxford was that of Edward Wells, *A New Sett of Maps of Ancient and Present Geography*, published in 1701. This consisted of maps of large areas, mostly continents. Geographically these were not as desirable as the Pitt maps, but they were obviously more successful, judging by the numbers in circulation. They were not intended to provide the most up to date information available at the period. Each country was provided with two maps in the atlas, one of the country as it was thought to have been previously, and the other of the country with contemporary detail. The atlas was dedicated to the Duke of Gloucester, whose arms appear on each map, and this may well have induced the public to buy the work. This Duke lived at the Royal Palace of Kensington and died there at a very early age. Apparently he refused to walk up the stairs, insisting that he should be carried, and he organised the local errand boys into his own personal army.

In the early part of the 18th century there were a number of fine atlases

Moses Pitt: the Low Countries. Published in 1681. The map is taken from Jansson, whose name appears on the map. Working in Oxford, Pitt published four volumes of maps taken mainly from the work of Dutchmen. He had hoped that the atlas would cover the whole world, but it was not completed.

Size: $17\frac{1}{3}$ by $21\frac{1}{2}$ in., 44 by 55 cm.

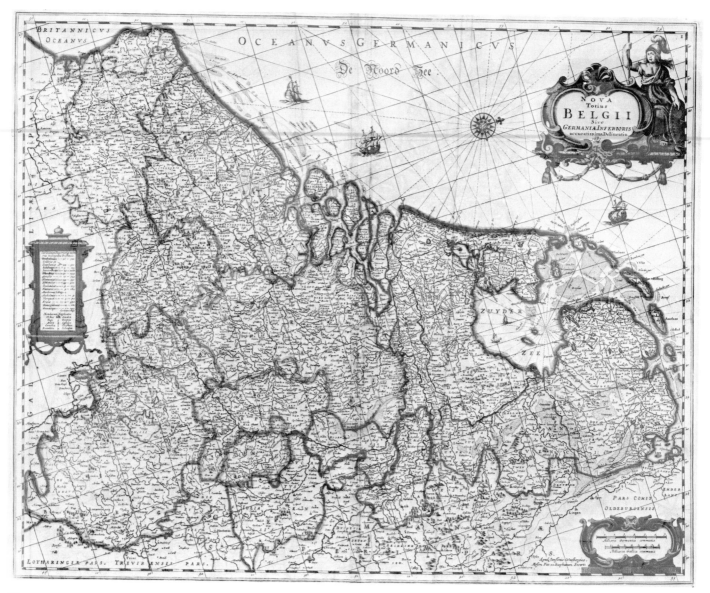

produced in England. Those of Moll and Senex have already been mentioned: others of note were by George Willdey, again not original surveys but nicely decorated maps with large cartouches. Laurie and Whittle published maps by many makers, including the later editions of Kitchin's large atlas. William Faden took over the business of Thomas Jefferys, and continued to produce excellent maps. The content of each atlas published by him varies, even in the number of maps, some of them containing over one hundred and covering all parts of the world. Faden's work is beautifully engraved and they were the finest maps being printed anywhere in the world at this time. He was soon supported by other map-makers. Cary's English maps will be mentioned in their place but in 1808 he published a fine collection of maps of the whole world, as did Pinkerton in 1815, Thompson in 1817, and later, Teesdale in about 1830. The last decorative series of maps was that of John Tallis, decorated with fine little vignettes of towns, scenery, the inhabitants and wildlife. There were several issues of the atlas from about 1850, and though the maps of Europe in the series are not expensive and easily found, the maps of America, Canada and Australia have a very large demand and usually cost about £10, $24, each. Also worthy of mention are the fine large maps made by Aaron Arrowsmith and his sons Aaron and John. They published several atlases from about 1800 up until about 1840, but of particular merit are the large scale maps of parts of America and Australia, all of them uncommon.

The finest county maps to be published in the 18th century were in the *Large English Atlas* with maps by Emanuel Bowen, Thomas Kitchin, and R. W. Seale, published in 1755. This was one of the few publications made by more than one cartographer, Bowen and Kitchin divided most of the maps between them, but the Middlesex map was made by Seale and is slightly different from the others in that the geographical content is less detailed and the sides are each decorated with four rows of arms of the City Livery Companies, ninety-two in number, and the arms of the City of London. All the other maps are elaborately detailed, and are by far the

Samuel Dunn: Switzerland. One of a series of maps published by Robert Sayer in 1774 and re-issued several times. All the maps are clearly engraved and well detailed. Dunn is probably best known for his map of North America, also published in 1774.
Size: 10½ by 14½ in., 27 by 37 cm.

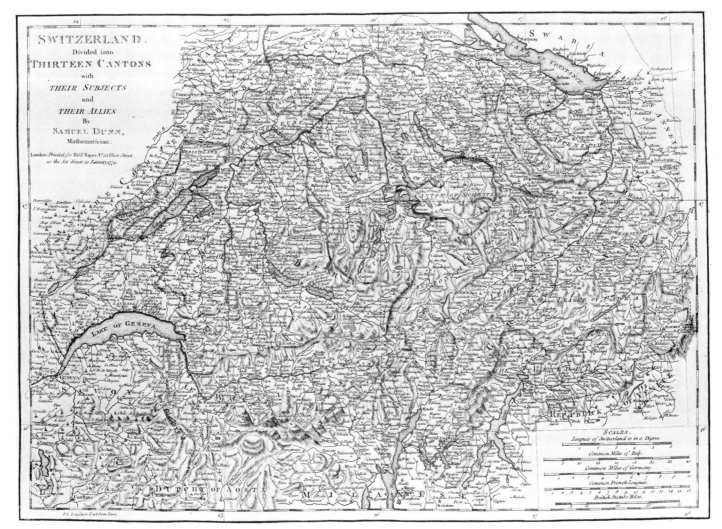

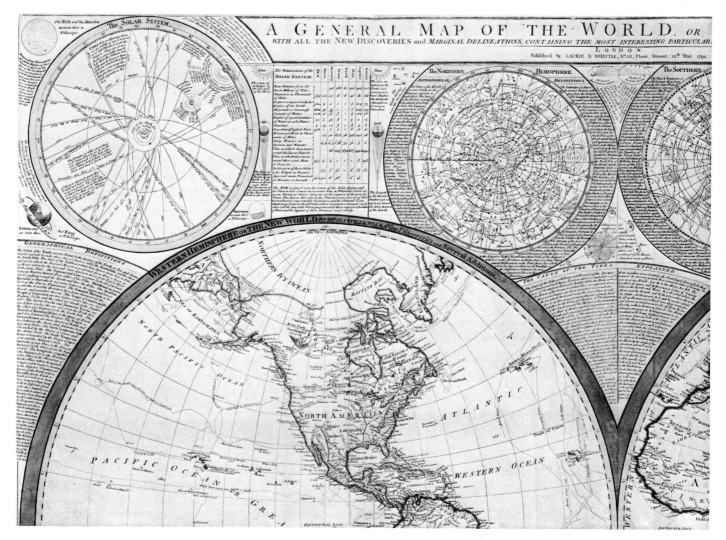

most accurate to have appeared to this time. They give notes on the features of the counties and items of historical interest, both on the map and round the borders.

The series consists of maps of each of the English counties, Gloucestershire and Monmouth together on the same sheet, and also Leicestershire and Rutland. North Wales was covered by one map, at a scale of a quarter of an inch to one mile, the South Wales maps were printed two to the page and are sometimes seen separated. Scotland and Ireland were not included in the first editions, but added to the edition of 1763. Each map has a key and shows castles, seats, rectories, vicarages, religious houses, post stages, charity schools, mines and so on. Market days are annexed to the towns and mileages are given in circles between each town. Each borough town is marked with stars which denote the number of its representatives in Parliament. Rococo cartouches illustrate the county's natural resources, and show scenes of harvesting, hop-growing, mining, fishing, dairy farming and various industries including steel and manufacturing fabrics. The large maps measure approximately 28 inches by 20 inches (71 by 51 cm), and are covered with notes, all finely engraved and very legible. For example the Bowen map of Bedfordshire is annotated: 'Tis remarkable that in January 1399, the 22nd of King Richard II, the year before the breaking out of those commotions between the Houses of York and Lancaster, which distracted and greatly afflicted this nation for ninety years afterwards, that the River Ouse, near Harrold in this county, suddenly stood still and only staid its usual course in so much that the channel appear'd dry, but the water retired for a space of three miles. This surprising Event was thought omenous by the people of that age, of the direful calamities that followed. Some affirm that the same thing happned in 1648 which was deemed by many as a prognostick of Charles's death.' The Surrey map records that: 'Norbury is remarkable for its orchard in which tis said is contain'd upwards of forty thousand walnut trees'. At this period walnut was important in the manufacture of English furniture. On the same map is a note concerning a lead pipe which

Laurie and Whittle: four sheet map of the world, bound in two pieces, the whole joins together to make a map measuring 41 by 49 inches, 104 by 125 cm, too large to store conveniently unless it is framed. Published in 1794, the map is after d'Anville, the notes by Samuel Dunn.

William Faden: the Northern Hemisphere, published in 1819. Similar to the counterpart of the Southern Hemisphere by Thompson.
Size: 23 by 22½ in., 58 by 57 cm.

was laid by Cardinal Wolsey to carry good water from Coombe Hill, through Kingston and under the Thames to Hampton Court, a distance of over three miles even in a straight line. The maps are not perhaps as decorative as some of the maps of the previous century, but they are the most interesting of any period. There were several editions of the maps up until 1787. They can be dated by the names of the publishers which can be seen in the centre beneath the lower ruled border. Only the first edition maps are dated, and as always, the date refers to the date of engraving from 1749 to 1755. All the maps are very good impressions and there does not appear to have been any re-engraving work carried out, an indication that there were not many of them printed. The cartouche on the top right hand corner of the Sussex map, showing surveyors at work, is usually very pale, even in the earliest issues, and technically this is the only adverse criticism that can be made of the series.

The atlas was published in smaller sizes. The *Royal English Atlas* was almost an exact reduction of the large atlas and about half the size, the annotations being similar but fewer. The maps are less common than the larger ones. They were first published in 1762 and were re-issued in 1778 and 1780. Finally, there was a further reduction of the atlas, published in 1765, quarto size, half the size of the Royal Atlas. The information is neces-

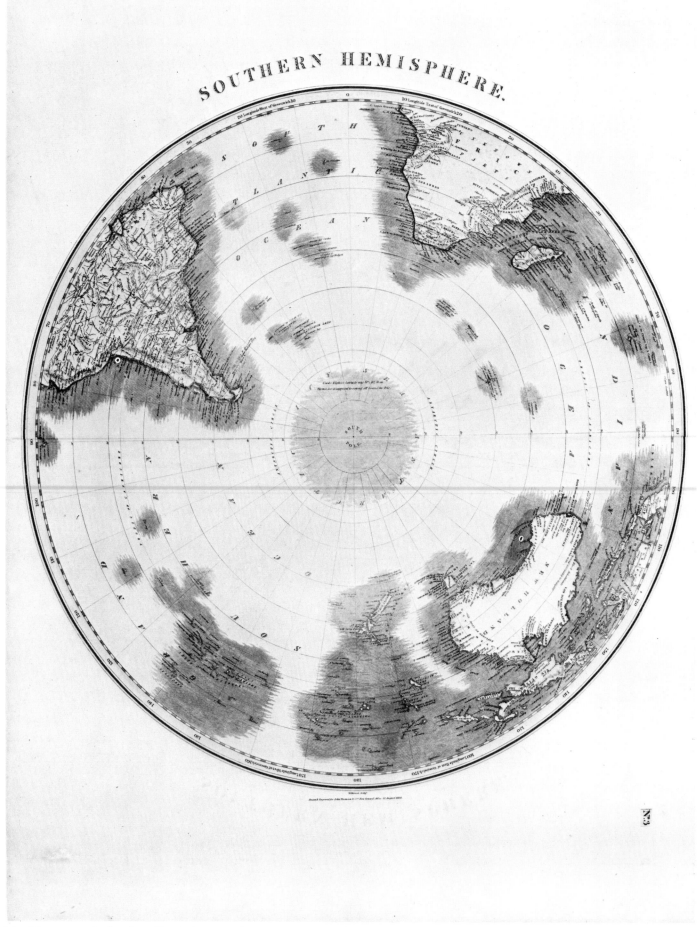

SOUTHERN HEMISPHERE.

John Thompson: the Southern Hemisphere,
published in the *New General Atlas* of 1814.

Though foreshortened by the projection, the
map shows good detail of Australia and New

Zealand.

Size: 21 by 20 in., 53 by 51 cm.

70

Emanuel Bowen: Lancashire. 1760. The series is unusual in that it was compiled by more than one maker. Bowen and Thomas Kitchin shared the counties almost equally, with the exception of Middlesex which was made by R. W. Seale. A very fine set of maps, the most interesting and the most original to be made in Britain since Christopher Saxton. All have notes about the main features of the counties and are decorated with cartouches depicting its industries.

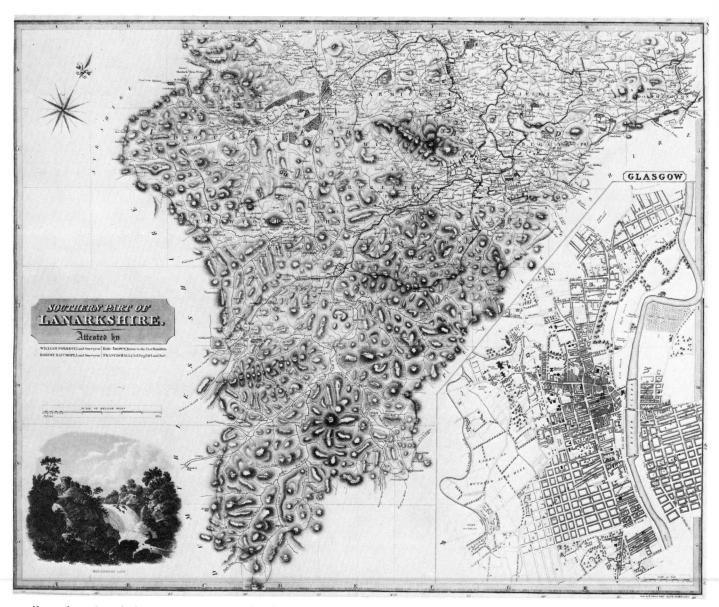

sarily reduced to fit into the space available but the maps are still filled with interesting notes of a similar nature to the earlier maps.

Bowen published a magnificent map of South Wales, as if to make up for the deficiency in the large atlas. Printed on six sheets at a scale of half an inch to one mile, the map was published in 1766. It is finely engraved and decorated with views of the most important towns. Unfortunately it is quite rare, probably selling for £80 to £100, $190-240, if one should come onto the market. He also published a reduced version of Ogilby's road maps with the assistance of J. Owen. Published in 1720 the octavo volume was titled *Britannia Depicta*. Too often this charming little book is broken for the county maps which look very attractive when framed. The roads were printed back to back and therefore it is not possible to frame the single sheets so that they can be properly viewed. Some of the earliest work by Bowen was the engraving of the large folio maps for the Willdey atlas of the world which was published in 1717. Bowen's name is credited to the map of Scandinavia which is strikingly like the Moll map of the same period.

Apart from the series of county maps, Thomas Kitchin is well known for his fine general atlas published in 1768 and containing magnificent four sheet maps of the continents, bound in such a way that the two northern sheets are joined together and the two southern sheets are joined. The whole can be joined for framing, in which case they measure overall about 50 inches square (130 sq cm). The maps are well detailed and engraved, decorated with large cartouches showing the inhabitants and their ways of life. The work was re-issued by Robert Sayer and by Laurie and Whittle several times and went on into the 19th century. The edition of 1800 includes an outline map of Australia which is an addition to the south part of the map of Asia and is engraved so that the sheets would join together. Kitchin

Southern part of Lanarkshire, published by Thomson in 1831: a separate sheet was printed to cover the northern part. All the maps in this series are well detailed and are in relief. Most of them include a small vignette but only a few of them contain a plan.
Size: 21 by 27 in., 54 by 68 cm.

Right
Christopher and John Greenwood, 1834. A fine, large map, beautifully engraved. The detail is better than previous maps and is comparable to the Ordnance Survey maps, even though the Greenwood Brothers lacked the resources of the army survey. Each map includes a large vignette, generally a view of a cathedral or a stately home. The hundreds are picked out in colour, the rest left in black and white. Often some offsetting occurs, here the impression of the title can just be seen on the opposite side.
Size: 22½ by 28 in., 57 by 71 cm.

Pigot & Co.: the counties of Leicestershire and Rutland. Several editions were published from 1829 up to 1846 when the production was taken over by Slater who continued the work until about 1860. The inset view is St Mary's Church, Melton Mowbray. Well detailed map usually in delicate wash colouring.
Size: 9 by 14 in., 23 by 36 cm.

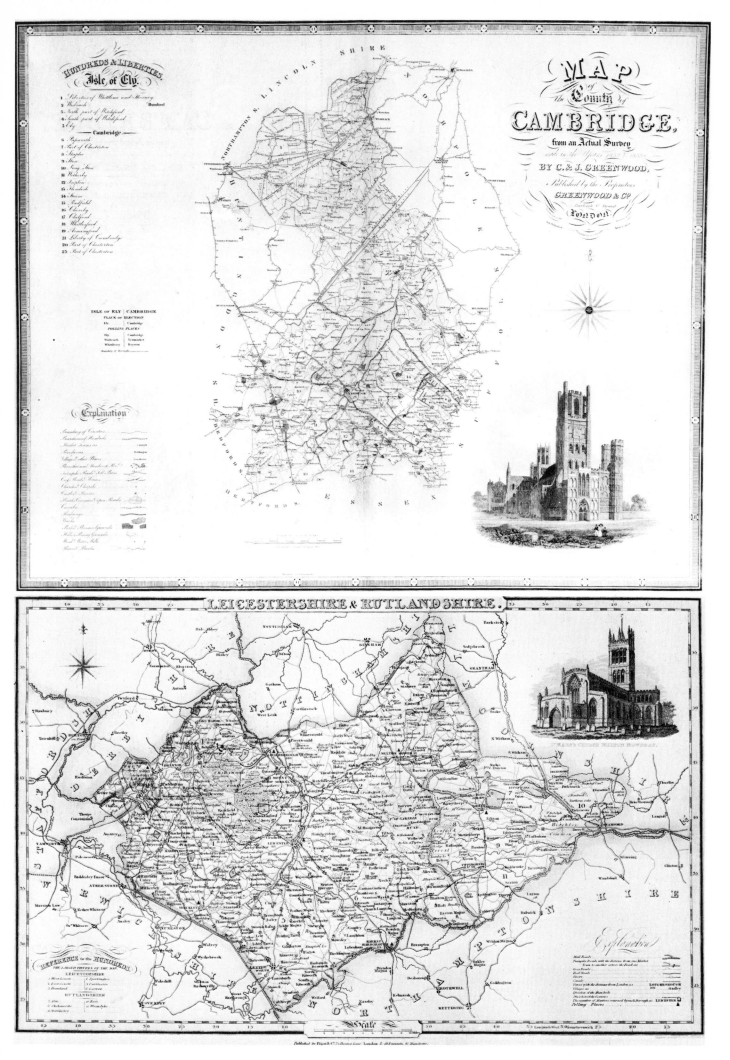

MAP of the County of CAMBRIDGE, from an Actual Survey made in the Years 1824 & 1825, BY C. & J. GREENWOOD, Published by the Proprietors GREENWOOD & Co. Burleigh St Strand London

LEICESTERSHIRE & RUTLANDSHIRE.

engraved a number of other maps of the English counties and also maps of other parts of the world which were included in atlases by other publishers.

The brothers Christopher and John Greenwood made a fine series of county maps of England and Wales. It was common practice for their predecessors to collect information from other maps and any other sources. The Greenwoods conducted a completely new survey, ignoring any of the maps that had been made earlier. The result was an accurate and well detailed set of

John Cary: Oxfordshire, one of a series of the English counties, published in several editions, from 1793. Though they are plain the maps are well detailed and well engraved. Size: 10½ by 8½ in., 27 by 21 cm.

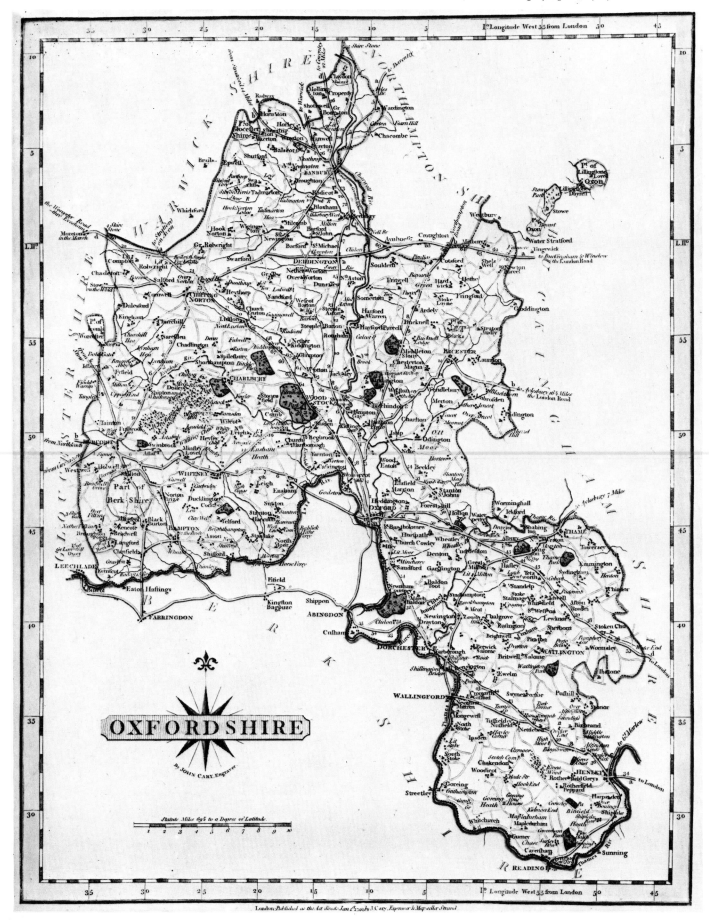

Hobson's Fox Hunting Map of Shropshire. The areas of the hunts are superimposed onto the earlier map by J. & C. Walker, mainly a map of the political divisions. Published in 1850 and re-issued many times after 1860.

Size: 13 by 15½ in., 33 by 39 cm.

maps, some of the finest engraving that had been carried out in England. Their work was in opposition to the Ordnance Survey, taking only seventeen years to survey, compared to almost one hundred years taken by the Ordnance Survey. All the maps have large titles, like the Cambridgeshire map illustrated, and give the dates of the survey. Each is provided with a key to the mapping symbols used, and shows a view of an edifice within the county. The maps are large, measuring 22½ inches by 28 inches (57 by 71

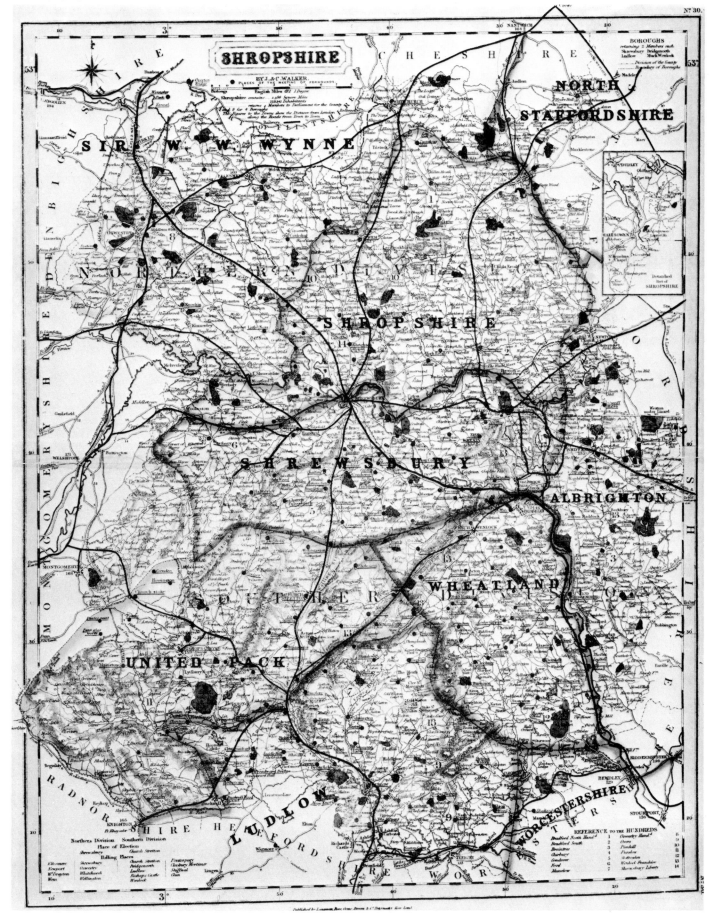

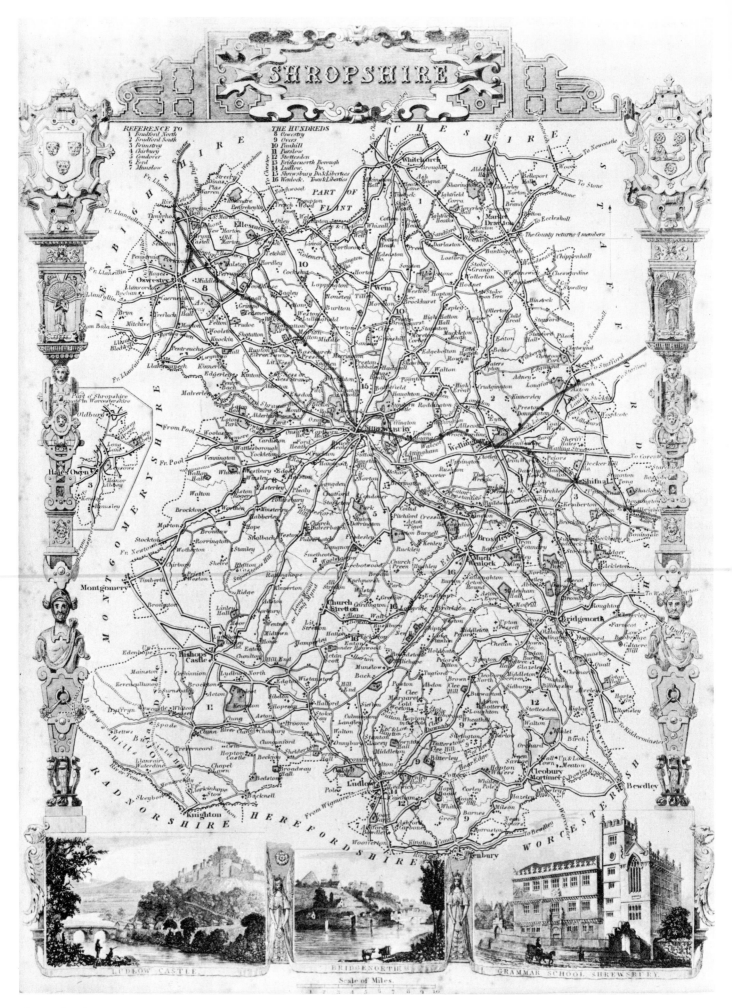

Thomas Moule: Shropshire, 1850. The first
edition was published in 1836 and is without
the railways. Engraved on steel, the views
and ornamentation are finely executed and
are very decorative in colour.
Size: 8 by 10½ in., 20 by 27 cm.

76

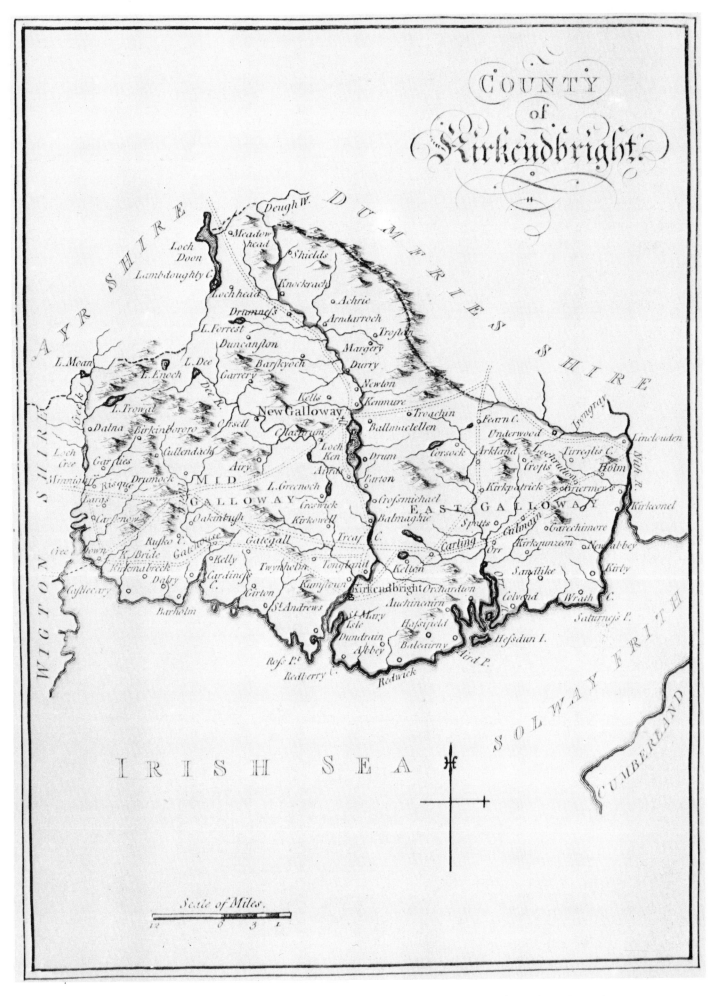

Mostyn Armstrong: Kirkcudbrightshire, 1777. Published by Sayer and Bennett. One of a series of thirty maps of Scotland. Unfortunately there are very few series made of Scotland, and although the maps are small this is a pleasant and well engraved series. Size: 7½ by 5½ in., 19 by 14 cm.

cm): an atlas of this size is perhaps a little unwieldy, but currently the atlas sells for about £150, $360, and offers a good investment. Apart from the county maps which were published in 1834, the Greenwoods also made some maps on a larger scale, mostly one inch to one mile, covering most of the counties and published separately during the 1820s. These are described in the chapter on large scale maps.

Contemporary with the Greenwood maps was another series on a smaller but similar style published by Pigot from 1829 up to 1860, though they are not so finely engraved or well detailed. Each map has a bold title and is decorated with a vignette.

The last of the decorative series of county maps of England was that published by Thomas Moule in 1836. The maps were printed from steel plates, and though the maps are not big, they are clearly engraved with decorative borders, coats of arms and vignettes of scenes within the county. There were several editions of the maps up until 1852, the year after Moule died: the only changes made to the maps were the additions of railways, which were gradually added to the plates during the various editions. They were obviously popular sellers when they were published, though from a geographical viewpoint they had nothing to add to the current maps of the counties. The illustration is taken from a black and white example but the early issues were generally coloured, or the map is coloured in outline and the embellishments are left plain. The maps are not easily found but are not expensive, currently the best are priced at about £6, $14, and are well worthy of inclusion in a collection.

At the end of the 18th century and the beginning of the nineteenth John Cary was a prolific map publisher. He made three atlases of particular merit, his first being *A New and Correct English Atlas*, published in 1787 in quarto size, containing forty-six maps, and went into several editions up until 1831. In 1809 the folio atlas was published titled *English Atlas*, the larger maps facilitating greater detail, and again continued to be published regularly until 1834. A small but interesting work is the *Travellers' Companion*, a series of road maps on the same lines as Ogilby but much reduced in size, first issued in 1790.

Cary was also an engraver and the maps that he published are all of a very high technical standard. They are mainly functional affairs, the decoration being reduced to the barest essential, the titles attractively combine with the compass roses. Cary is also well known for his globes, both celestial and terrestrial, and was the foremost maker of the period. A contemporary and rival of Cary's was Charles Smith who published a set of county maps in 1804 which are very similar to Cary's folio maps, equally plain and equally well engraved. Another Smith of the period was William Smith who published the first geological map of England and Wales, in 1815. This is a rare and important map on fourteen sheets, and the various strata are keyed by colours. It does not have the general appeal of most maps, but it is valuable to the collector and sells for over £1,000, $2,400.

An undecorated but beautifully produced set of maps made by J. & C. Walker were published in 1837. The detail is very thorough, matching the maps of Greenwood. Numerous editions were made and railways were included in the later maps. In 1850 the maps were used by Hobson for the basis of his fox-hunting maps, the areas of the hunts and the meeting places of the hounds were superimposed and usually the border lines are brightly coloured.

There were other series of maps which have not been mentioned so far and are of interest to the collector and investor alike. Most of the maps by the following makers can be bought inexpensively, either in volume form or by the single sheet.

Mostyn John Armstrong, map-maker and publisher. His most important work was his *Scotch Atlas*, a set of thirty maps of the Scottish counties published in 1777. He made some other maps of parts of Scotland which were published separately, and published a set of maps of the post road from London to Edinburgh.

Thomas Badeslade, surveyor and engineer. Mainly interested in mapping from an engineering point of view, including the reclamation of the Fens and the improvement of water ways. His best known published work is a series

of county maps of England in *Chorographia Britannia* of 1742, an octavo volume with maps engraved by W. H. Toms, each with a description of the county at the side.

Thomas Bakewell was mainly a map and print seller, but published a number of maps including an edition of the small maps of the counties by Richard Blome.

John Bill published an octavo series of maps in 1626 on the lines of the Peter Keere atlas. Unusual and difficult to find.

The Bowles family were prolific publishers. There were two Thomas Bowles, father and son, John was another son of the elder Thomas, and Carrington was the son of John. Thomas Bowles minor was the only engraver of the family. Between them they published a number of very important works, including the *Large English Atlas* by Bowen, the *Atlas Minor* by Moll and the English county maps by Moll, and an edition of the *Britannia Depicta* in 1764.

John Cowley made an attractive little series of the English counties in octavo, and though not profusely detailed, the maps show the chief towns, parks, rivers and roads. They were published in 1744.

William Darton published a number of maps: his main work was a complete set of the English counties, published in 1822.

John Ellis, engraver of maps and views, worked in conjunction with Palmer on the small atlas published in 1766.

Sidney Hall was a prolific engraver from about 1820. His general atlas published in 1830 contains some well engraved maps of the whole world. In 1832 he published a series of maps of parts of Scotland.

Alexander Hogg was a publisher and bookseller, not really concerned with the publication of maps, but more with illustrated histories. His *New British Traveller* published in 1794 included some small but attractive maps.

This map was engraved by Wenceslaus Hollar and was originally published by Richard Blome. It was later reprinted in the early 18th century by Thomas Taylor: this edition of 1715 was re-issued by Thomas Bakewell with the addition of roads and distances marked in the circles, taken from the maps of John Ogilby. This example shows some wear to the plate in the top left hand corner.

Size: 7 by 9½ in., 18 by 24 cm.

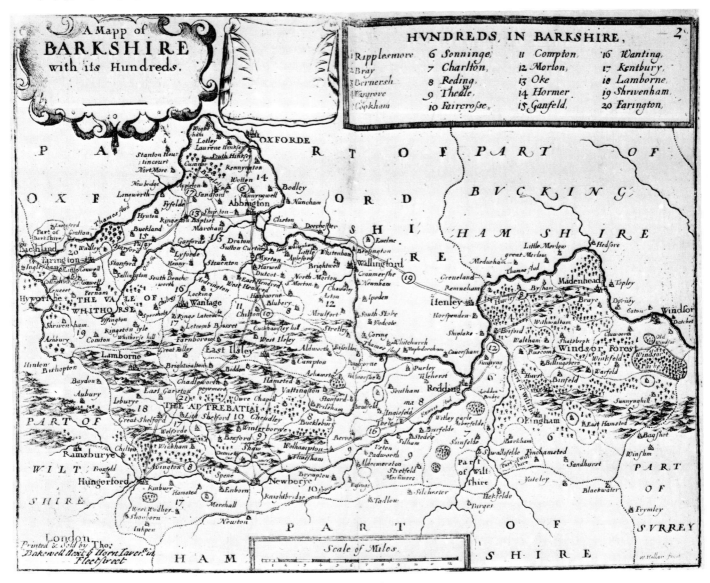

LINCOLNSHIRE

IS a maritime county, on the eaſtern coaſt of the iſland, included by the antient inhabitants in their principality of Coritani; but after the arrival of the Romans was belonging to the province of Flavia Cæſarienſis. On the eſtabliſhment of the Heptarchy it belonged to the Kingdom of Mercia, the laſt eſtabliſhed but by far the moſt extenſive, which commenced in 582 and ended in 827, having been governed by 18 kings. At preſent it is in the province of Canterbury, dioceſe of its own Biſhop, and is included in the Midland Circuit. It is of an oblong form, being bounded on the North by the Humber, which ſeparates it from York-ſhire; South by Rutlandſhire, Northamptonſhire, and Cambridgeſhire; Eaſt by the German Ocean; and Weſt by Yorkſhire, Nottinghamſhire, and Leiceſterſhire; being 70 miles long, 35 broad, and 160 in circumference, containing 1,740,000 acres, or 2162 ſquare miles divided into 30 hundreds, or wapontakes, having 630 pariſhes 256 vicarages, 1556 villages, 243,6000 inhabitants, 40,590 houſes, 1 city Lincoln, and 31 market towns, viz. Stamford, Boſton, Grantham, Gainſby, Gainſborough, Barton, Dunnington, Alford, Binbrooke, Bourne, Burgh, Saltfleet, Louth, Fol-kingham, Kirton, Burton, Caſtor, Crowland, Deeping, Glandford-Bridge, Hol-bech, Horncaſtle, Market-Raiſin, Sleaford, Spalding, Spilſby, Stanton, Tatter-ſhall, Wainfleet and Crowle; its remarkable places are Sunk Iſland, in the Hum-ber, Axholm Iſle, inland; Boſton and Lynn Deeps, Foſſe Dykes, Lincoln Heath,

Eaſt

81

Edward Langley, engraver and publisher, best known for his *New County Atlas of England and Wales* published in 1818. The maps are well engraved and are decorated with vignettes of local interest and with views of the towns.

Richard Palmer engraved maps for Richard Blome and also for John Seller's collection of County Maps of England published in 1680.

William Palmer assisted Ellis in the engraving of the small English atlas and the maps for Bernard Scale's *Hiberian Atlas* published in 1776.

Richard William Seale has been mentioned in connection with the splendid map of Middlesex which he made for the Bowen and Kitchin series. He was probably more important for his engraving of the Popple map of the British Empire in America, published in 1733.

John Stockdale, bookseller and publisher, particularly important for his large scale maps of England and Scotland engraved by Neele, but he published many other works, including *The American Geography* in 1794, Weld's *Travels through the States of North America* in 1799, Bryan Edwards' history of the West Indies in 1801, and the Gough edition of Camden's *Britannia* published in 1806, which contained maps by John Cary.

Andrew Skinner and George Taylor collaborated in the publication of *The Survey and Roads of North Britain or Scotland* in 1776, a work which is normally found in volume form because the maps are printed on each side of the page. They also published a similar work of the roads of Ireland, published in 1778.

Henry Teesdale was prolific in the early part of the 19th century, publishing a set of county maps in 1829, called the *New British Atlas*, and a travelling atlas in 1830. The following year he published *A New General Atlas of the World*.

William Henry Toms worked with Seale on the engraving of Popple's map of North America of 1733. He is best known for his engraving of the maps in *Chorographia Britannia* with Badeslade.

FRENCH &
GERMAN
MAP -MAKING

The history of French map-making can be traced back to the early part of the 16th century, but the few maps that were printed at that time are extreme rarities and do not really come into the scope of this book. Maps of France that were made at the end of the century, and which are available today, were those which were printed in the Low Countries by Ortelius and Mercator.

Prominent French map-makers of the 17th century were centred round the work of one man, Nicolas Sanson, in the same way that map-making in England had been fathered by Christopher Saxton. Sanson began to print maps in 1629, with a six sheet map of France, but it was not until the second half of the century that his atlases were made in comparative quantities, and like other map-makers, he gradually increased the number of maps contained in the atlas, until in 1664 it contained about one hundred and fifty maps. The volumes vary in content, some of them including maps from other sources. The style is unlike that of any other country, the nearest comparison being the maps by Bowen which were published in England almost one hundred years later, but the maps of Sanson are more finely engraved, and are decorated with fine cartouches ornamented with figures, trees, plants, fruit and fanciful sea-monsters against backgrounds of classical architecture. There is no other decoration. Sanson had two sons who became map publishers, Gillaume and Adrien, and after Sanson died in 1667, they continued with the business until Alexis Hubert Jaillot took over in the last decade of the 17th century. Jaillot continued to publish some fine maps, slowly improving on the maps of Sanson, not only in geographical detail but also in decoration. He published a number of sea charts, including the *Neptune Francais*, in 1693, a work which was later published by Mortier.

Many fine maps continued to be published in France during the 18th

Above right
Jean Covens and Corneille Mortier: *Le Royaume de Naples*. Covens and Mortier took over from Pieter Mortier and, in Amsterdam, published the maps of several of the French map-makers. This map is by Jaillot, published about 1730, and is typical of their fine maps. The cartouches are always decorative. Size: 19½ by 29 in., 50 by 74 cm.

Below right
Matthaus Merian: Spain. Published in 1646. A well engraved map, the detail of which is taken from the map by Ortelius, though most of his maps are copied from Blaeu. Size: 10½ by 14 in., 27 by 36 cm.

Below
H. Jaillot: France. Published in 1696. A prominent French cartographer, Jaillot took over from Sanson. Size: 20 by 24 in., 51 by 61 cm.

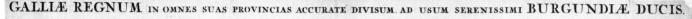

PARTIE SEPTENTRIONALE DU ROYAUME DE NAPLES

century, among them being those of Gillaume de l'Isle, probably the best cartographer in France during the century. His maps were published by Jean Covens and Corneille Mortier, usually signing themselves by their sur-names. De l'Isle's rival was Jean Baptiste Bourguignon D'Anville, who pub-lished atlases in the latter part of the century, but his first atlas was published in 1740 and continued to be re-issued until 1820. He died in 1782.

Some confusion is caused by the maps of Robert de Vaugondy, who is known as Sieur Robert or Monsieur Robert or, purely, as Vaugondy. He, too, published fine folio maps of all parts of the world: the *Universal Atlas* was first published in 1757, and was re-issued until 1799.

All these men produced some fine work, most of it in a similar style and some experience of their maps is necessary before one can easily determine their individual maps. Their maps were not as picturesque as the maps of the earlier Dutchmen, but they are all delicately engraved and have attrac-tive cartouches. Their surveys of France are especially fine and can be bought quite cheaply.

In Germany, after the initial successes of printing some of the early editions of Ptolemy's *Geography* and, later, the work of Sebastian Munster, followed by the epic work of Braun and Hogenberg, which is discussed in the chapter on town plans, there followed a period of relapse during the 17th century. There are, however, some map-makers who should be mentioned: among them Matthias Quad, who produced a small folio atlas in 1592, re-issued in 1594 and 1596. This was enlarged to a general atlas containing 82 maps, published in 1600 under the title *Geographisch Handtbuch*, and further enlarged to 86 maps in 1608. The maps are quite small, measuring about 10 inches

Robert de Vaugondy: the southern part of the States of Castille. Dated 1751 and pub-lished in 1754. Sometimes the 'Vaugondy' is dropped, the name appearing as 'le Sr Robert'.

Size: 19 by 22 in., 48 by 56 cm.

by 12 inches (25 by 30 cm), but they are executed with great care and attention and are charming to look at. Quad operated from Cologne, as did Braun and Hogenberg.

. An engraver of particular merit is Matthew Merian, who worked in Frankfurt. His main mapping work was an atlas published in 1646, the majority of the maps being taken from Blaeu. He also published a number of plans, but he is best remembered for his magnificent views of towns. Merian was one of the few German publishers of the period, but his maps were not his own surveys.

The work of Peter and Philip Apian, father and son, is of extreme rarity. Peter Apian's *Geographia* was first published in 1524, there were several re-issues until about 1600, and these later maps are occasionally on the market. Philip Apian made a very large survey of Bavaria which was published in 1568 on twenty-four sheets and this work was used as a basis for some of the later maps.

In the 18th century German map publication was revived and once again maps began to appear in quantities. Of particular note are two families, the Homanns and the Seutters. Johann Baptist Homann was an engraver and publisher of maps in Nuremberg. His first atlas was published from about 1720. When he died his heirs carried on the business. Their publications were numerous and their total output of maps was well over three hundred different maps. The maps are attractively engraved in a heavy style, the cartouches and extra decor remaining in black and white, the maps coloured in pale washes. Some of them have very fine detail and include small views of towns and buildings. The Norway map illustrated shows a mining scene

Johann Baptist Homann: part of Norway. Published in Nuremberg, 1730. Christiana is now Oslo, seen just under the cartouche. The scene on the right is a detail of mining, one of the treadles is operated by water, the other by a human.
Size: 18½ by 21½ in., 47 by 55 cm.

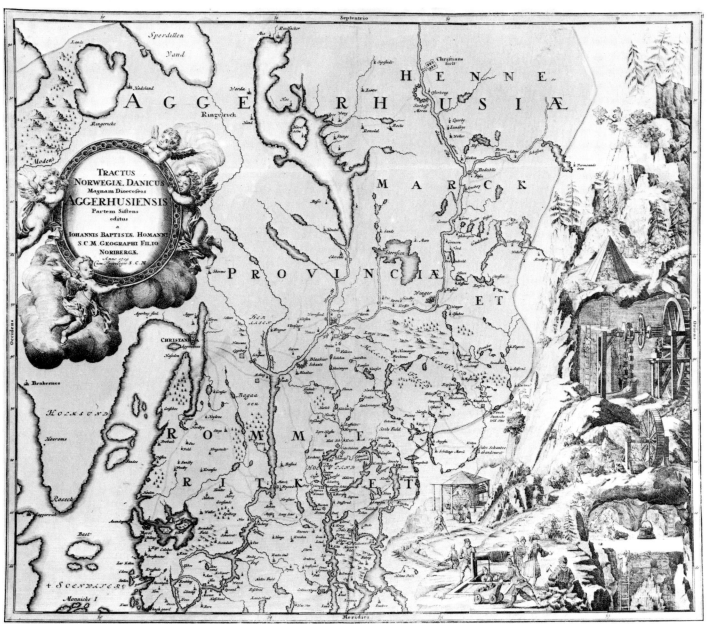

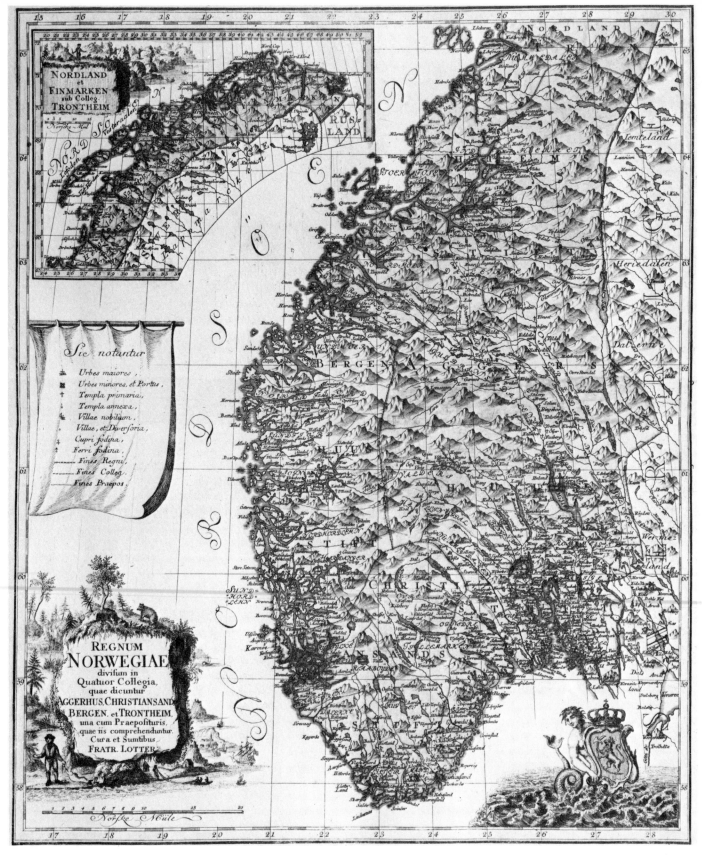

Tobias Lotter: Norway. An unusual map, published about 1750. Lotter was the son-in-law of Seutter and inherited the business, most of the maps being re-issues of Seutter's work.

Size: 22 by 19 in., 56 by 48 cm.

which is most interesting. Homann also published some maps by other makers, including the astronomical atlas by Doppelmaier, who was also a maker of terrestrial maps, some of which were published in the Homann atlas.

Matthew Seutter was a map publisher and engraver in Augsburg, having been originally apprenticed to Homann. He set up on his own in 1707 and Homann's influence is prominent in his maps, the engraving being in a similar style. Seutter's son Albrecht Karl went into the business, and when Seutter died the son was joined by his brother-in-law T. C. Lotter and then by G. B. Probst. Both Homann and Seutter produced general atlases of all parts of the world. Their maps can be obtained from as little as £10 or £15, $24-36, and an example would make an attractive addition to any collection.

SEA CHARTS

The earliest printed charts were made by the Spaniards but these are rare and are confined to museums. The first volume of sea charts is titled *Spieghel der Zeevaerdt* and was compiled by Lucas Jansen Waghenaer. Born in 1534 on the Zuider Zee, Waghenaer went to sea as a young man and eventually became a pilot. He retired from this position in 1575 and took up a post in his home sea port of Enchuysen. In 1582 he was out of work and it was only then that he began work on his important sea atlas, or 'waggoner'. During his career at sea he had collected information from all over western Europe, and his experiences at sea enabled him to make charts as an aid to a pilot, marking in detail which was essential for correct navigation. The plates were engraved by Johannes a Deutecum and were printed by Christopher Plantin, the printer of the Blaeu atlases, in Amsterdam in 1584. The first part of the atlas contained twenty-three maps, the second part contained twenty-two maps, and these parts were originally sold separately, but were bound together in the following year. Two further maps were added to the edition of 1591. The work was dedicated to the States General of Holland, who granted Waghenaer a sum of £500 to conduct the work. An English edition was published by Anthony Ashley in 1588, titled *The Mariners Mirrour*. The plates were new engravings, simplifying the place names by using their proper English titles, and these were engraved by various engravers including Theodor de Bry. The maps were the first to give information of the charted depths in fathoms, and also to show details of the tides. Buoys and beacons were systematically engraved to provide information for the sailor, and they each show elevations of the coastlines as seen from the sea, an innovation copied by some of the later map-makers. The maps are very picturesque, several monsters are shown on each as well as finely engraved shipping. Each has a most elegant cartouche. Place names are limited purely to the coastline: inland are seen sheep and cattle in idyllic countryside. There are eight charts of the British Isles, the others were made of the North Sea and the Baltic and the coast of western Europe as far south as Cadiz. A copy of the third issue of the work, 1586, containing forty-five maps, sold at auction in London in 1968 for £8,500, $20,400. Some of the plates were slightly rubbed but otherwise it was a magnificent copy, in fine original colouring. The single sheets are occasionally available, and sell

Above right
Captain Greenville Collins: Dartmouth. 1693. Collins was the first Englishman to publish a series of Sea Charts. The first edition is difficult to find but there were several subsequent editions made up until 1785 and the later editions are quite common. One should be careful to buy a good black impression. Not all his maps are as decorative as this but they are all very interesting and several include the profiles of the coastlines.
Size: 17½ by 22½ in., 44 by 57 cm.

Below right
Lucas Jansen Waghenaer: coast of Normandy and the Channel Islands. Another map from *The Mariners Mirrour*.
Size: 13 by 20 in., 33 by 51 cm.

Below
Lucas Jansen Waghenaer: south coast of Cornwall. Rare map from the first collection of sea charts to be published. Printed in Leyden 1584-86. New plates were engraved for the English edition of 1588, titled *The Mariners Mirrour*. Notice that depths and safe anchorages are marked and of particular interest are the profiles of the coastline, later elaborated on by Capt. Collins.
Size: 13 by 20 in., 33 by 51 cm.

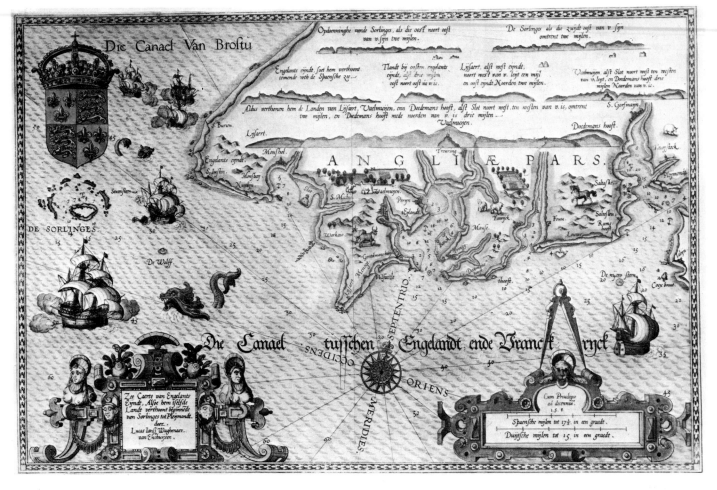

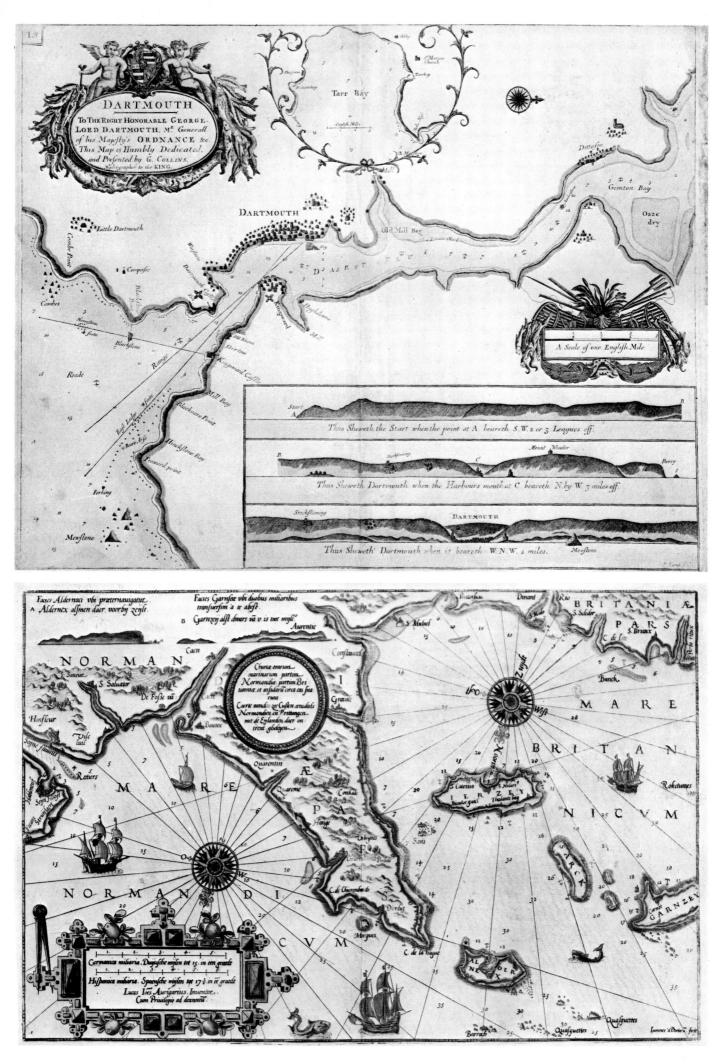

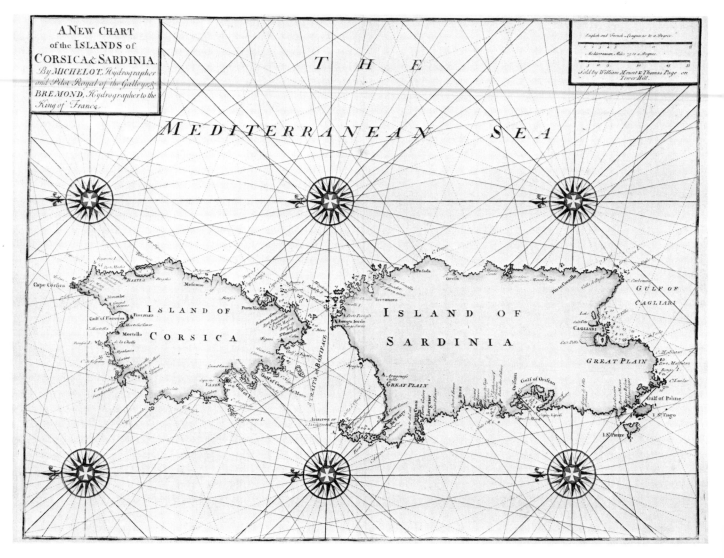

92

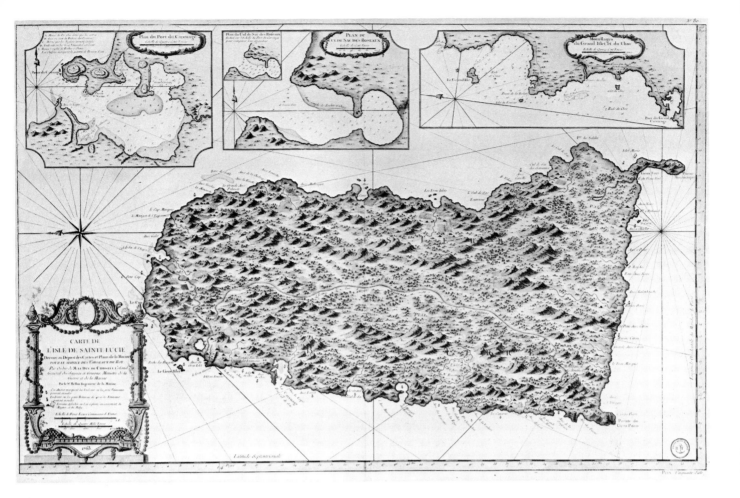

Above

Jacques Nicholas Bellin: chart of St Lucia in the West Indies. One of a series of over 550 charts covering all parts of the world, published in 1772.
Size: 22 by 34¾ in., 56 by 89 cm.

Above left

John Bowles: Sea Ports of Europe. Published about 1720. Engraved by Sutton Nicholls, and rather more elaborate than the majority of his work. Bowles published the large maps by Moll and this map is sometimes included in the Moll Atlas.
Notice that eleven different scales are given.
Size: 23 by 38½ in., 58 by 98 cm.

Below left

Mount and Page: chart of the islands of Corsica and Sardinia. 1745. Prolific chart publishers, this firm was begun by Richard Mount who published the Collins charts; his son was joined by Thomas Page and the business was carried on by the next generation, thus lasting over one hundred years. The style remained much the same throughout.
Size: 16 by 21 in., 41 by 54 cm.

for over £100, $240.

William Blaeu's atlas *Licht der Zeevaert* of 1608 was the first to be published by him. The maps are even more rare than those of Waghenaer. Undoubtedly Blaeu used Waghenaer's work for the basis of his own, the system of engraving and the method of marking detail are very similar. Blaeu's maps are plainer than the Waghenaer maps, and though they are decorated with fine cartouches and compass roses, they do not illustrate the particular gift for laying out a map which Blaeu was to show later on.

The Dutch dominated the manufacture of charts as they did land maps throughout the 18th century. The following are the most notable. J. van Keulen published charts from about 1680, the firm continuing into the 18th century. Pieter Goos, son of the engraver Abraham, published an atlas of forty charts in 1666. Anthonie Jacobsz published several volumes of charts from 1648, the business continued by his son until 1717. Henrik Donckers published a set of twenty-seven charts in 1660. A Frenchman, Loius Renard published a set of attractive maps usually in colour in 1715 in Amsterdam, and these were re-issued by Ottens in 1745. None of these is common but the van Keulen charts are the most readily available. A large and important work is the *Neptune Francais* published in Amsterdam by Pierre Mortier in 1700. Copies are not often found in contemporary colouring. Illustrated are the maps of the Mediterranean and the south coast of Cornwall, two of the most decorative maps in the series, engraved by Romain de Hooghe. Most of the other maps are plainer, some are without decoration of any kind. Maps of America were included in the set, the general map has an inset plan of Boston Harbour. The maps of Joannes Hugo a Linschoten can be defined as maps or charts, for they show detail of both the land and the sea. His maps were mainly of the south part of Africa, the East Indies, and the later editions included a map of South America. The volume is small folio, the twelve maps have to be folded into the volume and are often in poor condition. His maps are most striking, engraved as if he wished to fill the page with elaborate decoration. Each map has a large cartouche, a fine compass rose and is adorned with ships in battle or in full sail, whales and various sea monsters, and with animals on the land. The detail of the maps is almost

entirely confined to the coastlines, but he shows the important inland towns, rivers and ranges of hills and mountains, and sometimes shows the inhabitants. Also contained in the volume are thirty engraved double page plates depicting the inhabitants of Africa, India and the East Indies. This is a very difficult work to obtain in good condition, and such a volume would be priced at about £500, $1,200.

From France came a fine series of charts by Nicolas Bellin called the *Hydrographie Francoise*, published in Paris in 1765. The maps are beautifully engraved with carefully shaded coastlines, showing the type of terrain. They are not often found in colour but they are fine works of art in black and white. They have large rococo cartouches, but shipping and monsters have been dispensed with for the sake of more practical information. The charts numbered over one hundred and covered all parts of the world.

The English Pilot was first published in 1671 and also contained maps of all parts of the world, running into many issues up until 1803. The publishers alter from one edition to the next. They include Thornton and Mount, Mount and Page, who were prolific chart publishers, and lastly, Mount and Davidson. Early editions of the work are rare. Seller was one of the most important of the English chart makers and various other men were soon following his example: numerous charts began to appear from the workshops of leading map-makers.

In 1693 Captain Greenville Collins published the first national set of charts devoted to the British Isles titled *Great Britain's Coasting Pilot*. The set of forty-eight charts took seven years to survey and Collins published the charts as they became available. He made detailed maps of all parts of the country, paying particular attention to the ports and harbours, of course, and including the Scilly Isles and the Isles of Scotland. The work was re-issued during the 18th century; the later editions were printed on a coarse and thicker paper, not suitable for printing with worn plates, and therefore some of the later examples are very pale. Each map has a title cartouche and some of them are dedicated to important personages, including William III and Samuel Pepys.

Thomas Jefferys, whose *North American Pilot* of twenty-two charts was published in 1775, was another important chart maker. Sayer and Bennett published a complete *Channel Pilot* in 1777, and an *Oriental Pilot* in 1784. In 1801 William Heather published a set of charts of the harbours in the British Channel on five sheets, a beautifully engraved work. In 1805 William Faden published a *French Coasting Pilot*, a quarto volume, smaller than the majority of volumes of charts, containing a series of forty maps. Each map-maker made improvements and corrections to the charts as they were published, each collecting information from previous map-makers as was the case with maps of the land. Legend has it that a reef off the coast of Wales remained uncharted, much to the pleasure of the locals who profited by looting the ships that went aground. When the reef was eventually marked by William Morris other chart makers were quick to rectify the omission, thus, in the local view, destroying the livelihood of the area.

LARGE SCALE MAPS

Large scale maps are an important part of map collecting. They are not easy to find, because the size of them means that the mortality rate is much higher than the smaller maps protected within a volume. Some were mounted on canvas and rollers in the form of a wall map, usually fatal because they were originally varnished for their immediate protection, and this varnish makes the paper very frail and brittle. Some are found dissected into small sections and mounted onto canvas so that the map could be folded into a slip case. The best are those which are in volume form, but these are not easy to read, because of the difficulty of referring from one sheet to the next.

Many of the map-makers that have been discussed made large scale maps, including Mercator and Ortelius, though their work is extremely rare. Christopher Saxton made a twenty sheet map of England and Wales: the first issue is rare, but the later editions are occasionally found. The Dutchman Blaeu made some fine maps of the continents in the same style as his atlas, with views across the top and pictures of the inhabitants down each side.

By the middle of the 18th century there was a great demand for large scale maps. The Royal Society of Arts began an award scheme for the encouragement of such maps, offering an annual prize of £100 for the finest large scale map. The first prize winner was Benjamin Donn for his map of the county of Devon, published in 1765 by Thomas Jefferys, on twelve sheets at a scale of one inch to one mile, and with an index map. This map is usually found in volume form with an engraved title page, and is generally coloured in outline. Originally the volume sold for two guineas: now it is priced at about £100, $240. The first map to be submitted for an award was that of Dorset by Isaac Taylor, again on a scale of one inch to one mile, like the Donn map, but it did not come up to the standard required by the Society. The sum of £100 would not have been much assistance to a surveyor. It is recorded that Yeakell and Gardner required £2,400 for their survey of Sussex on a scale of two inches to one mile: this took six years to produce and was eventually published in 1783.

With the earlier and smaller maps of the counties we have seen how map-makers published individual maps of each county, but unfortunately no publisher completed a series of maps on a scale larger than the atlas by Bowen and Kitchin. Nearest to achieve this goal were Christopher and John Greenwood, the publishers of the atlas of the counties of England, already mentioned. Their large scale maps were printed on a scale of one inch to one mile and are therefore of varying sizes and printed on more than one sheet. The map of Devon is on nine sheets. The Yorkshire map is also on nine sheets, and because of the size of the county an exception to the one inch scale is made, and the Yorkshire map is reduced to three-quarters of an inch to one mile. The maps sold for three guineas each, the complete set was advertised at a private subscription rate of £125, but there seems to be some doubt whether the complete set was the maps which were published or whether it was intended to publish the last six maps to make up the set. The large maps were in serious opposition to the Ordnance Survey maps, even more than the smaller maps. The Greenwoods covered the country faster than the Ordnance Survey, who did not complete their survey of the north of England until 1873, but were the first to drop the system of mapping by county.

Unlike the smaller county maps, the large scale maps were generally made from new and up to date surveys. Their accuracy was very much better than the earlier maps, probably because the work was an individual survey and the financial success of such a map would depend on local purchasers, the inhabitants of the county, not always the case with a complete set of county maps.

There is a standard method of making these maps. The basic geographical detail is shown: county boundaries, divisions of the hundreds, roads and rivers, cities, towns and villages, hills, parks and woods. Apart from this, the degree of detail would depend on the quality of the map. By the 18th century roads had become imperative, some of the maps mark the mileages from place to place, the turn-pike gates, and so on. Early railways were marked as soon as they were constructed. Some maps show industrial detail, mills, potteries, furnaces and coal mines. Most of the 18th century maps

Colour illustrations on following pages:
Blaeu: Rutland, 1645.
Harris: Kent, engraved by Parker. 1719.
Plot; Staffordshire, engraved by Browne. 1682.

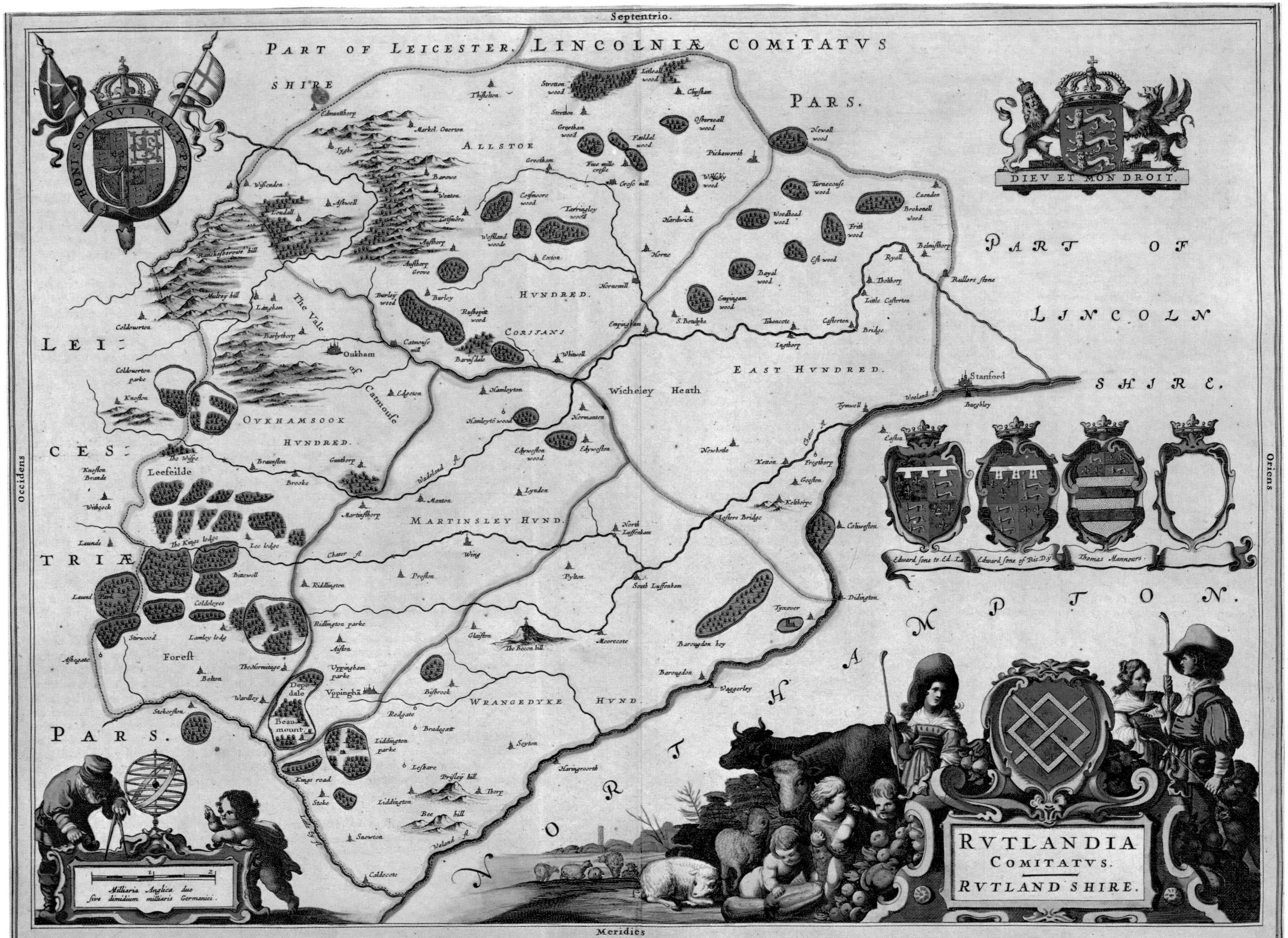

Septentrio.

DIEV ET MON DROIT

PART OF LEICESTER. LINCOLNIÆ COMITATVS

P A R T   O F

L I N C O L N

S H I R E.

PARS.

RVTLANDIA
COMITATVS.
RVTLAND SHIRE.

Edward Sons to Ed. Le. Edward Son of Rich D.Q. · *Thomas Mannners*

EAST HVNDRED.

Wicheley Heath

HVNDRED.

CORIFANS

ALLSTOE

The Vale

of

Catmoule

OVKHAMSOOK

HVNDRED.

MARTINSLEY HVND.

N O R T H A M P T O N

WRANGEDYKE HVND.

LEI-

CES-

TRIÆ

Foreft

HONI SOIT QVI MALY PENSE

P A R S.

Meridies

Milliaria Anglica duo
five dimidium milliaris Germanicum.

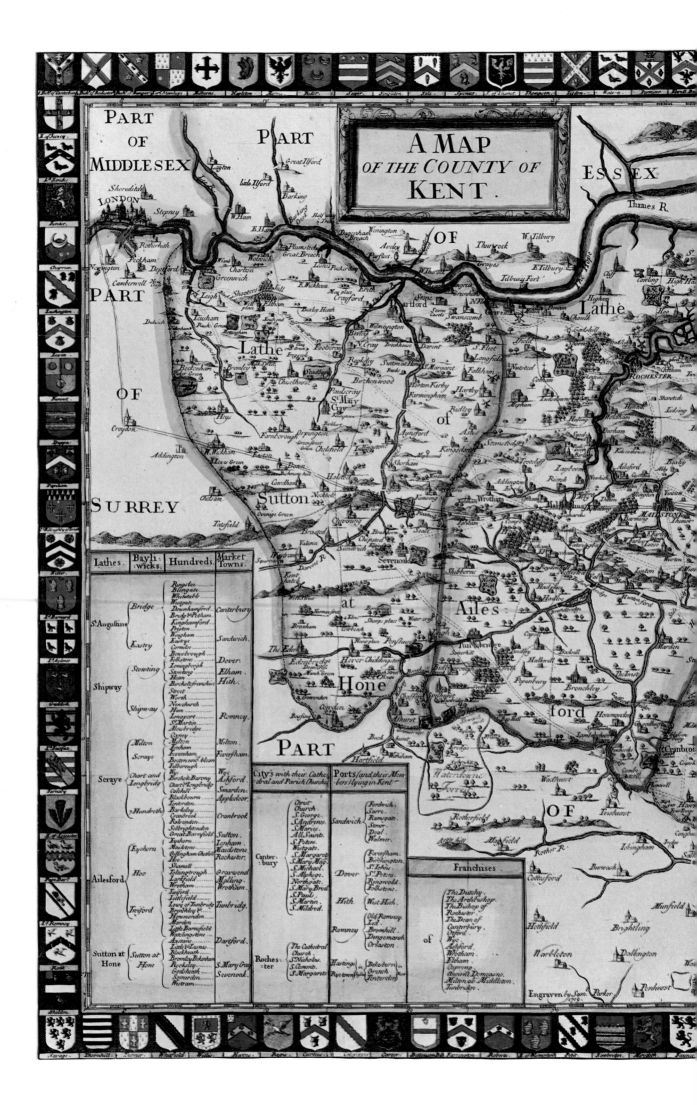

DOVER CASTLE and TOWNE

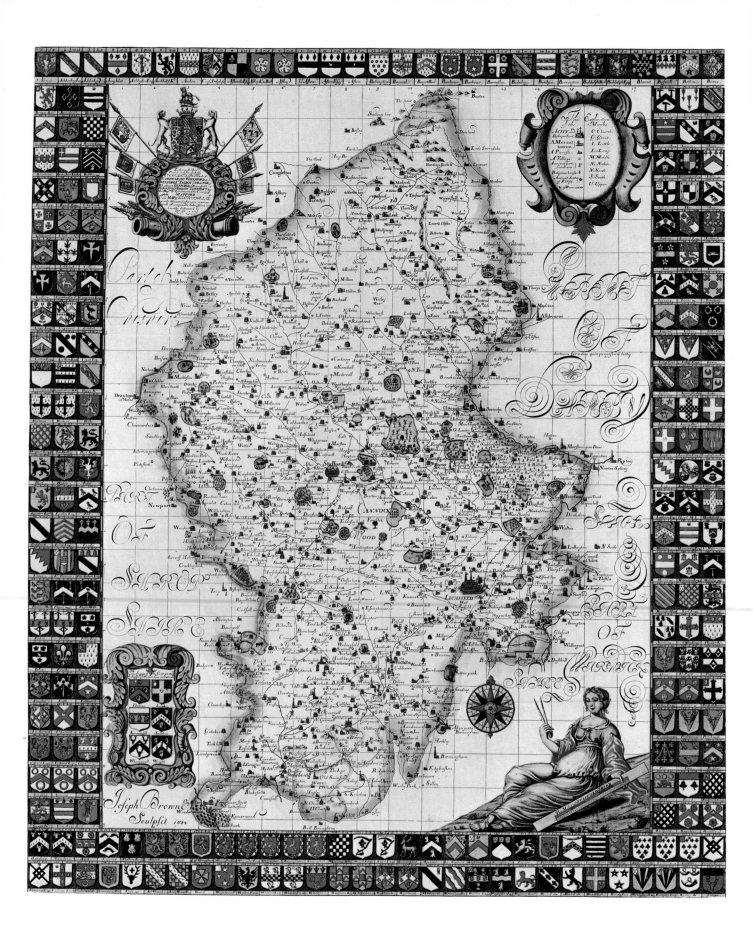

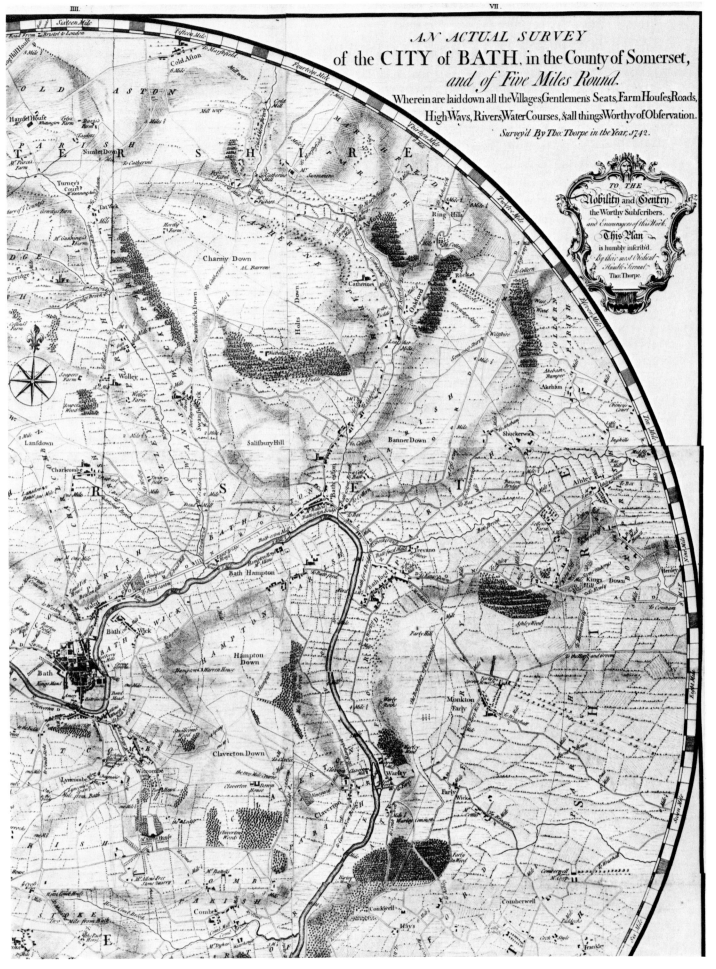

Section of the large scale map of the environs
of Bath, surveyed by Thomas Taylor in 1742,
in fine detail.
Overall size: 39¾ by 40 in., 103 by 104 cm.

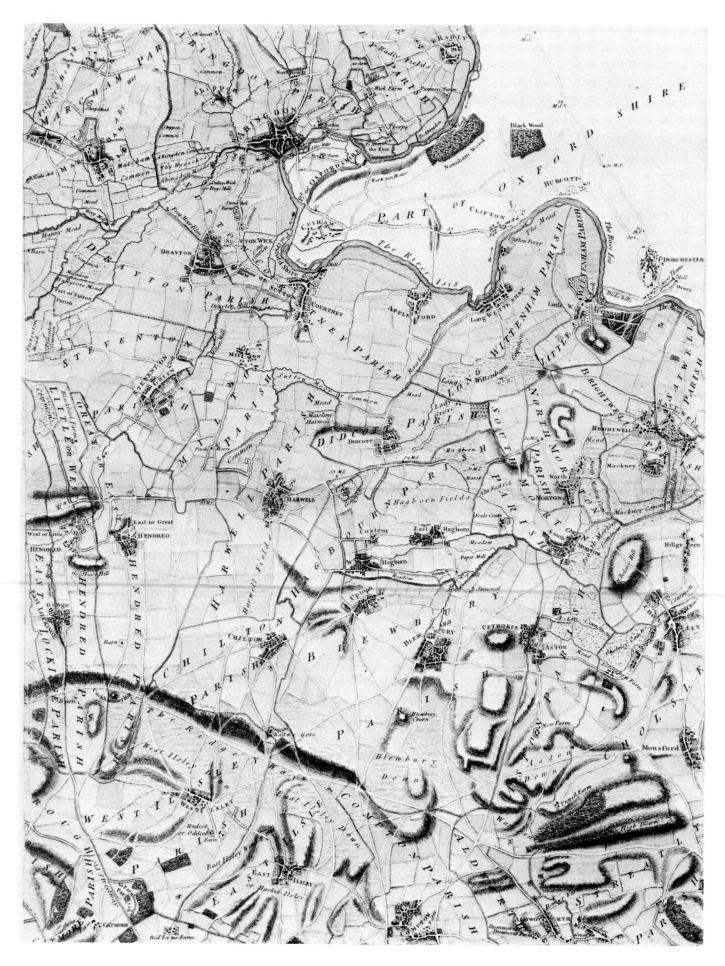

John Rocque: part of the 18 sheet map of
Berkshire published in 1761. The scale is
2 inches to 1 mile, one of the largest scale
maps. The detail is very good, each field is
clearly defined and the buildings in the
towns are marked. The method of showing the hills in relief is a great improvement
on the 'sugar-loaf' system of earlier years.
An interesting feature is the inclusion of the
milestones, marking the distances from London. They are not easy to see on the body
of the map but can be seen on the white
background of Oxfordshire, marked either
with a number or with the number and
M.S.

Size of each sheet: 25 by 19½ in., 64 by 50 cm.

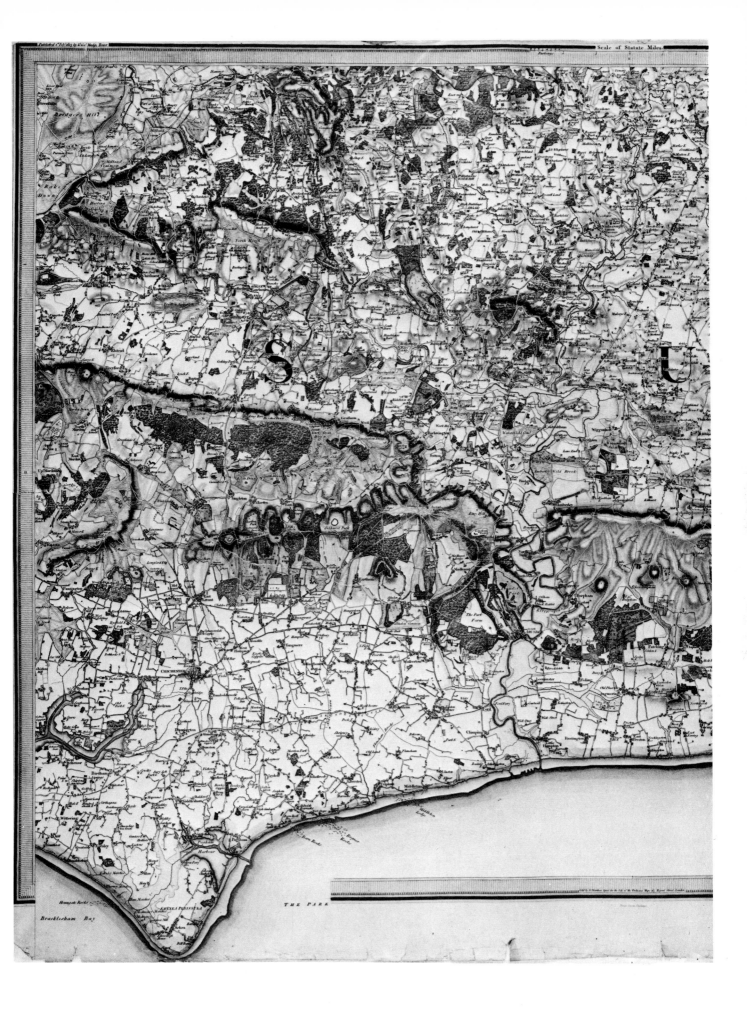

Section of the Ordnance Survey covering Sussex. This particular sheet was published in 1813. The makers of the Ordnance Survey were the first to dispense with the system of mapping the country by dividing the maps into counties.

Overall size of the sheet: 26 by 35½ in., 66 by 91 cm.

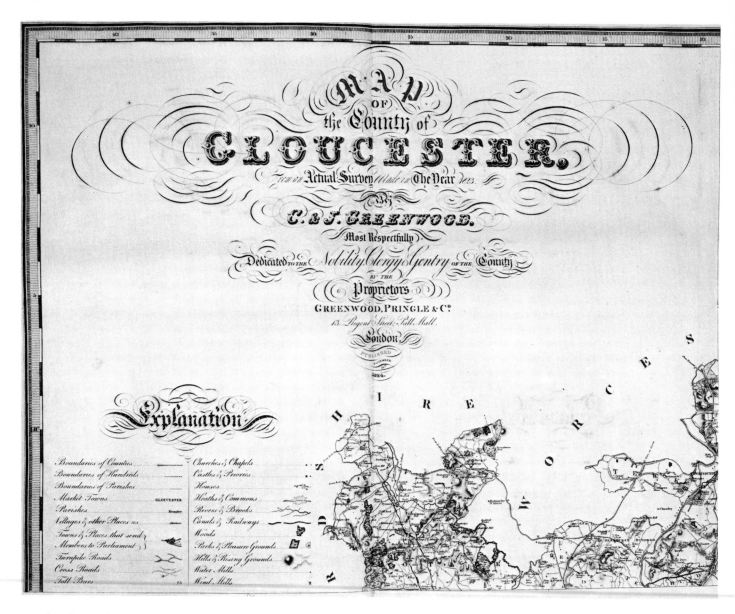

Detail of one sheet of the large scale map of Gloucestershire surveyed by the Greenwood brothers in 1823 and published in the following year. The key indicates the extent of the detail of the map. The map consists of six sheets, each measuring 19 by 25 in., 48 by 63 cm.

retain the style of decoration which is typical of county maps. Many of them have elaborate cartouches and are decorated with armorials, some have vignettes illustrating the local industries, similar to the large English Atlas by Bowen and Kitchin, including fishing, mining, cheesemaking and harvesting. The Martyn map of Cornwall has an attractive vignette showing a man using a theodolite, and another pushing a measuring wheel or 'waywiser'.

Among the other important large scale maps are those of John Rocque, who published maps of Surrey, Middlesex, Berkshire, and Shropshire. The detail of his maps is very fine, even the smallest buildings being marked. Chapman and André published a fine map of the county of Essex in 1774 on twenty-five sheets, another on twenty-five sheets was the Andrews and Dury map of Kent in 1769, and there were many others printed from about 1750, covering every county.

COUNTY
HISTORIES

All the English map-makers mentioned so far have been those who are particularly important, and with the exception of Saxton and Norden and the Anonymous series, all have made maps which the collector will come across regularly. These form the foundation of every collection of county maps, and if good examples have been selected, they will always be sound investments.

There are some historians and publishers who have devoted their attentions to one particular county. The earliest of these was Sir William Dugdale, whose history of Warwickshire, a folio volume published in 1656, contained maps of the individual hundreds. A second and somewhat improved edition was published in 1730, in which the original maps were augmented by those of Henry Beighton. These were re-issued in 1756 and as late as 1817, but the latter edition was reduced to octavo and therefore the maps were folded. A similar work was published of the county of Kent over one hundred years later, between 1778 and 1799, by Edward Hasted. Though the maps are plainly engraved, without any decorative titles or cartouches, they are extremely well detailed and, like the more attractive Beighton maps, they show every building and lane, though in the case of Beighton the importance he gave to private buildings seems to depend on the size of the owner's subscription to the work. A third work of this kind was P. Morant's *History and Antiquities of the County of Essex*, published in 1768, which included thirty-

Henry Beighton: Hemlingford Hundred of Warwickshire. Published in Sir William Dugdale's *History and Antiquities of Warwickshire*, 1729, one of the best county histories. Beighton was a surveyor of merit, the maps are well detailed and finely engraved. Size: 15 by 14 in., 38 by 36 cm.

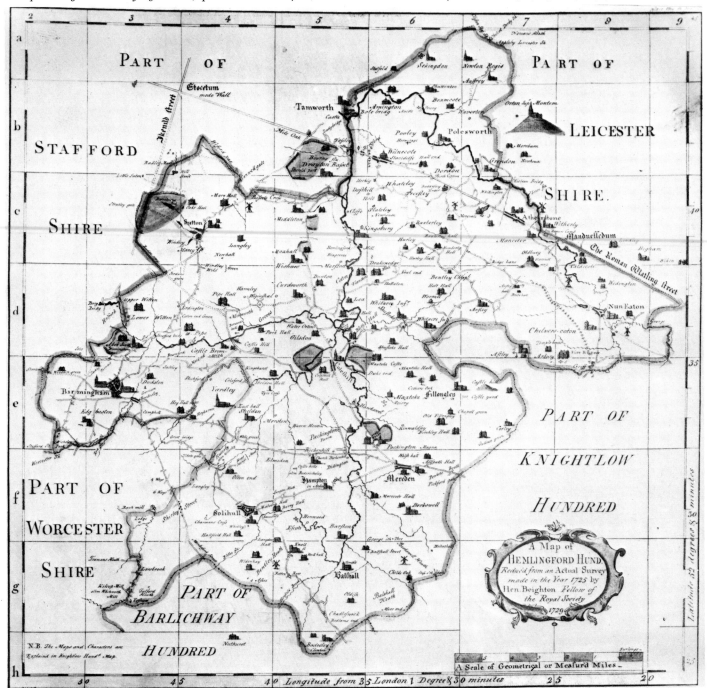

three plates, views of the historic monuments within the county and a series of maps of the hundreds. It is surprising that more comprehensive histories of this kind were not published, although there were many county histories illustrated with a map of the county concerned. Among the most important of these are the two volumes by Robert Plot, *The Natural History of Oxfordshire* and *The Natural History of Staffordshire*, published in 1677 and 1686 respectively, and both re-issued in 1705. The Staffordshire map is illustrated and is one of the most striking in this kind of work, with fine engraved cartouches and a wealth of armorials of subscribers. No indication was given to the colourist in order that the arms should be coloured correctly, a subject mentioned in the chapter on colouring, but it is possible that this map was coloured from a master copy. The Oxfordshire map is slightly smaller but in a very similar style, engraved by different hands—the Staffordshire map is by Joseph Browne and dated 1682—the Oxfordshire map is by Michael Burghers, who lived in Oxford and worked as the engraver to the University, but was originally from the Netherlands. He also engraved a number of plates for Edward Wells in *A New Sett of Maps*, published in Oxford in 1700. John Morton published *A Natural History of Northamptonshire* in 1712, containing an anonymous engraving of the county, measuring 28 inches by $15\frac{3}{4}$ inches (70 by 40 cm), which is again particularly attractive and is embellished with ninety-four armorials round the borders. When these works were originally published the maps were not the important part of the volumes, but today the histories are not prized very highly and it is the maps which make the volumes valuable, to such an extent that the loose maps are worth as much as the complete volumes.

A history of Kent which includes a very attractive map is by John Harris, published in 1719. The map was engraved by Samuel Parker and the scale of it is $5\frac{1}{4}$ inches to one mile. The borders are adorned with one hundred and eighteen armorials and in the lower right corner is a view of Dover and the Castle. It measures 23 inches by 32 inches (58.5 by 80 cm), and is folded into a folio volume. Also included are some fine views of the county's houses by John Kip. These enhance the value of the complete volume. The history

The Hundred of Hinckford, printed for the history of Essex by Morant, published in 1768. Well detailed with particular emphasis on halls and mansions. This example measures $11\frac{3}{4}$ by 11 in., 30 by 28 cm., the other maps in the series are larger.

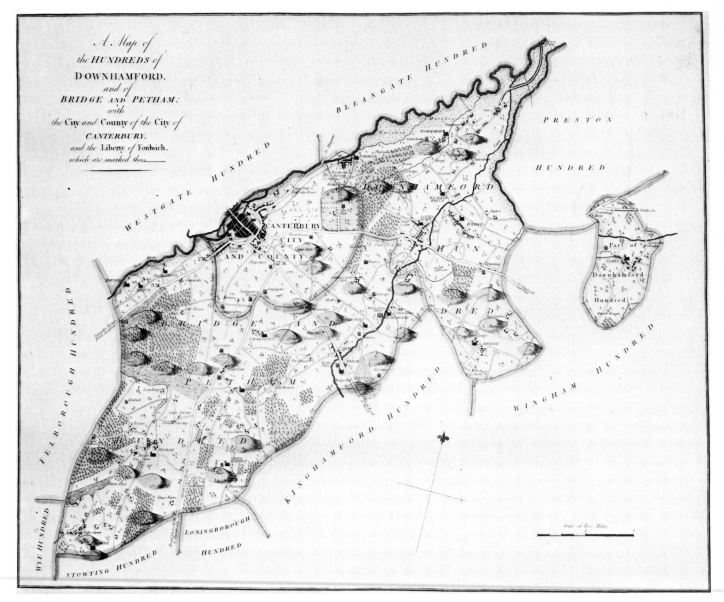

One of the maps of the Hundreds published by Hasted in his History of Kent, 1799. All the roads and lanes are marked, and most of the buildings.
Size: 17 by 21 in., 43 by 53 cm.

of Gloucestershire by Sir Robert Atkyns also has views of houses by Kip and the work is usually sold for these prints rather than the map, which is quite plain. It was engraved by Herman Moll and names all the houses mentioned in the history. Dated 1714, it is one of the earliest of Moll's maps. Sir Henry Chauncy published a history of Hertfordshire in 1700. Again this contained numerous house views but there were also some maps of the county and plans of Hitchin and St Albans. This list is by no means complete, but the books mentioned have been selected because they are representative of the histories which were made of most of the counties.

A number of maps were included in other topographical books purely for illustrative purposes. For example, Archibald Robertson published *A Survey of the Road from London to Bath and Bristol* which comprised some views taken along the road and was accompanied by a set of eleven maps covering the route. W. G. Tombleson's attractive series of views of the River Thames, published in 1834, is sometimes seen with an interesting map of the whole length of the river, beautifully engraved in the form of a bird's eye view, and although in minute scale, the whole river is shown on a page 51 inches long, buildings and bridges shown are recognisable even though they appear so small on the print.

Like atlases, these volumes have been broken up over the years, the single maps are by no means common, and possibly the complete works are more easily obtained, although they involve a larger capital outlay. One would expect to pay at least £50, $120, for any of the most decorative maps mentioned here, and more if the condition and colour is especially good. The value of the complete books depends on the number of plates in the volume and are priced according to the value of the individual prints. If the binding is particularly good the value will be considerably increased.

TOWN PLANS

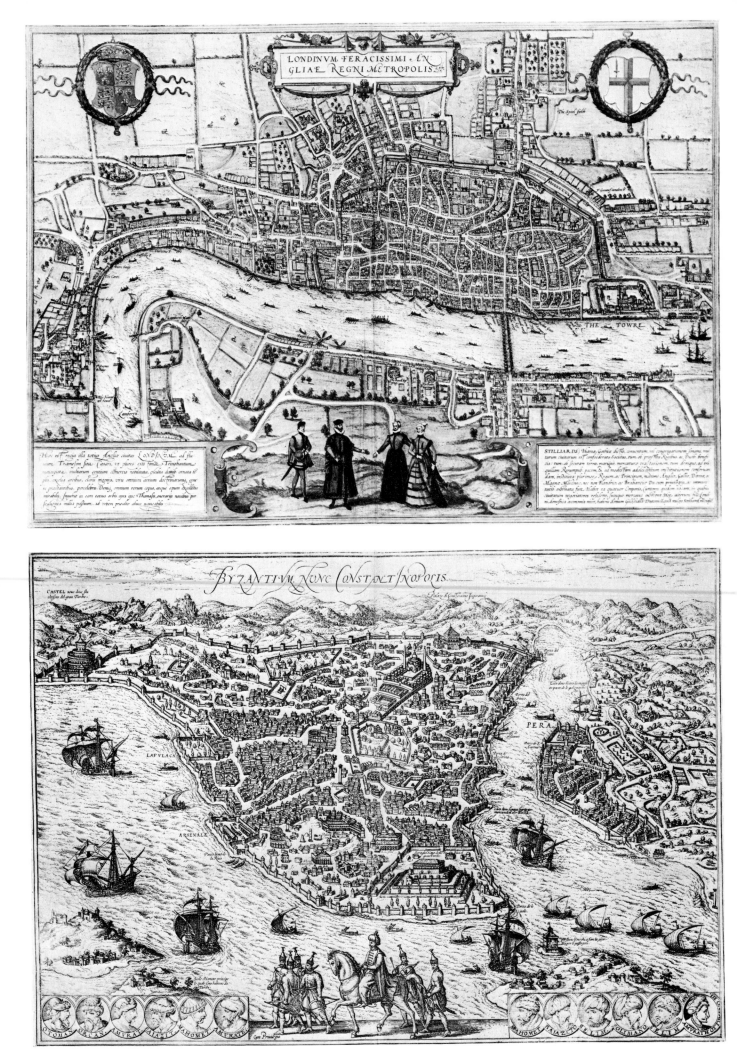

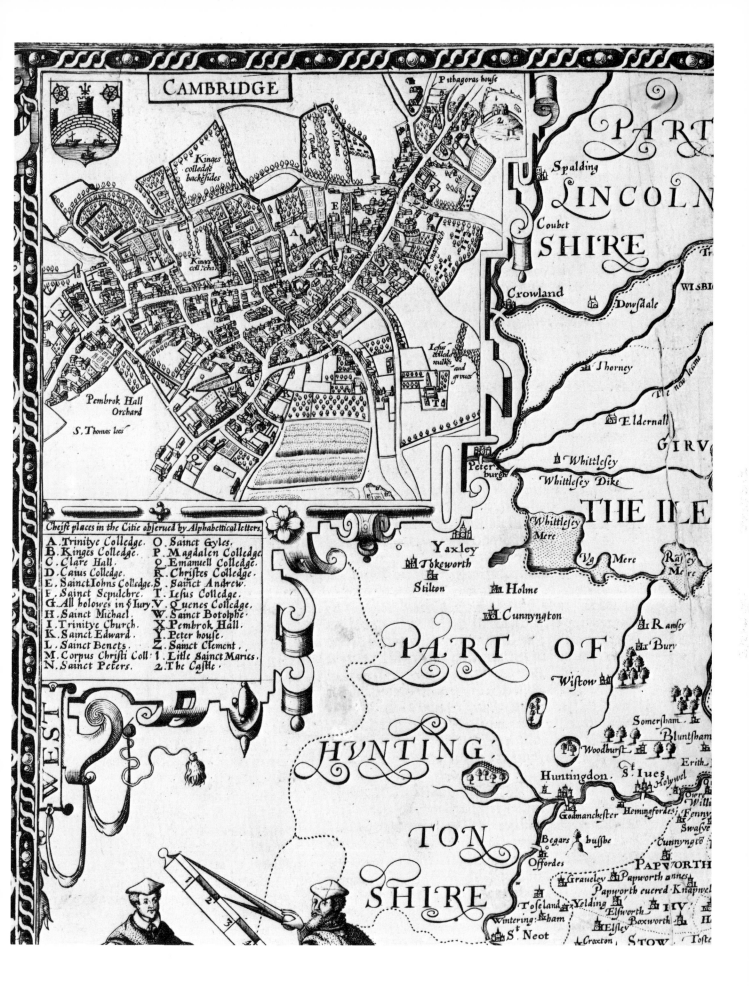

Left
Braun and Hogenberg's plans of London and Constantinople, from the *Civitates Orbis Terrarum* of about 1580.
Size: 13 by 14 in., 33 by 48 cm.

Above
Detail of the plan of Cambridge from the Speed map of Cambridgeshire. The key below indicates the colleges and important buildings in the city. In many cases Speed's plans of towns are the earliest to be printed.

Town plans can be as fascinating as any other maps. Being on a large scale, they show detail of the formation of a town or city at the period of mapping, some of them even number the houses. It is unfortunate that there were not many towns and cities of which plans were made. Many places did not have maps printed of them until the 19th century.

The earliest town plans were made in the form of bird's eye views, the

Richard Blome: Plan of London. Published in 1673. The engraving is by Wenceslaus Hollar who was responsible for several different plans of London. With the arms of some of the City Livery Companies this is one of the most decorative.

Size: 7 by 11 in., 18 by 28 cm.

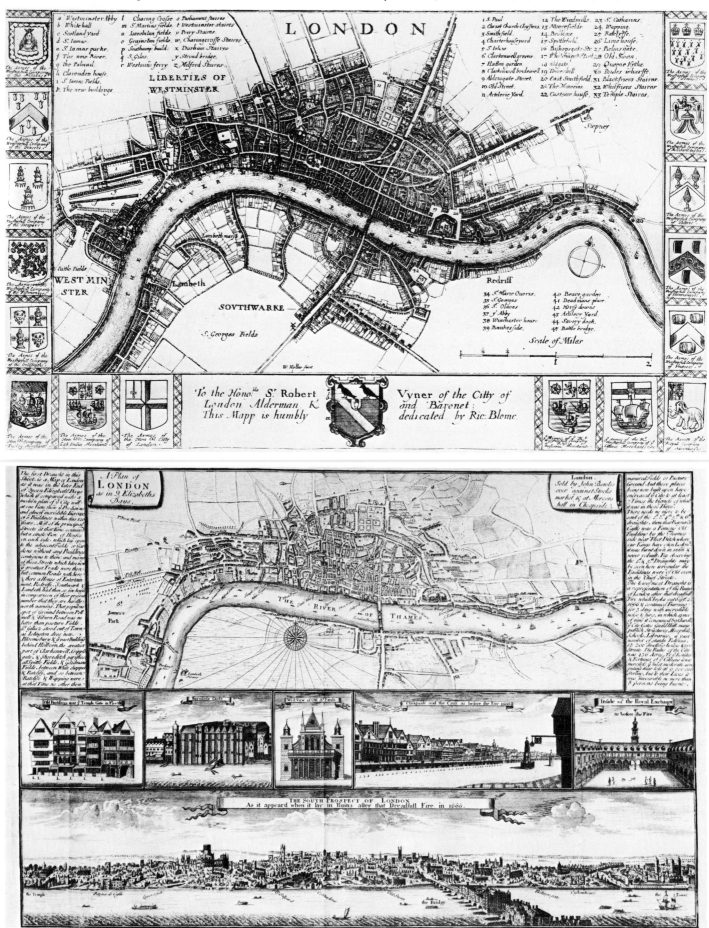

Johann Baptist Homann: Stockholm. Published in Nuremberg, 1730. Most of Homann's work was not as detailed as this, but the figures and the cartouche are typical. Usually the decorative detail is uncoloured, and the map itself is coloured in pale washes. Size: 19 by 22½ in., 48 by 57 cm.

buildings picked out in perspective. George Braun and Frans Hogenberg published a large series of plans titled *Civitates Orbis Terrarum*, first issued in 1572. The monumental work consisted of over three hundred double page plans, mostly covering the cities of Europe, though there were some of Asia and a few of central America included. The plans that they made of Britain were: London, which is illustrated, Oxford and Windsor, being two views

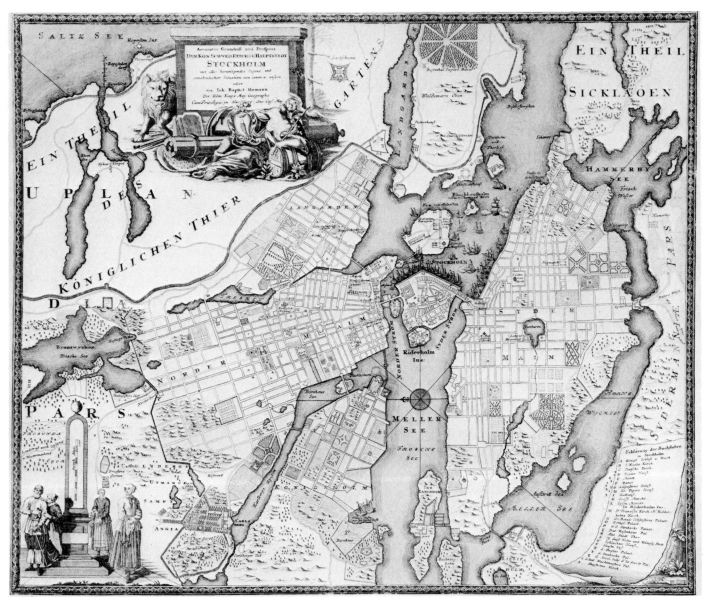

on one sheet, Bristol, Chester, Norwich, Canterbury, Edinburgh, Exeter, Cambridge and Nonsuch Palace at Ewell in Surrey. This last is an odd man out, and there is no apparent reason for the view to have been included. However it is an attractive scene, with figures in period costume. In 1618 two more plans were added to the series in a rather different style, laid out four to the sheet. One covered Ireland, the other depicted the northern cities of York, Shrewsbury, Lancaster and Richmond. These were engraved by George Hoefnagel, a Belgian, but his name does not appear on all of them. Though there were earlier plans of these places, these are the earliest which can be found on the market.

John Bowles' plan of Elizabethan London, published about 1740. Contemporary maps of Elizabethan London are expensive and difficult to find, and the later editions are therefore a good substitute. The 18th century maps of this kind are very acceptable, this one has the added attraction of the panorama showing the damage caused by the Great Fire of 1666, taken from the print by Wenceslaus Hollar. The buildings shown in the middle of the print were all damaged in the fire.
Size: 14½ by 22 in., 37 by 56 cm.

Sebastian Munster had been making similar plans in Basle from about 1550, slightly reduced in size and, as all his work, they were printed from wood blocks. He copied the detail for his plan of London from Braun and Hogenberg, and apart from the fact that Munster was not able to include as many street names as did Braun and Hogenberg, the two plans are virtually identical. The Munster print was first published in 1598. Another wood-cut which was copied from Braun and Hogenberg was that of Francois de Belle Forest, whose *La Cosmographie Universelle de tout le Monde* was published in 1575. His London plan is rarer than the Braun and Hogenberg version.

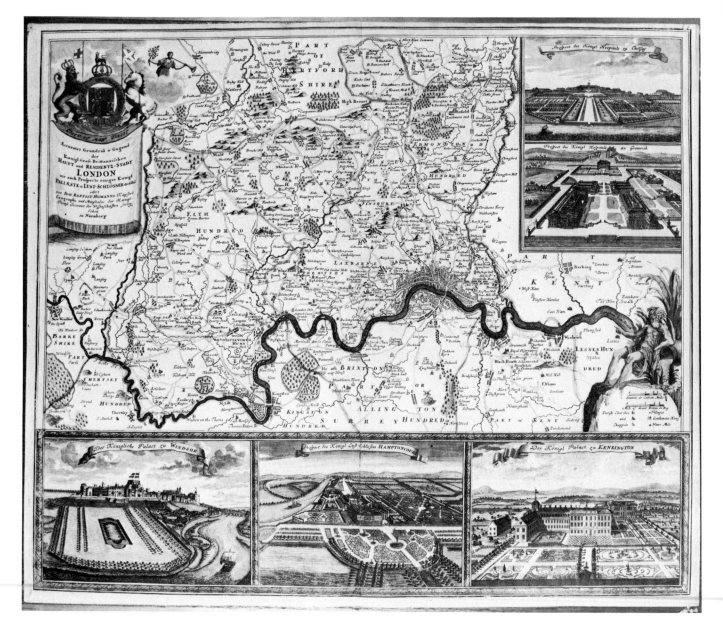

There were more plans made of London than of any other city in the world. The book *The Printed Maps of London from 1553 to 1852* by Darlington and Howgego, is the standard work on London plans. There are no fewer than four hundred and twenty-one entries without counting the variant issues. Despite this great number of maps made within those three hundred years, they are not easy to find because of the enormous population of London.

The other towns and cities in Britain were not mapped nearly as thoroughly. The first series of plans were those included on the county maps by John Speed. These were taken from the manuscript maps of William Smith in most cases, the rest he possibly made himself during his travels. On his complete set of maps there were no less than seventy-three insets and most of them are plans, a few being elevations of buildings. The plans were made in the familiar bird's eye view style. Because of their size they do not contain many place names, but this difficulty was overcome by lettering or numbering the buildings and supplying a key beneath. Although the city arms are pleasing to look at, a compass rose would undoubtedly have served a more useful purpose. Though not shown on the Cambridge map which is illustrated, most of the plans are given a scale of 'pases' (paces), in itself an unreliable way of making a map. Nonetheless, these plans were an important start and it is therefore rather surprising that no one followed Speed's example.

It was not until the 18th century that town plans began to be printed in quantity. In contrast to Speed's town plans which occupied a small corner of a page, large and magnificent plans began to be printed as separate publications. Pierre Mortier of Amsterdam published a fine series of uniform

Johann Baptist Homann: London. Published in Nuremberg about 1740. The views are of the hospitals of Chelsea and Greenwich, and the palaces of Windsor, Hampton Court, and Kensington. Though the map is titled 'London' the area covered was the whole of Middlesex. The advantage of this sort of map is that it shows the outlying parts of London which are now heavily populated but do not figure on the early plans of central London.

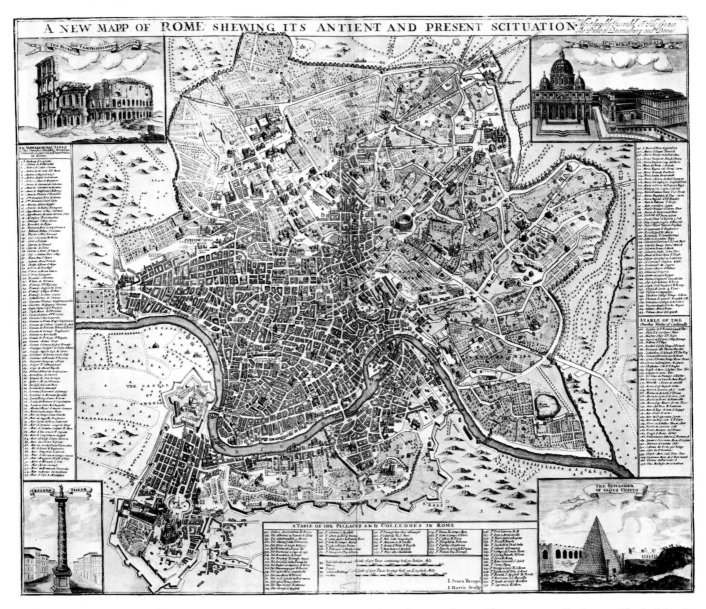

John Senex: Plan of the City of Rome. Senex was one of the best of the 18th century plan engravers. Listed are 252 landmarks. Size: 19 by 22½ in., 48 by 57 cm.

plans which are occasionally seen bound but are usually loose. Probably they were sold separately in order that the customer could make up his own set. These covered Europe mainly and were printed from about 1700. In 1720 John Kip published a number of plans in his *Britannia Illustrata*, the most important of these being the plans of London and Edinburgh.

John Rocque emigrated from France in the 1730s. Two of his earliest plans were those of Kensington Gardens and Hampton Court but they can hardly have been financially successful, because the demand for such specialised plans would have been very limited. Probably his intention was to bring his work before Royalty in the hope that this would spur on the sales of his work. In 1737 he started a survey of London which took nine years to complete and engrave. The engraving was carried out by Richard Parr and was published in 1746, printed on sixteen sheets at a scale of 5½ inches to one mile and was titled *An Exact Survey of the Cities of London, Westminster and the Borough of Southwark and the Country near Ten Miles round*. This was followed by a twenty-four sheet map of the more central part of London at a scale of 26 inches to one mile, Rocque's most important work, which was engraved by John Pine. In 1755 Rocque published an eight sheet map, again of central London, at a scale of 13 inches to one mile. All these maps were enclosed within ornamental borders and have large and elaborate cartouches. They had key maps which were printed and sold after the large maps were published but are often included in bound sets. Rocque also published large scale plans of Bristol in 1750 and Dublin in 1756, similar to his London maps and probably even more difficult to find. In about 1770 he published a less important series of plans of many of the British cities.

Another extremely fine map of London is that of Richard Horwood. Like the largest Rocque map, it is printed on a scale of 26 inches to one mile. The

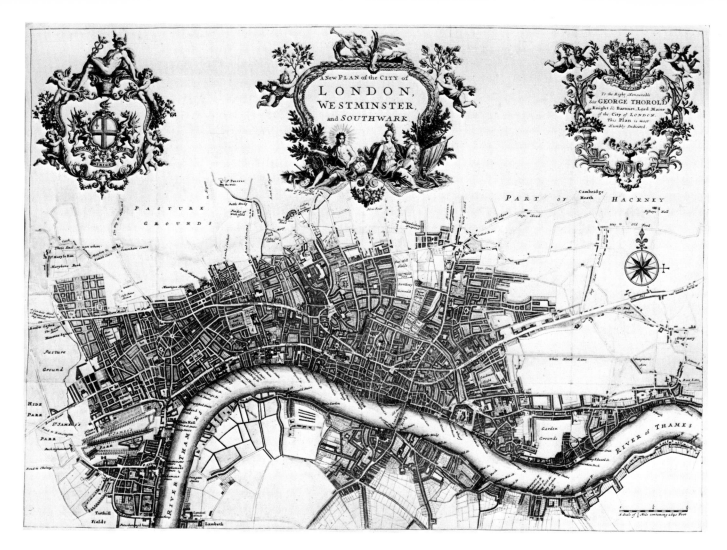

work was under the auspices of the Phoenix Assurance Company to whom the work was eventually dedicated. Horwood was continually in financial difficulties, as a survey of this kind would have been a very expensive business. It may well be that the Phoenix lent him money on the basis that he produced the map to their specification. The map shows and numbers every building, a remarkable achievement. For an insurance company this would have been very valuable: there was no National Fire Brigade at this time and

Above
John Strype: Plan of London and Westminster, published in 1720. A well engraved map, naming the main roads, squares, and stairs—the river crossing points. The churches and important buildings are shown in semi-elevation, like a bird's eye view. The cartouches are very decorative, and are sometimes found in colour.
Size: 19 by 26 in., 48 by 66 cm.

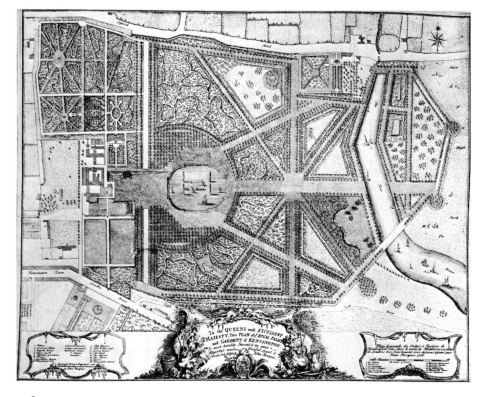

Left
John Rocque: Plan of the Palace and Gardens of Kensington. 1736. One of the earliest of the plans that Rocque made in England after he arrived from France. Judging by the comparative rarity of the map, the venture cannot have been very successful. A year later he began work on the large scale maps of the whole of London for which he is now famed. This map is typical of the fine engraving of all the work produced by Rocque.
Size: 20¾ by 25¾ in., 53 by 65 cm.

Right
Plan of Cambridge engraved by J. Roper from a drawing by G. Cole and published by Vernor & Hood in 1809. All these plans are very attractive with vignettes and arms on each. They are often coloured but the standard of colouring varies enormously, and is executed with little attention to detail.
Size: 9½ by 7 in., 24 by 18 cm.

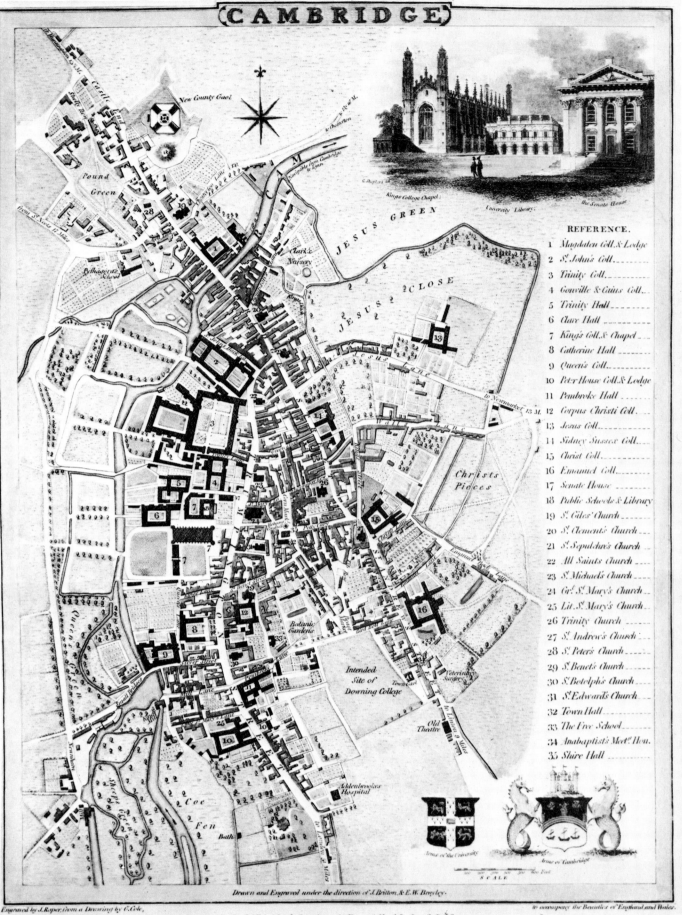

CAMBRIDGE

REFERENCE.

1 Magdalen Coll. & Lodge
2 St. John's Coll.
3 Trinity Coll.
4 Gonville & Caius Coll.
5 Trinity Hall
6 Clare Hall
7 King's Coll. & Chapel
8 Catherine Hall
9 Queen's Coll.
10 Peter House Coll. & Lodge
11 Pembroke Hall
12 Corpus Christi Coll.
13 Jesus Coll.
14 Sidney Sussex Coll.
15 Christ Coll.
16 Emanuel Coll.
17 Senate House
18 Public Schools & Library
19 St. Giles' Church
20 St. Clement's Church
21 St. Sepulchre's Church
22 All Saints Church
23 St. Michael's Church
24 Gr.t St. Mary's Church
25 Lit. St. Mary's Church
26 Trinity Church
27 St. Andrew's Church
28 St. Peter's Church
29 St. Benet's Church
30 St. Botolph's Church
31 St. Edward's Church
32 Town Hall
33 The Free School
34 Anabaptist's Meet.g Hou.
35 Shire Hall

Kings College Chapel.

University Library.

the Senate House

Arms of the University

Arms of Cambridge

Drawn and Engraved under the direction of J. Britton & E.W. Brayley.

Engraved by J. Roper, from a Drawing by C. Cole.

London: Published for the Proprietors by Verner & Hood, Poultry, Oct.r 1.st 1804.

to accompany the Beauties of England and Wales.

each company had its own brigade which was called to a fire only when the burning house was insured by one of its subscribers. This is why some houses are seen with an insurance company's plaque fixed to the front wall. Some contemporary prints show rival insurance companies hindering fire fighting attempts. The map was published in 1799, and re-issued in 1800, 1807,

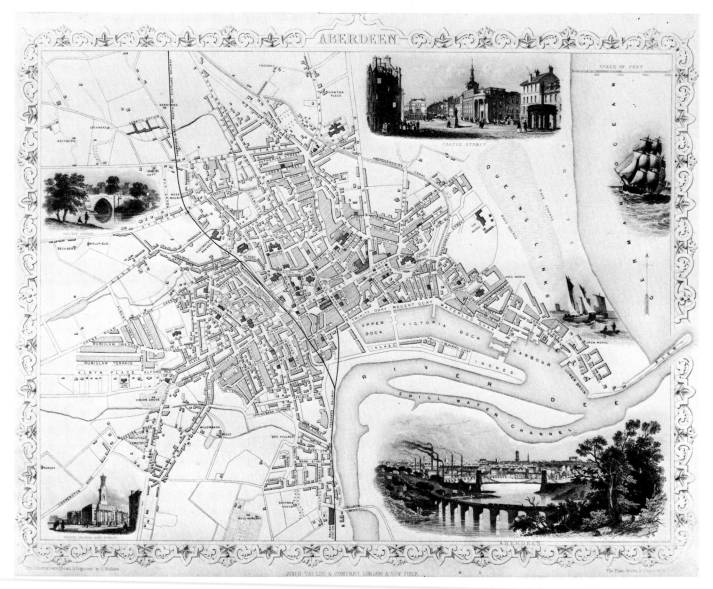

Tallis: Plan of Aberdeen published about 1850. Most of these plans are similar in style, with vignettes of the town and other decorative scenes.
Size: 10¼ by 13 in., 26 by 33 cm.

1813 and 1819. It would seem that once Horwood had managed to complete the survey it was a successful publication. However he died in utter poverty.

Among those who made series of town plans was John Andrews, who had previously combined with Andrew Dury to make the large scale map of Hertfordshire in 1766. In 1772 he issued the plans, small maps decorated with cartouches, covering all parts of the world, entitled *The Collection of the Plans of the most Capital Cities in every Empire* and re-issued in 1792. In the 19th century a comprehensive series was published for Baldwin and Craddock by 'The Society for the Diffusion of Useful Knowledge'. This was issued between 1833 and 1850, and covered all the main cities throughout the world, some of them on two sheets. The maps were included in a general atlas. John Tallis included some plans in his atlas of 1850 which are rather more decorative than the maps by Craddock and Baldwin, with elaborately engraved borders and some with views of street scenes in the vignettes. Similarly Thomas Moule published a few plans in his county atlas of 1836, but particularly attractive are the maps by G. Cole and J. Roper published by Vernor and Hood in 1809, the maps being dated earlier. They were engraved on copper plates, decorated with arms and vignettes. The Cambridge plan is illustrated and it is interesting to compare it with the plan by Speed.

ODDITIES

Many maps were made which were not intended to be a serious attempt at geographical accuracy. Countries have been portrayed as caricatures of people and animals: the most famous animal is the 'Leo Belgicus', first made as early as 1588, and adapted by many later publishers. It shows Belgium and Holland in the form of a lion, its head in the north eastern corner of France, the Frisian Islands forming the tail. This is done without distorting the geographical detail of the map, over which the lion is superimposed.

There is an uncommon series of English county maps which were made as playing cards by Robert Morden, the idea stemming from a set made in 1590 which is extremely rare, the only complete set being in the British Museum. The Morden series was published in 1680 and 1750, and again it is unlikely that a complete series should be found, as the single maps are only occasionally available. Some games were made using maps, probably to further children's education in preference to snakes and ladders, but these are mainly late Victorian and out of our period. Jig-saws were also popular, particularly those of the British Isles, the counties forming the pieces.

An intriguing series of novelty maps was published in 1612 to illustrate the poems of Michael Drayton's *Poly-Olbion*, blank verse extolling the beauties of the English and Welsh countryside. Hardly a city or a town is named, but the rivers and the hills are predominant, each river adorned by a Goddess. The map covering Oxford shows a delightful scene of the marriage of the rivers Thames and Isis. The map of the Severn area is illustrated with a choir on the Welsh side and an orchestra on the Somerset side. In the edition of 1612 there were eighteen maps in the series, and this was enlarged to thirty maps in the 1622 edition, the additions covering the northern part of the country. The *Poly-Olbion* took many years to complete. Drayton is reported to have been writing it in 1598 and he completed the second part in 1619. He had some difficulty in finding a publisher. The maps were engraved by William Hole, a famous engraver, already mentioned in con-

Michael Drayton, 1612. An unmistakable set of maps, engraved by William Hole to illustrate the poems of Drayton's *Poly-Olbion*. The information is confined to the natural geographical features, the hills, rivers, and forests. Sometimes these are seen in contemporary colour, usually executed in autumn shades which gives the print the appearance of early needlework. They are quite uncommon but are priced comparatively cheaply, around £20, $50.
Size: 10 by 13 in., 25 by 33 cm.

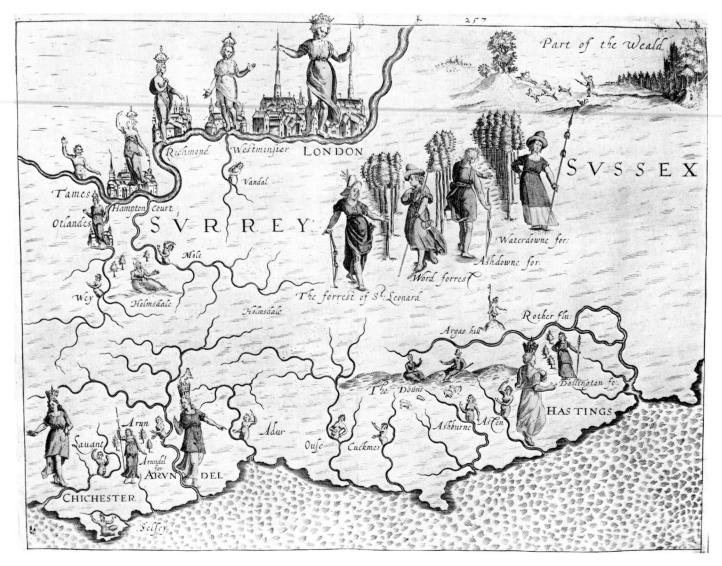

nection with his engraving of the Saxton maps for William Camden's *Britannia*. The maps are not often found in colour, particularly those in volume form. The coloured examples have a predominance of greens and browns, giving them the appearance of tapestries.

Equally unusual and charming is the series of bird's eye county maps by George Bickham published in 1743. Each of the counties is shown from above, and although there is little or no perspective they are more like a view than a map, the county conveniently coming to an end at the top of a hill in the distance. Some of the places depicted are not positioned accurately on the map, but moved a few miles to make more room for the lettering. George Bickham is renowned for his mastery in the art of calligraphy, his *Universal Penman* is one of the standard works on the subject of copper plate lettering. Though the bird's eye views were sold separately they were intended to be included in a greater work called *The British Monarchy*, consisting of fine copper plates describing each of the counties, decorated with views

George Bickham: bird's eye view of Sussex; not a serious attempt at geographical accuracy. The plates were published separately from 1743 to 1754, and thereafter complete sets were bound together. This is the re-issue of 1796. The earlier issues have an elaborately engraved title and a dedication at the top, and below a list of distances between towns within the county.

Andreas Cellarius: one of the prints from *Atlas Coelestis seu Harmonia Macrocosmica*, a set of charts of the heavens published by Jansson in 1660. Most of the charts are purely of the heavens, some show vague outlines of the earth.

See also colour illustration on page 136.

and arms. The Shropshire sheet is surmounted by a scene of some children playing cricket, one of the earliest prints on the subject. The third part of the book is *The Description of the Dominions of Great Britain*, which unfortunately did not contain maps but followed the same format as the *Monarchy*, describing the American Colonies. The complete work published in 1754 is rare, but the single parts are to be found, and also the separate counties which were published in parts at sixpence each. The views are now sold for about £12, $30. There is a later and slightly altered edition of 1796, in which the views were published with simplified titles at the top and the table of distances below is omitted.

George Bickham had a son of the same name who collaborated with him on the *Monarchy*, and also published a work called *The Musical Entertainer*, a book of songs set to music. Though this and the *Penman* are not strictly within the scope of this book, it is recommended that they should be closely examined, if the chance arises, to show the fine quality that could be achieved in the art of engraving.

Charts of the heavens do not strictly come into our scope either, but they are well worth mentioning here because the majority of them were made by eminent map-makers. Some of them are very fine works of art. The most important series was published by Jansson in 1660 from the charts of Andreas Cellarius—a magnificent set of twenty-nine folio maps of the constellations shown as figures and animals. The maps are circular within a rectangular border, the corners are decorated with geographers and surveyors at work, the ornamental titles, and cherubim. These are normally in fine original colour and are often heightened in gold. They were engraved by van Loon, many of them depicting the cosmographical surveys of Ptolemy and

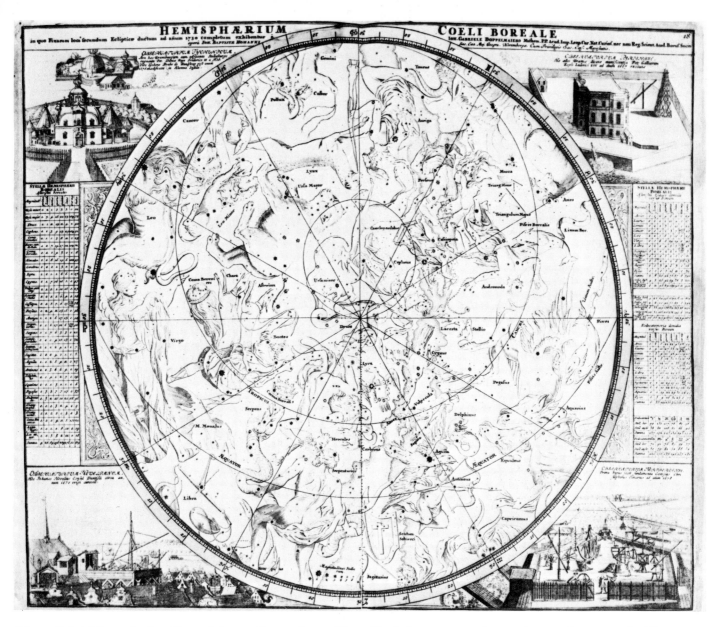

Johann Gabriel Doppelmaier: Chart of the Heavens. Published by Homann in Nuremberg in 1742. Though these charts are not as decorative as those of Cellarius, they are very colourful. This one shows observation instruments in use in the lower corners. Size: 19 by 22½ in., 48 by 57 cm.

Copernicus. Not all of them are as decorative as the example illustrated, some of them being more technical and scientific, but still embellished with attractive borders. A fine bound set sold at auction in London in 1968 for £2,200, $5,280.

A similar work was that of Johannes Gabriel Doppelmaier, not as spectacular as the Cellarius and about one quarter of the price. The set comprises thirty double page charts, again founded on Ptolemy and Copernicus, and was published by Homann in Nuremberg in 1742. The charts are not as finely engraved as the Cellarius maps, and they are usually coloured in pale washes, the cartouches remaining in black and white.

A charming little work which was made as a school atlas was the set of English county maps by Reuben Ramble, published in 1845. The small maps are surrounded by an ornamental border showing rural and industrial scenes according to the county in question, considerably more of the page being taken up with these matters than with the map itself. The maps are quite uncommon: they were probably not appreciated sufficiently to be preserved by their early owners.

THE
CONTINENTS

The atlases that have been mentioned were intended for a European market, but all the general atlases included maps of the other continents which were quickly improved upon as more information became available and they were mapped in detail. It is interesting therefore to follow the progress in the development of the maps of each of the continents, and to mention some of the maps which can be found.

AFRICA

The north coast of Africa is shown in the earliest editions of Ptolemy, printed and published in 1477. His map of the world, as he knew it, shows land along the south side of the Mediterranean. It was not until 1508 that the whole of the continent of Africa is shown on a map. The first map of the continent which is likely to be found on the market is the map by Sebastian Munster, published in 1540. A wood-cut map, it is decorated with elephants, trees with exotic birds and cyclops, and crowns and sceptres mark various kingdoms. Geographically the map is very plain, and although the shape of the continent is reasonable, only the names of the kingdoms appear round the southern part. Thirty years later the map by Ortelius shows great improvement in the information provided. The source of the Nile is shown well down in the south, and the River Niger is shown to be flowing the wrong way, a mistake common to most of the early maps. Mercator's atlas published in 1595 contained a similar map to that of Ortelius, and both of them are fine and decorative maps, illustrated with colourful cartouches, animals, ships

H. Hondius: Africa. Dated 1631. Published afterwards in the Mercator-Hondius Atlas.
Size: 15 by 19½ in., 38 by 50 cm.

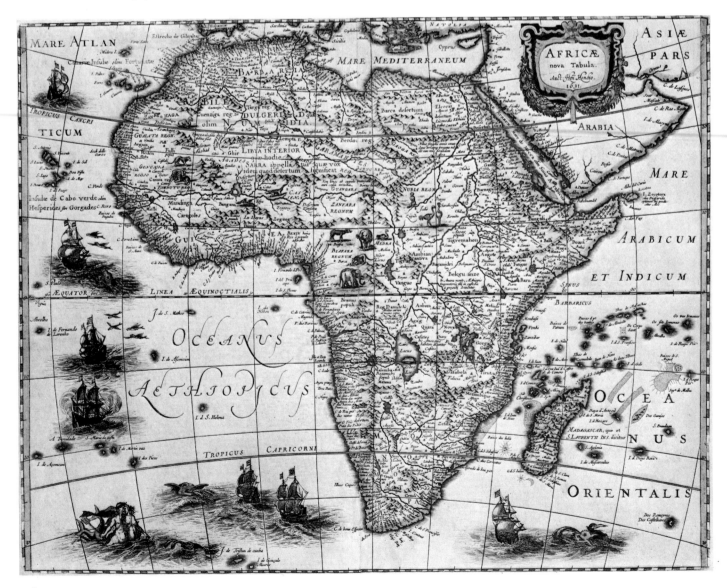

and monsters. In the early part of the 17th century several maps were printed which were even more decorative than those of Ortelius and Mercator. John Speed's map was published in 1627, a spectacular work with views of towns across the top, with an emphasis on northern areas, and views of the inhabitants in their national costumes down each side. This was the first English map of Africa. The style of it was soon copied by other makers, including Blaeu, in 1648, and Visscher in 1636. The later edition of the map in the Mercator atlas was engraved by Mercator's successor, Hondius, and is illustrated. From 1600 maps of the continent became more common, and each of the publishers of world atlases included at least one map.

Maps of parts of Africa were first printed at the end of the 16th century. Ortelius published two maps in his atlas of 1572, one of north Africa and one of Abyssinia, the land of the mythical Prester John. Linschoten published two maps which covered all the land from the West Coast to the Cape, and the East Coast, the maps joining at the Cape. They are highly decorated with ships and monsters on the seas and animals on the land, both of them giving more space to the decoration of the map than to the geographical content. Linschoten's maps were used as the basis for many future maps.

In the 17th century maps of the regions were more abundant: all the important map-makers made fine maps of the parts, which they divided usually by the north coast bordering the Mediterranean, the west coast, the east coast which is titled Abyssinia, and the southern part. Blaeu, Jansson, Sanson and Ogilby all followed the example set by Ortelius and Mercator, though one of the most attractive maps by Ortelius is his map of Morocco which is not included by the others. All these men made fine maps both of the whole continent and of the parts. They are decorated with pictures of African animals—elephants, monkeys, giraffes and crocodiles being those most commonly found. They showed the inhabitants, and the kings surrounded by their entourages. The detail of the coastlines of these maps is

Map of West Africa by Jacob Meurse. It was published in two separate histories of Africa, that of John Ogilby in 1670, the most common, and that of Dapper in 1668. Size: 10¼ by 13¾ in., 26 by 35 cm.

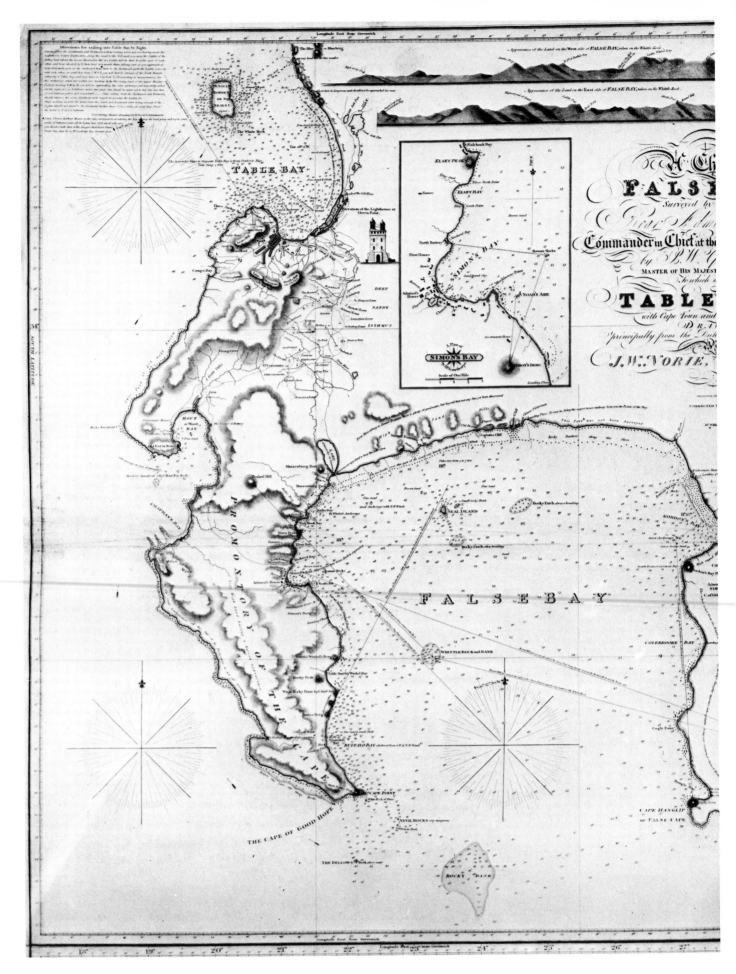

A fine detailed chart of the extreme south west part of Africa, published by J. W. Norie in 1837. The lower part of the map which is not shown shows the southern coast of Africa. Norie admits to the parts of the coastline that he has not surveyed. The parts which are surveyed are shown in good detail, to the extent of describing geographical formations, safe anchorages and depths. At the top are views of the coastline as seen from the sea, a useful piloting innovation dating back to Waghenaer.

Overall size: 38 by 25 in., 97 by 65 cm.

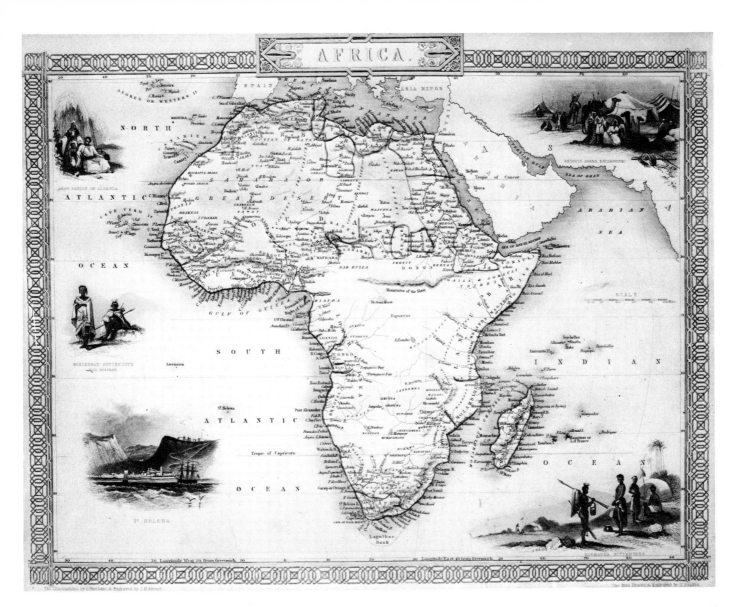

A small but attractive map of Africa, published in 1850 by John Tallis. The vignettes are usually in black and white, the map is coloured in outline.

Size: 12½ by 10¼ in., 32 by 26 cm.

strikingly good in view of the limited resources available. The inland detail was less accurate, particularly noticeable being the size and position of the lakes, and the River Nile commencing well to the south of the Equator.

In the 18th century the maps become more accurate but less decorative. Herman Moll published a fine map in 1720 which has a view of Cape Town in one corner, as had some of the later maps. Mainly the maps which were published from 1720 onwards came from the English and French presses, and the improvements in the inland geography become obvious as the settlements were made. Of particular merit are the maps of Senex, de l'Isle, Vaugondy, d'Anville, Sayer, Thornton, Seller, de la Rochette and Faden. From Germany there came the maps of Homann and Seutter. Homann also published a large map of the continent on four sheets, with a particularly fine cartouche of a group of inhabitants.

In keeping with the general trend of the time the 19th century African maps are less decorative. It had become necessary to have detailed and accurate maps, and the embellishments were not needed to help the sales. The Tallis map is one of the few exceptions and is well ornamented, showing groups of Arabs and Hottentots, and a view of St Helena.

The early maps of Africa are quite difficult to find and the demand for them is perpetually increasing. Any of the maps which show the gradual development of the hinterland are most sought after. Of the regions, the maps of the south are the most hard to find, but currently there is little demand for maps of the north part and of Egypt.

AMERICA

The earliest known printed map to show America is one of the world by Matteo Giovanni Contarini, printed in 1506. The only known copy is now housed in the British Museum. South America is shown as an unrecognisable mass of land at the south of the page, the West Indies are outlined but there seems to be some confusion about the area to the north, while the east coast appears to be an extension of the east coast of Asia.

The first printed map which is likely to be found by the collector is the *New World* of 1540 by Sebastian Munster. Although it is still very inaccurate, the shape has become recognisable, particularly the east coast, and great improvement has been made over the short period from 1506. There are some other maps which were made before the Dutch atlases appeared, but they are mostly very rare indeed and are unlikely to be found.

Both Ortelius and Mercator included maps of the whole continent in their atlases which have already been mentioned. America was covered by part three of Mercator's atlas, published in 1595. The north-west part is outlined and a few Spanish settlements are named along the coast, but the land immediately to the north of California is left blank. Mercator cleverly filled the space by noting that Christopher Columbus discovered America in 1492. The rest of the continent is well mapped.

In 1597 Cornelius Wytfliet published a volume which he called *A Supplement to Ptolemy's Geography*, the first atlas devoted to the American continent. In 1605 the atlas was enlarged to include four maps of the East Indies, and now contained twenty-three maps. This edition is more common than the

Hondius: America, published from 1631, the date in the cartouche in the lower right-hand corner, in the Mercator-Hondius Atlas. A fine engraving, in a very different style to the map in the previous editions which was superseded by this map. This is one of the early maps showing California correctly joined to the mainland: later there was a period of about a hundred years when it was thought to be an island.

Size: 15 by 19½ in., 38 by 50 cm.

one with nineteen maps, and is worth about £1,000, $2,400.

In the beginning of the 17th century there were a number of maps printed of parts of America, which, although they are rare and are not often on the market, played an important part in forming the basis for the maps which were to be printed later. Speed, Blaeu, Jansson, Visscher and de Wit all made decorative maps of the whole continent, and though they are scarce, they are not impossible to obtain. Blaeu and Jansson published maps of the separate parts of the continent in about the middle of the century, and Speed included four maps of North America in his atlas of 1676. Previously there had been only a general map in the editions published from 1627.

Speed was one of the first to show California as an island. Though the maps of Mercator and Ortelius had presented it correctly as a peninsula, there followed a period of about one hundred and twenty years when practically every map-maker showed it as an island, Blaeu being one of the exceptions.

Every publisher included maps of the continent in their atlases of the 17th century, but there was very little new surveying work carried out until the 18th century when the improvement in detail become more apparent. Herman Moll's maps are more accurate than those of his predecessors, though he continued to map California as an island. His world atlas which was published in several undated editions, all about 1720, contained three maps of North America, one of the South and one of the West Indies, two sheet maps each measuring about 22 inches by 38 inches (56 by 97 cm). These are well engraved, with clear lettering. The map of the British Dominions in North America shows the east coast in detail. One of the captions reads: 'The Western Post setts out from Philadelphia every Fryday leaving letters at Burlington and Perth Amboy and arrives at New York on Sunday night . . .'. An inset shows 'A View of ye Industry of ye Beavers of Canada in making dams to stop the course of a Rivulet, in order to make a great Lake, about which they build their habitations. To effect this, they fell large

W. Blaeu: Brazil. About 1650. The detail is confined to the coastline, while the rivers and hills are vaguely put in as if to fill in the blank spaces. The scenes of the cannibals operating on their colleagues are macabre and probably as inaccurate as the geographical detail. Blaeu did not usually use the lines radiating from the compass roses, a habit of his contemporary and rival, Jansson. Brazil is the most sought after of the South American countries and therefore tends to be more expensive: the example illustrated is in very good condition and would sell for about £30, $75.
Size: 15 by 19½ in., 38 by 50 cm.

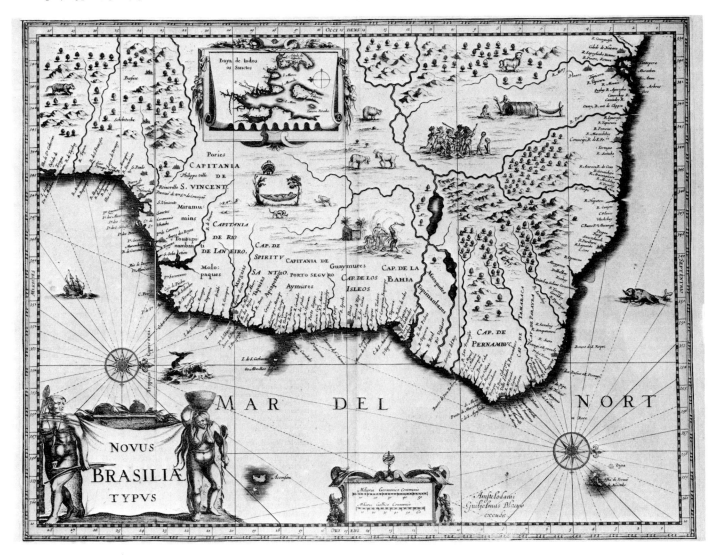

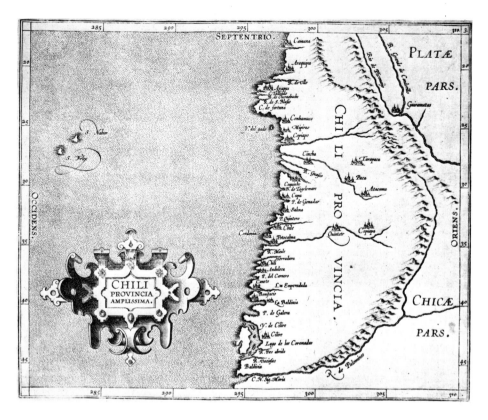

Wytfleit: Chile, 1597. Part of the first atlas devoted to the American continent. The style is very similar to the maps of his contemporary, Mercator, though smaller in size. All are quite rare, but the maps of the northern continent are particularly difficult to find.

Size: 9 by 11½ in., 23 by 29 cm.

Below

Joanne de Laet: the West Indies, published in an atlas of American maps. This is the edition of 1633. There is an earlier edition with Dutch titles of 1625.

Size: 11 by 14 in., 28 by 36 cm.

Colour illustrations on following pages:
De Hooghe: South-west England, published by Mortier. 1700.
De Hooghe: The Mediterranean. 1700.
Cellarius: Map of the Heavens. 1661.

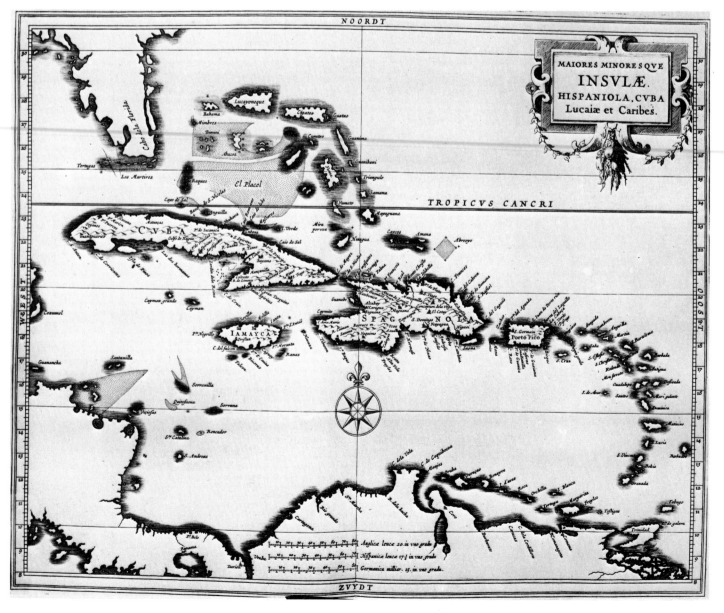

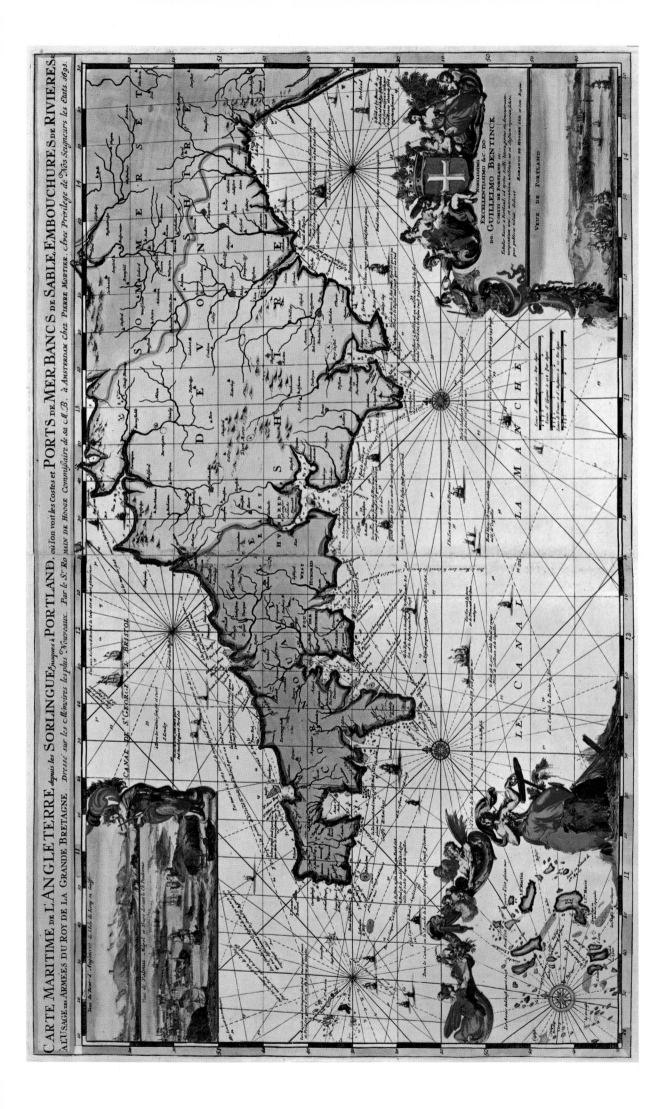

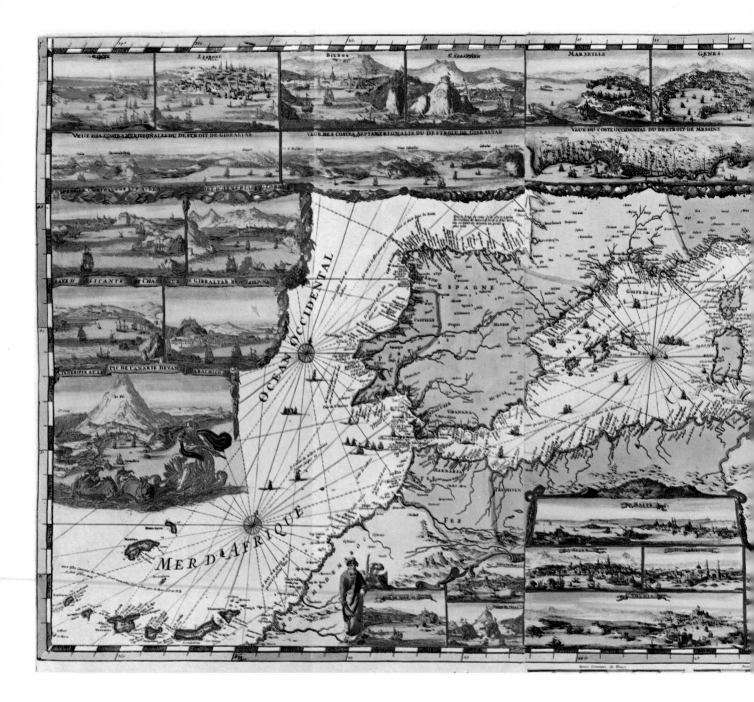

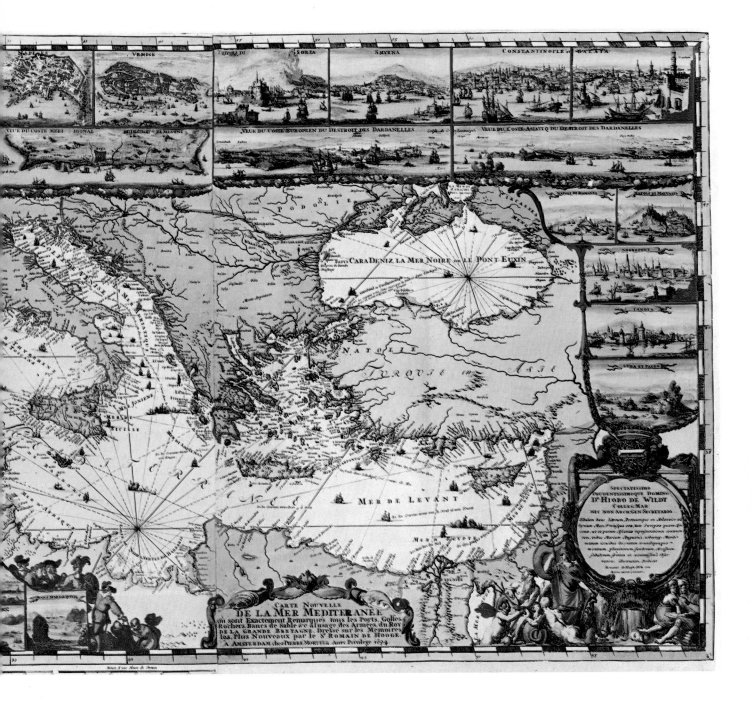

NAPLES · VENISE · L'ILE DI · SORIA · SMYRNA · CONSTANTINOPLE et GALATA

VEUE DU COSTE MERI DIONAL · DU DESTROIT DE MESSINE · VEUE DU COSTE EUROPÉEN DU DESTROIT DES DARDANELLES · VEUE DU COSTE ASIATIQ. DU DESTROIT DES DARDANELLES

NAPOLI DI ROMANIA · NAPOLI DI MALVASIA

NEGREPONT

CANDIA

SUDA ET PALEO

PODOLIE

MOLDAVIA

CIRCASSES MER

Turcis CARA DENIZ, LA MER NOIRE ou LE PONT EUXIN

NATOLIE

TURQUIE ou ASIE

MER DE LEVANT

MER D'EGYPTE

CARTE NOUVELLE
DE LA MER MEDITERANÉE
ou sont Exactement Remarqués tous les Ports, Golfes,
Rochers, Bancs de Sable &c a l'usage des Armées, du Roy
DE LA GRANDE BRETAGNE. Dressé sur les Memoires
les Plus Nouveaux par le Sr ROMAIN DE HOOGE.
A AMSTERDAM chez PIERRE MORTIER Avec Privilege 1694

SPECTATISSIMO
PRUDENTISSIMOQUE DOMINO
Dno HIOBO DE WILDT
COLLEG MAR
NEC NON ARCH GEN SECRETARIO

trees with their teeth in such a manner as to make them come across ye Rivulet, to lay ye foundation of ye Dam; they make Mortar, work up, and finish ye whole with great order and wonderfull Dexterity.' The map of the whole of North America is equally well annotated and both are illustrated. The geographical content of the maps is based largely on the maps of Sanson but extra place names have been added. Sanson included rococo cartouches which give the maps an earlier appearance.

Similar to both the maps of Sanson and those of Moll were the maps by John Senex, though the quality of the engraving of the maps was not up to the standard set by Moll. There are no inset views on the maps but he does include some notes about the country. On the North America map, dated 1710, is a caption 'The head of the Mississippi according to the report of the savages'. Senex also published some maps of America in his folio atlas of 1724 which are preferable as works of art, and probably less common than the large maps.

In 1733 a fine important map of America was published, a set of twenty sheets and a key map, the most detailed work of America that had yet been published. It was by Henry Popple and titled *A Map of the British Empire in America*. It is a rare map and one would be fortunate to own a copy. It was reduced and re-issued but even these cannot be described as common. The set on seven sheets is the one most often found, however, published by Covens and Mortier in Amsterdam. It consists of a general map, four parts which would join together, one sheet of plans of the forts and harbours, and one sheet of four views of New York, Mexico, Niagara and Quebec. Each page measures 21 inches by 25 inches (53.5 by 63.5 cm). Although on a much smaller scale, all the information contained on the separate sheets is also covered by the general map. One should expect to pay in excess of £200, $480, for this set. The map was influential on the later maps of America, though not often credited to Popple.

Other large scale maps soon appeared, among the most important is

John Speed: New England and New York. Published in 1676. Although this is a late edition of the atlas, it is the first in which the parts of America were included.
Size: 15 by 19¾ in., 38 by 51 cm.

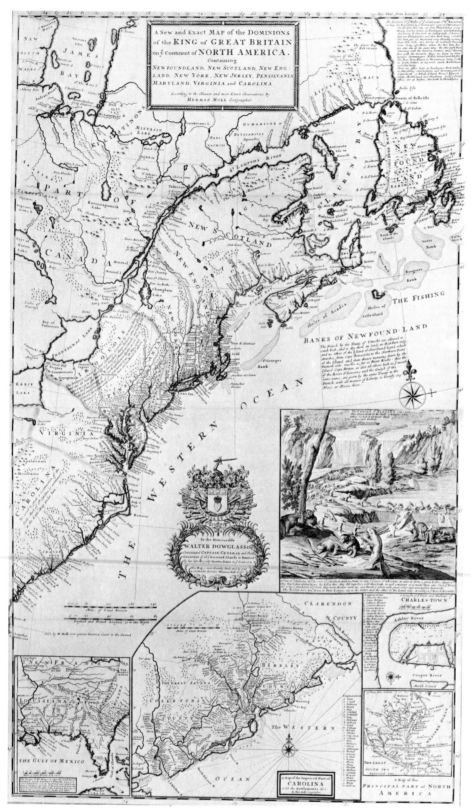

Herman Moll: North-East America and part of Canada. 1720. A large map generally found folded three times and consequently not often in good condition. Because of the limitations of paper and printing press sizes, the maps were printed on two pages and joined together, and they do not always meet perfectly. Here it can be seen that the 'O' of Ocean has been slightly cut off where the pages were joined. The illustration of the beavers has been referred to in the text. Size: 38 by 22 in., 97 by 56 cm.

Right

Thomas Jefferys: Barbados. Published by Sayer, 1775. The map was surveyed by William Mayo and is one of a series of sixteen of the West Indian Islands. In 1779 Sayer was joined by Bennett in publishing another atlas of the West Indies, this time there being 40 maps on 20 sheets. The engraving is very clear and precise, typical of the work produced in England at this period. Size: 23¾ by 18½ in., 60 by 47 cm.

Evans' map of the Middle Colonies and John Mitchell's of the British and French Dominions in North America. Some fine maps were published by Sayer and Bennett from about 1765. In 1776 an important atlas was published by Thomas Jefferys called the *American Atlas*, containing thirty maps devoted to the American continent. Jefferys was one of the most important map-makers of this period, and apart from the *American Atlas* he published a *West Indian Atlas*, first issued in 1775 and quite rare, but the later editions from 1780 are more readily available. The maps of this period are particularly interesting because they show the development which was taking place in the country, and they were in great demand during the War of Independence.

Another rare work is the remarkable *Atlantic Neptune*, compiled by J. F. W. des Barres and comprising maps, charts and topographical views. All copies are slightly varied, their value therefore depending on the content, but copies rarely come on to the market.

BARBADOES,
SURVEYED
BY WILLIAM MAYO,
ENGRAVED and IMPROVED
BY
THOMAS JEFFERYS,
Geographer to the KING.

Appearance of Barbadoes when the North Point is W.N.W.9 Leagues off.

Appearance of Barbadoes when it bears W.N.W. 7 Leagues off.

THE AREA of EACH PARISH IN ACRES.

Names of the Parishes.	Acres.
1. CHRIST CHURCH	14310
2. ST PHILIP	16010
3. ST MICHEL	9580
4. ST GEORGE	10795
5. ST JOHN	9600
6. ST JAMES	7805
7. ST THOMAS	8500
8. ST JOSEPH	6010
9. ST ANDREW	8780
10. ST PETER	8580
11. ST LUCY	9735
Total	100170

One Sea League of 20 in a Degree.

Statute Miles 69½ in a Degree.

William Faden took over the business of Thomas Jefferys and continued to publish atlases of America of some merit, especially those on a large scale. Similar to these are the maps by Arrowsmith which he began to publish in 1796.

The Americans began printing their own maps with the atlas by Carey and Lea published in 1822. Once they had established themselves they took over publication of their own maps and they were soon providing information for the maps which were printed in Europe.

ASIA

The history of the mapping of Asia is as ancient as the history of the mapping of Europe. The continent was well covered by the maps of Ptolemy, though these are less recognisable than his maps of Europe. India appears to be very foreshortened and Ptolemy drew Ceylon as a much larger island than in fact it is.

As with the maps of Africa and America, the earliest examples which may come on to the market are the Munster maps of 1540. His Asian map is very imaginative, showing the continent quite square, and surrounded by small islands as if to complete the picture. He notes that there are 7,448 islands in the Archipelago roughly where Japan should be.

The early maps from the Low Countries showed much more detail of the western part of Asia, especially Palestine and Persia. The geographical content of them fades as they proceed further to the east. The maps of Linschoten show the coastlines in detail and his maps formed the basis of many subsequent works. His map of Eastern Asia is illustrated and it can be seen that the islands are clearly defined in the south part, gradually becoming less accurate in the north, Korea being shown as an island.

It was not until 1655 that a set of maps devoted to China was published by Blaeu. It was titled *Atlas Sinensis* and was the work of Martin Martini, an Italian Jesuit missionary, collected from local maps. The series consists of seventeen maps, including one of Japan, and they are much plainer than Blaeu's usual work. Some of them are decorated with figures in national costume which assist to embellish the cartouches, but that of Japan, which is illustrated, will be seen to be void of decor. It was eighty years before the

Linschoten: Eastern Asia. Engraved by Langren in 1595 and published in the same year. The north point of the map is on the left-hand side.
Size: 15¼ by 20 in., 39 by 51 cm.

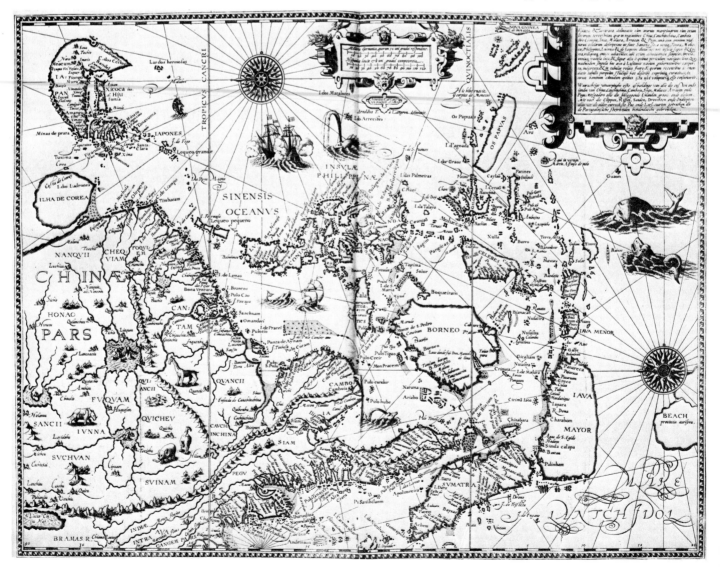

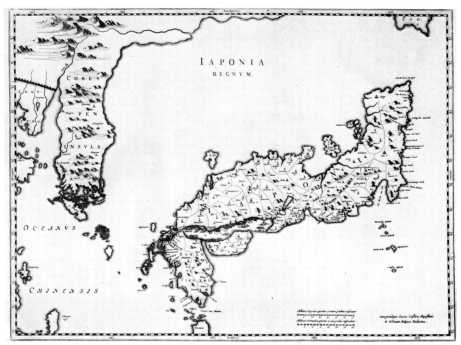

Blaeu: Japan. Published in 1650. Though this is one of the plainest maps ever to be published by Blaeu, it is still very attractive, and the absence of any cartouche seems to draw attention to the fine lettering.
Size: 16½ by 22½ in., 42 by 57 cm.

work of Martini was improved upon. An atlas was published in 1735 by du Halde and included maps and view of China, an important work. Two years later another atlas was published of China by d'Anville, titled *Atlas de la Chine*. The work of these two was used thereafter by the later map-makers until the 19th century.

The first maps to be made of India covered a large area. Ortelius and Mercator included the East Indies in their maps and this was the practice of the majority of 17th century map-makers. It was not until detailed maps were required for trading purposes, in particular by the East India Company,

Mercator: East Indies. Included in the Mercator-Hondius Atlas, this particular example was published in 1630. Like all Mercator maps, the lettering is clearly engraved and the decor finely executed.
Size: 13½ by 18¾ in., 34 by 48 cm.

that a thorough survey of India was carried out. Major James Rennel published a map of the whole of India in 1782, but this was preceded by some fine maps of parts of India which were published from 1779. His maps were issued by Laurie and Whittle, William Faden and James Wild. From then on maps were made by other military men and appeared in many of the English atlases.

AUSTRALIA

The illustration of the Ortelius map of the Pacific Ocean shows a huge mass of land right across the south, which is marked 'Terra Australis, sive Magellanica, nondum detecta'. Ortelius was the first cartographer to show the strait between New Guinea and Australia. His successors were not so certain about this, and over a hundred years later, New Guinea was shown joined on to Carpentaria. The first maps to give a more accurate outline of the coastline were made after 1770. Captain Cook charted New Zealand and Eastern Australia between 1768 and 1771, and cartographers were quick to add Cook's findings to their maps. Their accuracy quickly developed, but most of the maps which showed Australia before 1800 were in fact of the East Indies. A good impression of the development of Australia can be gained by looking at maps of the world and Asia to see how the shape gradually took its form. Some of the maps made before Cook's discoveries show Australia as an island, being a shrewd guess, the more reliable map-makers only marking the coastline that had been discovered. After 1800 more interest was taken in the country as a whole and maps began to be printed purely of Australia. These are now not easily found and in fact some buyers prefer to have a map which shows the development of the country rather than

Right
New South Wales, published in 1850 by John Tallis. All the maps in the series are by Rapkin and the vignettes by various artists, in this case by H. Warren and engraved by J. Rogers. Generally the maps are coloured in outline with the borders and the vignettes left black and white. The maps in the series of the British Colonies are very popular, being one of the few decorative series made at this period.
Size: 14 by 10 in., 36 by 25 cm.

Abraham Ortelius: Pacific Ocean. Dated 1589 and published in the subsequent atlases by Ortelius. The map was composed from the best available information and illustrates how little was known of the area.
Size: 13½ by 19½ in., 35 by 50 cm.

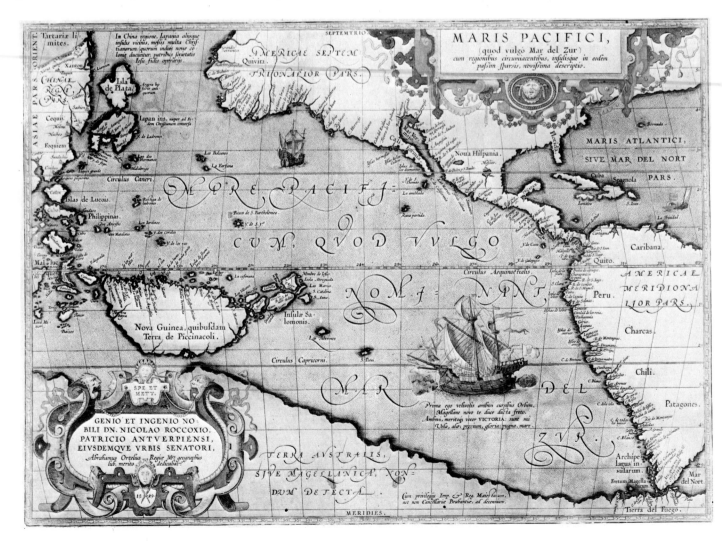

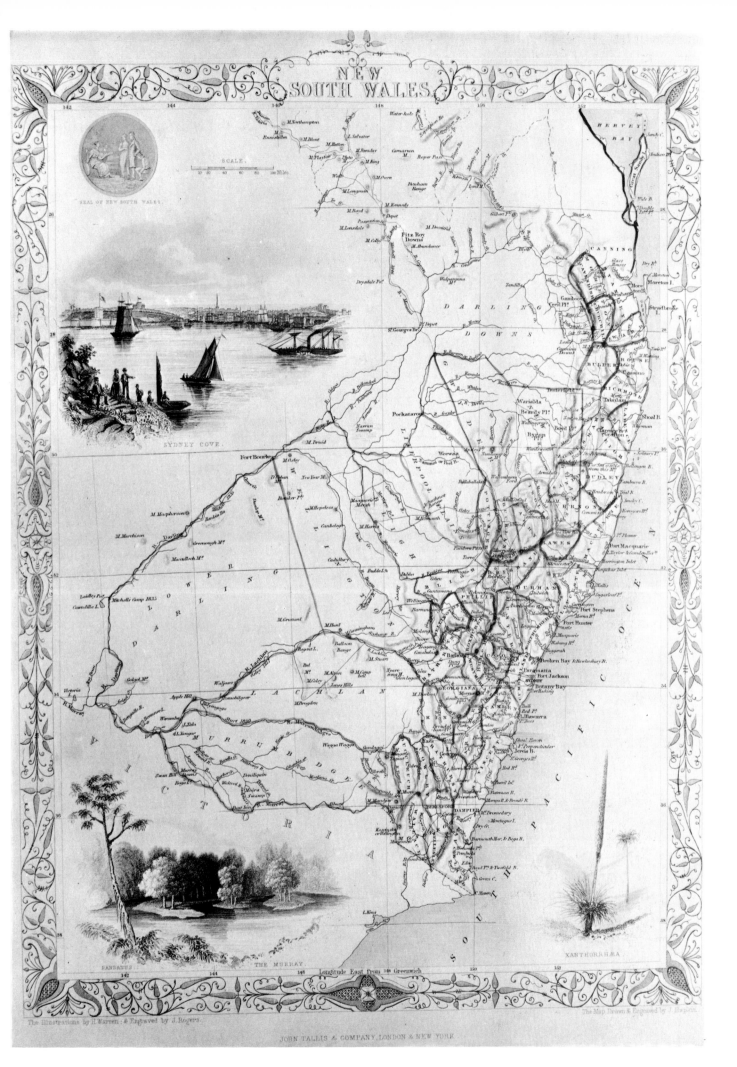

NEW SOUTH WALES.

SCALE

SEAL OF NEW SOUTH WALES.

SYDNEY COVE.

PANDANUS.

THE MURRAY.

XANTHORRHÆA.

Longitude East from 14th Greenwich

The Illustrations by H. Warren; & Engraved by J. Rogers.

The Map Drawn & Engraved by J. Rapkin.

JOHN TALLIS & COMPANY, LONDON & NEW YORK.

an earlier map which shows the country in outline only. There were no maps which showed any inland features until the 19th century—the map by Thompson in 1814 indicates the mountains on the east and the states begin to appear at about that date. All the map-makers working at the period made maps of the country because it was a recent discovery, but few of them had any new information to add. Among those who published up to date maps was the Society for the Diffusion of Useful Knowledge in about 1830, and the maps by Tallis, the last series of decorative maps, with views of the towns, inhabitants, animals and birds decorating the borders, show the inland features, mountains, rivers and boundaries of the states. In this short period the whole history of the country is portrayed in maps, well inside the period of printed maps which are generally available. It should not be supposed, however, that maps of Australia are easily obtained—the supply is far too limited to meet an ever increasing demand. The museums are still anxiously looking for maps to make up their collections and they are willing to pay high prices in order to complete their collections. It may mean that the prices of rarities are very high, and the not so rare are probably above the price range of the individual who is looking for something to hang on the wall of the dining room. Pre-19th century maps are difficult to find at any price, and the later maps are usually rather plain. The vignettes on the Tallis maps give them an attractive appeal but there are no maps of Australia which are a match for the 17th century European maps.

FRONTISPIECES

An integral part of map collecting is the study of frontispieces and title pages of atlases. They are usually very elaborate affairs, engraved by the finest craftsmen available, not only announcing the title of the volume, but enticing the viewer to look further into the pages.

Some of the earliest atlases included portraits of the publishers, two of the best being those of Ortelius and Mercator. Camden, the historian, had his portrait in the editions of the *Britannia* with the county maps. Speed's portrait was in the *Prospect of the most Famous Parts of the World* and also in his *History of Great Britain*, published in 1632, but not in the earliest editions with county maps.

Apart from atlases a number of books include maps and globes in the title pages, especially in the early part of the 17th century. The history of the world by Sir Walter Raleigh published in 1614 shows the world including America, and *The Divine Weekes and Workes* by du Bartus, published in 1621 and engraved by Renold Elstrack shows a similar globe and also a chart of the heavens. William Hole engraved the title page to Aaron Rathbone's *The Surveyor* published in 1616, again showing terrestrial and celestial globes and also two men carrying out surveys. The title page of Samuel Purchas's

John Speed's frontispiece to *The Theatre of the Empire of Great Britain*, published in 1627, and engraved by Jocodus Hondius. This is priced at about £15, $36. Examples in original colour are rare, and would be more expensive.

Purchas his Pilgrims published in 1625 is not signed but is probably the work of Henry Hondius who engraved a number of the maps contained in the work. This also shows two globes, one of America, Africa and Europe, the other of Asia and the north-west part of America. These pages are essentially from narrative books and are therefore not likely to be found loose: one has to buy the volume to obtain them. Conversely the title pages and frontispieces of atlases seldom show maps. An exception is Camden's *Britannia* which has a map of England, Wales and Scotland and is surrounded by several figures including Neptune. Some atlases show surveying instruments, and particularly important among these is the frontispiece of John Ogilby's *Britannia*, engraved by Wenceslaus Hollar after Francis Barlow. Barlow is better known for his prints of sporting subjects, the first to be made in England, and the huntsmen are in similar apparel to that which is worn in the illustration. He has been tempted to show a hunting scene in the background.

The English edition of Linschoten's *Discours of Voyages*, published in 1589, was engraved by William Rogers and shows attractive shipping scenes surrounded by figures and the Royal Coat of Arms. The English edition of

John Speed: the arms of King James I, published in 1614, in the front of *The Theatre*. Like the frontispiece this is not often found in colour. Notice the letters on the armorials which are a guide to the correct colours, referred to in detail in the text.

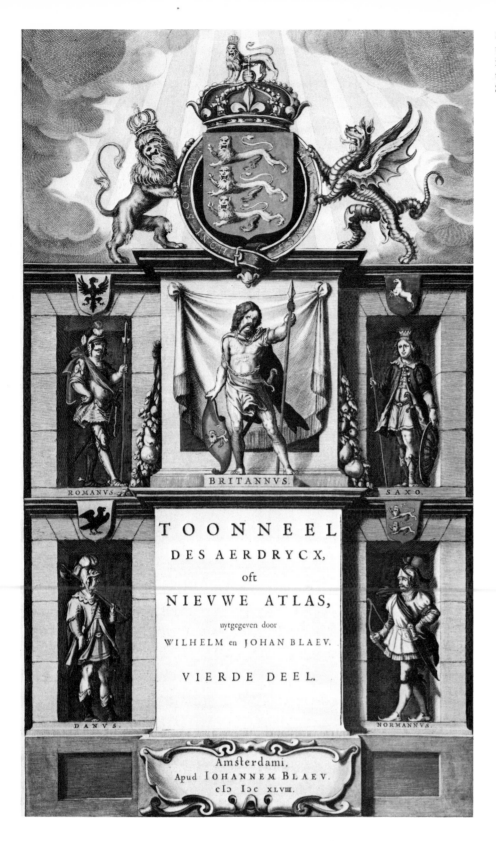

the *Mariners Mirrour* is also particularly pleasing, engraved by Theodore de Bry and adorned with various navigational instruments around the title tableau.

The frontispiece of the Ortelius atlas *Theatrum Orbis Terrarum* of 1570 is finely engraved but unexpectedly plain. In the foreground a figure is holding a severed head of a man. Undoubtedly one of the finest frontispieces is that of the Saxton atlas, which is reproduced in colour. It illustrates the rich colouring which was applied at this period. There are two editions of this frontispiece: it is the second state that is illustrated. In the first state jewels on the front of Queen Elizabeth I's dress are more elaborate, and other alterations were probably made because the dress did not hang naturally over her knees. The title page of Blaeu's English Atlas is equally fine, and

See colour illustration on page 25.

The frontispiece to Ogilby's *Britannia*, engraved by Hollar. The scene shows some interesting surveying instruments, including a way-wiser, or measuring wheel, in use. Size: 14 by 8½ in., 35 by 22 cm.

not so difficult to find. Each of his volumes bore a different title page. The colouring was usually done in Blaeu's own workshops and was always superbly executed.

In the 18th century title pages were less elaborate. One of the last of the really decorative examples is that of Mortier's *Neptune Francois*, also illustrated. It is normally found in black and white but coloured copies are occasionally seen. The engraving is so fine, particularly in the detail of Neptune and the horses heads, that any colouring has to be carefully applied in order to prevent any obscuring of the print. Generally this is a print which is preferable in black and white.

The value of these pages depends mainly on the rarity of the atlas. Camden's title is cheaply priced at about £5, $12, and the prices range to about £25, $60, for the Ogilby and Neptune pages and about £40, $100, for the Saxton title.

PRICES

In this book a number of maps and atlases have been priced according to their current values and it is emphasised that these prices are only a rough guide.

The rise in prices in the last decade has been phenomenal. The examples picked to illustrate the trend have not been chosen at random, but are atlases which turn up regularly, and it is therefore possible to choose examples of similar works in similar condition. Of necessity these prices are all London auction prices.

An outline of the value of Speed's atlas since 1900 has already been given. Closer examination shows that in 1961 a good first edition copy sold for £360, $908; in 1963 a similar atlas sold for £600, $1,680, and in 1965 a third copy sold for £870, $2,440. Three years later in 1968 another first edition sold for £2,100, $5,040. It is interesting to note that in 1967 a copy in old colour sold for £1,400, $3,920, and at the time the price was thought to be very high.

The prices of Camden's *Britannia* with the Saxton and Norden maps have risen in the same proportion. In the latter part of 1960 a copy sold for £62, $174, and in 1968 an equal copy made £400, $960. The rise in price of the Morden maps has been even greater, no less than ten times increased in eight years, from around £20, $48, in 1960 to over £200, $480, before the end of 1968. The Bowen and Kitchin atlases have also risen to the same extent, and are still underated, from £38, $106, in 1961 to over £400, $960, before the end of 1968. It has been the same with the Ogilby *Britannia*, from £44 in 1960 to £420 in 1968 ($123-$1,008), and £600, $1,440, for an average first edition in 1969.

The Moll atlas of the *World Described* has always been popular, and as explained previously, it is unusual to find the atlas in good condition because of the folds in the maps. These examples are therefore of copies which are above average and with the folds in good order. In November of 1961 a copy sold for £110, $308, moving only to £180, $504, for an excellent example in 1965. It rose to £400, $960, at the end of 1968, and then leapt to £580, $1,390, in February of 1969.

The Ortelius atlas is extremely difficult to compare because of the variant copies. Over twenty different atlases sold in London auctions from 1963 to 1968, the best comparison being editions of the 1608 atlas selling in 1964 and 1968 for £1,200 and £1,800 respectively ($3,360 and $4,320). The value of this atlas is higher for the later editions because of the increase in the number of maps contained in the volume. In 1968 a first edition of 1570 with fifty-three maps sold for £900, $2,160, and in 1964 the last edition, of 1612, sold for £1,150, $3,220, almost the same as the edition of 1608.

These prices give a fair indication of price trends. It would be possible to show other examples without regard to their overall condition. Every now and then a copy of an atlas comes onto the market which is in the finest possible condition, has hardly been touched since the day it was printed and is in fine original colour. Such copies are almost impossible to value, the price depends only on how much a buyer is willing to pay. More often a copy of an atlas turns up in very bad condition and the price of this would depend on whether or not it would be possible for a restorer to put it into a saleable condition, and whether the restorer would charge more for his services than the value of the print in good condition.

It is unlikely that the Camden *Britannia* with the Morden maps will continue to rise in price at its present rate. The maps are not particularly difficult to find and should they continue to increase at the same rate they would be over-priced in comparison with other maps. The Bowen and Kitchin is

quite uncommon, the maps are very fine and it is not possible to compare them with any other work. Whether one likes the maps or not is a personal matter, but these should prove to be a good buy.

The individual maps from the small atlases made after 1750 will not increase in value to the same extent as the complete volumes, as dealers have to make a fair profit, which is in a higher proportion for a small item, and therefore they cannot allow a high price when the owner wishes to re-sell. The complete atlases of the makers like Owen and Bowen's *Britannia Depicta*, and Cary and Moule county maps are bound to increase steadily.

If the investor can afford to go to the extent of, say, a Speed or Blaeu atlas, then this is certainly the safest investment of all. The single maps from atlases made before 1750 are also good investments, but their prices depend largely on the demand for the part of the world which they depict.

Among the areas where there is room for speculation are the histories devoted to one country, for example Ogilby's Africa and America, and de Laet's America, all containing fine maps. A good copy of Ogilby's Africa can be bought for £150, $360, and should prove worthwhile. A good copy of Thomson's Scottish maps can be bought for less than £100, $240, a fine work which is worth investing in.

The maps which are most likely to rise rapidly in a few years are the British Ordnance Survey maps, which were printed from the end of the 18th century. These, too, are fine works of engraving, though they are completely unadorned. They can be found for less than £2, $5, and will most certainly become collectors pieces.

The value of a collection of maps is slightly higher than each single map, providing that the collection has a theme, for example, maps or plans of one particular place. A comprehensive collection of a subject is therefore worth making.

The following is a list of the inscriptions found on maps, and will be useful in determining origins.

Apud=after

Auct., *auct*[d]., or *auctore*=author

Autographum=copied from

Caelavit=engraved by

Cum privilegio=with permission of

Del., *delt.*, *delin.*, or *delineavit*=drawn by. This applies to title pages and frontispieces mainly, sometimes seen on vignettes

Descripsit=described=mapped by . . . (cartographer)

Eng., *Engr* or *engd*=abbreviations of engraver

Et., *etched*=a system of engraving using resin and acid, usually confined to titles and frontispieces when applied to mapping

Ex., or *excudit*=engraved by

Fec., or *fecit*=drawn and engraved by

Incidit, *incidente* or *incidebat*=engraver

Invenit=made by . . . (cartographer)

Performed by=made by . . . (cartographer)

Pub., *pubd.*=abbreviations for published

Sc., *sculp.*, or *sculpsit*=engraved by

Vulgo (seen in titles and occasionally in the body of the map)=more commonly . . .

BIBLIOGRAPHY

There have been many books written on the subject of old maps, and most of them are very creditable. The majority are very technical, assuming some experience on the part of the reader. Some are concerned mainly with the maps which one would only find in museums or are extreme rarities. Among the books which are recommended are:

Leo Bagrow—*History of Cartography*
Sir H. G. Fordham—*Maps; their History, Characteristics and Uses*
A. E. Humphries—*Old Decorative Maps and Charts*
Raymond Lister—*How to Identify Old Maps and Globes*
Edward Lynam—*British Maps and Map-Makers*
R. A. Skelton—*Decorative Printed Maps of the Fifteenth to Eighteenth Centuries*
R. V. Tooley—*Maps and Map-Makers.*

There are several specialised catalogues which are essential for further and more detailed examination of maps, the most notable being the *Catalogue of the Library of Congress*, which ran into four volumes published from 1909 to 1920 and was compiled by Phillips. This is the most comprehensive list of printed atlases. The collection of British maps in the British Museum was catalogued by Thomas Chubb and first published in 1927, titled *The Printed Maps in the Atlases of Great Britain and Ireland, a Bibliography, 1579-1870*. In 1927 the stock of atlases in the British Museum being rather smaller than it is today, a revised edition is nearing completion.

An ambitious work gradually being compiled is the series of authoritative booklets published regularly by the Map Collectors Circle, begun in 1963. Designed to assist collectors, librarians and book sellers, they are very technical and they are not economic for the small private collector. Nearly all the English counties have been covered by various bibliographers through the ages, too many to list here, but local libraries always carry these books in stock. Among the most notable of these are those compiled by Chubb, Fordham, Skelton and H. Whittaker, all of them making fine comprehensive catalogues of the printed maps of various counties. Many works are available dealing with specialised subjects or about one map-maker and his work and several theses have been written about single maps. The collector should make enquiries of his local library or a map dealer to find details of the literature which is available to assist in making a collection.

INDEX

This index of cartographers, engravers, publishers and others connected with the history of maps contains a number of map-makers, and their better known works, to whom direct reference is not made in this book. They are included as an aid to identification of maps which may be encountered by the reader.

The page numbers in roman type refer to the text, those in italic to the illustrations.

AA, Pieter Van der: 38
Dutch publisher; *Galerie agréable du monde*, 1729, 66 vols.

ADAIR, John
British surveyor; maps and charts of Scotland, c. 1700–1722.

ADAMS, John
Improved map of England and Wales, based on Saxton, published by Philip Lea, c. 1690.

ALLARD, Hugo: 38
Dutch publisher, 1628–1666; followed by his sons, Abraham and Karel, who continued until c. 1710.

ANDRE, Peter: 104
Surveyor; Chapman and André map of Essex, 25 sheets, 2 inches to 1 mile, 1777.

ANDREWS, Peter
British engraver; Rocque's map of Surrey, 9 sheets, 2 inches to 1 mile, 1754.

ANDREWS, John: 104, 118
British surveyor; Andrews and Dury map of Hertfordshire, 9 sheets, 2 inches to 1 mile, 1766, re-issued in 1777 and 1782; *Plans of the Principal Cities of the World*, 1792; and others.

ANONYMOUS: 44
Extremely rare maps of some of the English counties, 1603–1605, of unknown origin; re-issued by Peter Stent c. 1650 and John Overton c. 1690.

ANSON, George
Voyage autour du Monde, 1751, 4to, maps and views, some by N. Bellin.

ANVILLE, Jean Baptiste d': 68, 86, 129, 141
French cartographer, born 1697, died 1782; several atlases published from 1737 to about 1840; much of his work was used as a basis for other maps.

APIAN, Peter (Petrus Apianus): 87
German cartographer; rare wood-cut maps.

APIAN, Philip: 87
Son of Peter.

ARCHER, J.
British engraver; Atlas of ecclesiastical maps, 8vo, 1841; Dugdale's *British County Atlas*, 8vo, 1843, re-issued to 1865.

ARMSTRONG, Andrew
British surveyor; maps of North England and South Scotland, 1768–1796.

ARMSTRONG, Mostyn John: 77, 78
Son of Andrew; surveyor; main work: *A Scotch Atlas*, 1787, 30 maps, 4to, published by Sayer with maps engraved by H. Ashby.

ARROWSMITH, Aaron: 67, 139
British cartographer and publisher; large scale maps of the world, 1794–1819; *New General Atlas*, 1817, folio.

ARROWSMITH, Aaron, junior: 67
Cartographer, 1828–1830.

ARROWSMITH, John: 67
Nephew of Aaron senior; cartographer and publisher, 1834–1840.

ARROWSMITH, Samuel
Son of Aaron senior; cartographer.

ASHBY, H.: 78
Engraver; Armstrong's *Scotch Atlas*.

ASHLEY, Sir Anthony: 90
Publisher; *Mariner's Mirrour*, English edition of Waghenaer's charts, 1588, 45 charts, folio.

ATKYNS, Sir Robert: 108
The Ancient and Present State of Gloucestershire, 1768, with map by H. Moll, folio.

ATKINSON, J.
Publisher; Seller's *English Pilot*, 1677, folio.

AUSTEN, Stephen: 137
Publisher; M. H. Popple's *Map of the British Empire in America*, 1732.

AYROUART, Jacques
French cartographer; charts and plans of the Mediterranean, 1746.

BADESLADE, Thomas and Henry: 78, 82
British surveyors; *Chorographia Britannia*, 1742, 46 maps engraved by W. H. Toms, 4to; re-issued in 1745 and 1747; original price, bound and coloured – 12 shillings.

BAILLEUL, Gaspar: 47
French cartographer; map of the world and the four continents, c. 1750, folio, scarce.

BAKER, Benjamin
British publisher; *Universal Magasine*, 1797 and other editions.

BAKEWELL, Thomas: 79
British publisher; Blome's *England Exactly Described*, with Ogilby's roads added, 1715.

BALDWIN & CRADOCK: 118
British cartographers; atlases published by the Society for the Diffusion of Useful Knowledge, 1829–1850, folio.

BANKES, Thomas
British cartographer; *Complete System of Geography*, c. 1790, folio.

BARCLAY, Rev. James
Complete and Universal Dictionary of the English Language, c. 1840–1850, folio, contains English county maps by Thomas Moule.

BARLOW, Francis: 147, 149
Sporting artist; drew frontispiece of Ogilby's *Britannia*, 1675 (first two editions).

BARRES, J. F. W. des: 138
Cartographer and publisher; *Atlantic Neptune*, published for the Royal Navy of Great Britain, 1776–1781, large folio.

BASIRE, James
British engraver, c. 1760–1800.

BASSETT, Thomas: 6, 53, 54, 56, 137
With Richard Chiswell, publisher of Speed's atlas, 1676, folio.

BEIGHTON, Henry, F.R.S.: 9, 106, 106
British surveyor; Warwickshire maps; four-sheet map published from 1722; later editions published by Elizabeth, his wife; provided maps for Dugdale's *Antiquities of Warwickshire*, folio, 1725 and later editions.

BELLE FOREST, François de: 113
French cartographer; *La Cosmographie Universelle de Tout le Monde*, 1575, woodcut plans taken from Braun and Hogenberg.

BELLIN, Jacques Nicolas: 17, 18, 93, 94
Cartographer and publisher; *Hydrographie Francoise*, from 1772, large folio; *Atlas de l'Histoire des Voyages*, c. 1752–1754, 4to; G. Anson's *Voyage autour du Monde*, 1751, 4to.

BENNETT, John: 94, 138
With Robert Sayer published many maps and atlases, 1770–1810.

BERRY, William
British cartographer; published 38 maps c. 1680, subsequently bound, large folio.

BERTIUS, Petrus
Belgian cartographer and publisher; folio maps 1600 to c. 1650.

BICKHAM, George: 121, 121, 122
British engraver; *A Curious Antique Collection of Bird's Eye Views*, 1754, 46 plates, folio; re-issued in 1796 by Laurie

and Whittle; also engraved American Colonies, 1794, and *Musical Entertainer*.

BILL, John: 79
British publisher; set of English county maps, 1626, 8vo.

BLACKWOOD, William, and Sons
Atlas of Scotland, 1839, 31 maps, 4to.

BLAEU, Willem or Guiljelmus: 9, 13, 32, *34*, *35*, 37, 38, 56, 66, 93, 96, *97*, 127, 131, *131*, 140, *141*, 148
Dutch; founder of the Blaeu publishing house; father of Cornelius and Johannes; many atlases from 1635, extending to twelve volumes.

BLOME, Richard: 9, 56, 57, *58*, 65, 79, *112*
British cartographer; *Britannia*, 1673 and 1691, 50 maps, folio; *Speed's Maps Epitomised, or England Exactly Described*, 1681, 1685 and 1715, 8vo; *Cosmography*, with county maps and maps of other parts of the world, 1682 and 1693, folio.

BOAZIO, Baptista: *33*
Italian cartographer, settled in London; map of Ireland, 1599; re-engraved and published in Ortelius' *Theatrum Orbis Terrarum*.

BODENEHR, Hans George
German engraver and publisher; Atlas of Germany, 1677; *Atlas Curieux*, 1704; publication continued by his sons Gabriel and Moritz.

BONNE, Rigobert
French cartographer; atlases and charts from 1760 to 1785; maps usually signed M. Bonne.

BOSWELL, Henry
Antiquities of England and Wales, 1786, with 50 maps by T. Condor and T. Kitchin, published by Alex. Hogg, folio.

BOTERO, Giovanni
Italian cartographer; *Relationi Universali*, four maps of the continents, 1595, 4to.

BOUGARD, René
French cartographer; *Little Sea Torch*, 1801, 24 charts and 20 sheets of coastlines, folio.

BOWEN, Emanuel: 9, *62*, 67–9, *71*, 72, 79, 96, 104
British engraver and publisher; many atlases, including the *Large English Atlas*, 1755, folio, with T. Kitchin, and *Atlas Anglicanus*, 1767–1777, 45 maps, folio, with Thomas Bowen.

BOWEN, Thomas: *see* Bowen, Emanuel

BOWLES, John: 79, *92*, *112*
British publisher; many atlases, including those of Bowen and Moll, *c.* 1714–1750.

BOWLES, Thomas: 79
British engraver and map-seller; brother of John.

BOWLES, Carrington: 79
British publisher; *Bowles' New English Atlas*, 1785, 44 maps, 4to; *Bowles' Pocket Atlas*, 1785, 57 maps, 8vo.

BRAUN, George: 21, *28*, 29, 86, 87, *110*, 113
German cartographer; with Hogenberg published *Civitates Orbis Terrarum*, 1572

and re-issues, folio, a collection of bird's eye views.

BRION DE LA TOUR, Louis
French cartographer; *Recueil des Côtes Maritimes de France*, 1757, 51 charts; *Atlas General*, 1766.

BROWNE, Joseph: *100*, 107
British engraver; Plot's map of Staffordshire, 1686.

BRY, Theodore de: 90, 148
Engraver and publisher; Waghenaer's *Mariner's Mirror*, English edition, 1588.

BRYANT, A.
British surveyor; large scale maps, 1820–1831.

BURGHERS, Michael: 107
Dutch engraver, settled in Oxford; Wells' *A New Sett of Maps*, 1700; Plot's map of Oxfordshire, 1677.

BUTLER, Samuel
British publisher; *A General Atlas of Ancient and Modern Geography*, 1826, 43 maps by Sidney Hall.

CAMDEN, William: 49, 50, *50*, *51*, 146, 147
British historian; *Britannia*, 1607, 1610 and 1637, 57 county maps after Saxton and Norden, engraved by William Hole and William Kip; *Britannia*, 1695, 1722, 1755 and 1772, 50 maps by Robert Morden; *Britannia*, 1789, 60 maps by John Cary.

CAREY, Henry Charles and Isaac Lea: 139
American publishers; *American Atlas*, 1822, 1823 and 1827.

CAREY, Mathew
American cartographer; *American Atlas*, 1795; *American Pocket Atlas*, 1796 and several re-issues; *General Atlas*, 1796 and several re-issues.

CARY, John: 67, *74*, 78
English engraver and publisher; prolific; many general atlases and county maps, 1786–1834.

CARY, George, John II, William
Publishers

CELLARIUS, Andreas: 122, *136*
Astronomer; *Harmonia Microcosmica seu Atlas*, 1660, 1661 and 1708, 29 charts of the heavens.

CELLARIUS, Christopher
Historical cartographer; *Geographica Antiqua*, 1774, folio.

CHAPMAN, John: 104
British surveyor, engraver and publisher; map of Nottinghamshire, 1776, 1 inch to 1 mile; engraved Yates' map of Staffordshire, 1775; published Armstrong's map of Durham, 1768; Chapman and André map of Essex, 1777, 25 sheets, 2 inches to 1 mile.

CHATELAIN, Henri Abraham
French cartographer; *Atlas Historique*, 1705–1720 and 1732–1739, folio.

CHAUNCY, Sir Henry: 108
Historian; *The History and Antiquities of Hertfordshire*, 1700, map by H. Moll, plans and views, folio.

CHETWIND, P.
British cartographer; maps, mainly of the continents, *c.* 1666.

CHISWELL, Richard: 6, 53, *54*, 56, *137*
Publisher and bookseller; with Thomas Bassett, publisher of Speed's Atlas, 1676, folio.

CHURCHILL, Awnsham and John: 52
Publishers and booksellers; with Abel Swale, publishers of Camden's *Britannia*, 1695 and 1722.

CLUTTERBUCK, Robert
The History and Antiquities of the County of Hertford, 1815, maps, plans and views.

CLUVERIUS, Philip
German cartographer, 1580–1623; historical maps published posthumously.

COLE, G.: *117*, 118
British cartographer; co-operated with J. Roper on *British Atlas*, 1810, 79 maps, 4to, published by Vernor and Hood.

COLLINS, Captain Greenville: *91*, 94
Surveyor and cartographer; Hydrographer to the King; *Great Britain's Coasting Pilot*, 1693 and several editions to 1792, various publishers and engravers.

COLOM, Arnold
Dutch cartographer and publisher; sea atlases from 1656 to 1669.

COLOM, Jacob Aertz
Dutch cartographer, publisher, and bookseller; sea atlases from 1632 to 1669.

CONDER, Thomas
British engraver; some of the maps in Boswell's *Antiquities of England and Wales*, 1786, folio.

CONTARINI, Giovanni Matteo: 130
Italian cartographer; map of the world was the first printed map to show America, 1506.

CORONELLI, Vincenzo Maria: *31*
Italian cartographer; main work: *Atlante Veneto*, 12 vols., 1697–1701.

COVENS, Jean: 38, *85*, 137
Dutch publisher with Corneill Mortier; printed and published maps by many cartographers, 1714–1761.

COWLEY, John: 79
British cartographer; with Dodsley, *Geography of England*, 1744, 55 maps, 8vo; re-issue 1745.

CRADOCK AND BALDWIN: 118
Cartographers; atlases published by the Society for the Diffusion of Useful Knowledge, 1829–1850, folio.

DALRYMPLE, Alexander
British publisher and cartographer, 1737–1808; many maps and charts of all parts of the world.

DANCKERTS, Cornelius: 38
Dutch engraver and publisher; many maps published from 1670 to 1710; some maps signed by his sons, Danker and Justus, and Justus' sons, Theodorus and Cornelius.

DAPPER, Oliver: *127*
Published *Description de l'Afrique*, 43 maps, 1668, folio; maps similar to those

of Ogilby's *Africa*, includes map of Africa by Meurse.

DARTON, William: 79
British publisher; complete atlas of the English counties, 1822, 42 maps, folio, further editions 1830, 1833, 1848.

DAVIDSON: 94
Mount and Davidson, chart publishers, late 18th century.

DEUTECUM, or DOETECUM, Baptista van
Dutch engraver and cartographer; engraved maps by Plancius.

DEUTECUM, or DOETECUM, Johannes ('van' or 'a') and Lucas van, brothers: 90, *90*
Dutch engravers; worked for Plantin from 1599, engraved maps for de Jode, Ortelius and Waghenaer.

DICEY, Cluer: 44, 56
British publisher; Speed's atlas, 1770 folio edition. Saxton's atlas, 1770 folio edition.

DIEST, Gilles Coppens van: 23
Dutch printer; printed early editions of Ortelius' *Theatrum Orbis Terrarum*.

DONCKER, Henrik: 93
Dutch publisher of charts; *De Zee Atlas Ofte Water-Woereld*, 1660–1666.

DONN, Benjamin: 96
British surveyor; map of Devonshire, 1765, 12 sheets, 1 inch to 1 mile, engraved by T. Jefferys.

DOPPELMAIER, Johann Gabriel: 88, 123, *123*
German cartographer and mathematician; charts of the heavens, published in 1742 by Homann.

DRAYTON, Michael: 120, *120*
Poet; *Poly-Olbion*, Part I, 1612, 18 maps, folio: Part II (with part I), 30 maps, folio, engraved by W. Hole.

DUDLEY, Sir Robert
British cartographer; *Arcano del mare*, three volumes of charts, published in Venice, 1646–1647.

DUGDALE, James
British cartographer; *The New British Traveller*, 1819, 45 maps, 4to, engraved by Neele.

DUGDALE, Thomas
British historian; *British County Atlas*, 1835, 58 maps by Archer, 8vo.

DUGDALE, Sir William: 104, *106*
British historian, surveyor and publisher; *Antiquities of Warwickshire*, 1656, enlarged editions 1730 and 1765, maps by Henry Beighton; large scale map of The Fens, 1662, and Romney Marsh, 1662.

DUNCAN, J.
British publisher; *New British Atlas*, 1819, 45 maps, 4to.

DUNN, Samuel: 67, *67*
British cartographer and astronomer; *New atlas of the Mundane System*, 1774, published by Sayer, 1789 by Laurie and Whittle.

DURY, Andrew: 104, 118
British cartographer and publisher; *A New General and Universal Atlas*, 1761, 45 maps, 8vo.

EDWARDS, Bryan
British geographer; *History, Civil and Commercial, of the British Colonies in the West Indies*, 1794 and 1801, 16 maps and views, 4to.

ELLIS, G.
British publisher; *New and Correct Atlas of England and Wales*, 1819, 44 maps, 4to; *General Atlas of the World*, 4to, 1823.

ELLIS, John: 79
British engraver; *Ellis' English Atlas*, 1766, 50 maps, 8vo; re-issues 1768, 1773 and 1777, maps by Ellis, Jefferys, and Palmer.

ELSTRACK, Renold: 146
British engraver; engraved some of the maps for Saxton and Speed.

EVANS, Rev. John
British cartographer; map of North Wales, 1795; *A New Royal Atlas*, 1810.

EVANS, Lewis: 137, 138
British surveyor; maps for Thomas Jefferys' *American Atlas*, 1776, folio; *Map of the Middle Colonies of America*, 1755.

FADEN, William: 67, *69*, 94, 129, 139, 142
British cartographer, engraver and publisher; successor to Thomas Jefferys; many maps and atlases from about 1770 to about 1845.

FER, Nicolas de
French cartographer, engraver and publisher; many maps and atlases from 1693, mainly of France.

FINDLAY, Alexander George
British cartographer and engraver; three atlases published by W. Tegg, all about 1850.

FISHER, Son & Co.
British publishers; county atlas of England and Wales, 1842, 43 maps, 8vo.

FOOT, Thomas
British engraver; worked on early Ordnance Survey maps.

FOWLER, William
British surveyor; large scale maps of South Scotland, 1825–1845.

FULLARTON, Archibald
British printer and publisher of several atlases in the 19th century.

GARDNER, Thomas
British engraver; *English Traveller*, 100 road maps taken from Ogilby, 1719, 8vo.

GARDNER, William: 96
Surveyor; map of Guernsey, 1787, engraved by J. Warner; Yeakell & Gardner, map of Sussex, 1778, four sheets, 2 inches to 1 mile.

GASCOYNE, Joel
British surveyor; large scale map of Cornwall, 1700, nine sheets, 1 inch to 1 mile, engraved by J. Harris.

GASTALDI, Giacoma: 21
Italian cartographer; map of the world, 1546, copied by subsequent publishers; made maps for Ptolemy's *Geographia*, 1548, and for Lafreri's atlases.

GIBSON, Bishop Edmund: 52

Translated Camden's *Britannia*, published 1695, 1722, 1755 and 1772.

GIBSON, John
British engraver. *New and Accurate Maps of the Counties of England and Wales*, 1759, 53 maps, 12mo.

GOOS, Abraham
Dutch engraver; work includes maps for Speed and Visscher.

GOOS, Pieter: 93
Dutch cartographer; several atlases, mainly charts, 1654–1666.

GORDON, Robert of Stroloch: *35*, 37
British cartographer; improved Pont's maps of Scotland for Blaeu's atlas, folio, 1654, and subsequent editions.

GORTON, John
British topographer; with S. Hall, *Topographical Dictionary of Great Britain and Ireland*, 1833, 54 maps, 4to.

GOUGH, Richard: 82
Translated Camden's *Britannia* published 1789 and 1806.

GREENWOOD, Christopher and John: *73*, 74, 78, 96, *104*
British cartographers; *Atlas of the Counties of England* (and Wales), 1834, 46 maps, folio. Large scale maps of most counties, from 1818, 1 inch to 1 mile, Yorkshire ¾ inch to 1 mile.

GREVILLE, Sir Fulke: 9, 53
Sponsor of John Speed.

GRIERSON, George
Irish cartographer and publisher; *English Pilot*, 1749, folio.

GROSE, Francis: *81*
British historian; J. Seller and Grose Antiquities of Great Britain, 1777–1787, 52 maps, 4to.

GUEDEVILLE, Nicholas
French cartographer; *Atlas Historique*, 1708–1714, published by Chatelain Libraries.

GUTHERIE, William
American geographer; *System of Geography*, editions from 1795, 29 maps by J. Russell.

HALDE, J. B. du: 141
French cartographer; 51 maps of China, Tibet and Korea, 1738–1741.

HALL, Sidney: 79
British cartographer and engraver; *New British Atlas*, 1833, 54 maps, 4to; *Travelling Atlas*, 1842, 46 maps, 8vo; *New County Atlas*, 1847, 4to; engraved maps in Gorton and Hall's *Dictionary of Great Britain and Ireland*, 1833, 54 maps, 4to.

HARRIS, John: *98*, 107
British historian; *History of Kent*, 1719, map engraved by Samuel Parker, and forty views.

HARRIS, John: *115*
British engraver; c. 1720.

HARRISON, John
British publisher; maps of the English counties, 1791, 38 maps, folio; 2nd edition, 1792.

HASIUS, Johann Matthias

German cartographer; some maps published in the Homann atlases.

HASTED, Edward: 106, *108*
British historian and publisher; *History of Kent*, 1778–1799, map of Kent, hundreds, and views, folio.

HEATHER, William: 94
British cartographer; several charts and sea-pilots, 1795–1811.

HEYLIN, Peter
British cosmographer; *Cosmographie*, four maps of the continents by Henry or Anna Seile, 1657, 1666 and 1677, folio.

HINTON, John
British publisher; published 1st edition of Bowen and Kitchin's *Large English Atlas*, 1754, folio; *Universal Magasine*, 1773, road maps.

HOBSON, William C.: *75, 78*
Fox Hunting Atlas, 1850, 42 maps, folio, re-issued to 1880. Published by J. & C. Walker.

HOFNAGLE, OR HOEFNAGLE, Georg: 113
Belgian cartographer; collaborated with Braun and Hogenberg, *Civitates Orbis Terrarum*, 1572.

HOGENBERG, Frans: 21, *28*, 29, 86, 87, *110*, 113
Flemish engraver and publisher; worked in Cologne; engraved maps for Ortelius and others; with Braun published *Civitates Orbis Terrarum*, 1572.

HOGENBERG, Remigius: 42
Flemish engraver; worked in England; engraved some of Saxton's county maps, published in 1579.

HOGG, Alexander: 79
British publisher; *Boswell's Antiquities*, 1770, folio. *Walpole's New British Traveller*, 1784.

HOLE, William: 50, 120, *120*, 146
British engraver; engraved some of the maps for Camden's *Britannia*, 1607, 1610 and 1637; maps for Drayton's *Poly-Olbion*.

HOLLAND, Samuel, Capt. or Major
British cartographer and surveyor; maps of North America, published by Faden, Jefferys, and Laurie and Whittle from 1775 to about 1820.

HOLLAR, Wenceslaus: 60, *112*, 147
Bohemian engraver; worked in England; engraved some maps in Blome's atlases from 1673; Ogilby's *Britannia* frontispiece, 1675, first two issues only; some plates in Ogilby's *Africa*, 1670; several plans of London.

HOMANN, Johann Baptist: 87, *87*, 88, *113*, *114*, 123, 129
German cartographer, engraver and publisher; worked in Nuremberg; published many atlases from 1707 which were continued by his heirs after his death in 1724.

HOMANNISCHE ERBEN
The title used by the Homann publishing firm after Homann had died. The atlases included maps by many cartographers, and continued into the 19th century.

HONDIUS, Henry: *7*, 31, *126*, 127, *130*, 146
Dutch cartographer, engraver and publisher; took over publication of the Mercator Atlases and included many of his own maps in the work.

HONDIUS, Jodocus: 31, *53*, 54, *54*, 127
Dutch engraver and publisher; engraved Speed's county maps.

HOOGHE, Cornelius de: 42
Dutch engraver; engraved some of Saxton's county maps, published in 1579.

HOOGHE, Romain de: 93, *133*, *134*
Dutch cartographer; some of his maps were published in Mortier's *Atlas Maritime*, 1693.

HORN, Georg
Dutch cartographer; an historical atlas published by Jansson, 1644.

HORWOOD, Richard: 115, 116, 118
British surveyor; large scale map of London, 32 sheets, published in 1792, re-issued in 1800, 1807, 1813 and 1819.

HUMBLE, George: 54, 55
British publisher and book-seller; published editions of Speed's *Theatre* from 1611 to 1627 and *Prospect* in 1627.

HUTCHINS, John
British historian; *History and Antiquities of the County of Dorset*, general map by J. Bayley, maps, plans and views, 1772, folio.

ISLE, Guillaume de l': 86, 129
French cartographer; many maps and atlases from 1700, published by Covens and Mortier after his death.

ISLE, Joseph Nicolas de l'
French cartographer, brother of Guillaume; *Atlas Russicus*, 1745.

JACOBSZ, Anthonie: 93
Dutch publisher; charts and sea-pilots from 1648 to 1707.

JAILLOT, Alexis Hubert: 84, *84*, *85*
French cartographer and engraver; maps and atlases from 1689, some published by Covens and Mortier.

JANSSON, Jan or Joannes: 9, 31, 32, *36*, 38, 56, 66, 122, 127, 131
Dutch printer and publisher; collaborated with his brother-in-law, Henry Hondius, on the *Novus Atlas* in 1637, before publishing his own atlases, extending to six volumes in 1647, covering all parts of the world.

JANVIER, Antide
French cartographer and publisher, *c.* 1800–1835.

JEFFERYS, Thomas: 44, 67, 94, 96, 138, 139, *139*
British publisher and engraver; maps and atlases from 1746, including *West India Atlas*, 1775, 16 maps, folio; *A General Topography of North America and the West Indies*, 1762; Kitchin & Jefferys *Small English Atlas*, 1749, 50 maps, 4to, and editions to 1787.

JENNER, Thomas
British publisher and engraver, from 1623 to about 1666.

JODE, Cornelius and Gerard
Dutch cartographers and publishers; *Speculum orbis terrarum*, 1578, re-issued 1593.

JOHNSTON, Andrew: 52
British cartographer; two maps of Scotland in Camden's *Britannia*, 1722, 1753, 1772.

JOHNSON, Thomas
British publisher; *Atlas of England*, 1847, 41 maps, 4to.

JORDEN, Mark: *28*
Danish cartographer; map of Denmark, reduced for *Civitates Orbis Terrarum*, 1585.

KEERE, Peter van den, or Petrus Kaerius: 56, *57*
Dutch engraver; collection of 37 English maps, 1599, 8vo, re-issued by Speed's publishers and increased to 63 maps in the 1627 edition; 20 maps of other parts of the world added to the 1676 edition.

KEULEN, Johannes van: 93
Dutch cartographer and publisher; published many charts from 1682; the business was continued by his son, Gerard, and his grandson, Johannes.

KIP, John: 107, 115
British engraver and publisher; published several plans of British cities and towns about 1720.

KIP, William: 50, *50*
British engraver; engraved maps with William Hole for Camden's *Britannia*, 1607, 1610 and 1637.

KITCHIN, Thomas: 67, 68, 69, *71*, 72, 96, 104
British engraver and publisher; Kitchin & Jefferys *Small English Atlas*, 1749 and editions; Bowen and Kitchin *Large English Atlas*, 1754; *Pocket Atlas*, 1769, 47 maps, 8vo; *General Atlas*, 25 maps mostly four-sheet, 1773–1801, folio.

LAET, Johannes de: *132*
Dutch geographer; *NieuvveWereldt*, 1625, 10 maps of America, Latin edition, *Novus Orbis*, 1633, increased to 14 maps, folio.

LAFRERI, Antonio: 21
Italian cartographer and publisher; made many maps from about 1540, subsequently bound.

LAMB, Francis: 137
British engraver and publisher; some Speed maps, including New England and New York and East Indies; Ogilby and Morgan's map of Essex.

LANGLEY, Edward: 82
British engraver and publisher; *New County Atlas*, 1818, 53 maps, 4to.

LAPIE, Alexander Emile
French cartographer; *Atlas Universel*, 1833.

LAPIE, Pierre
French cartographer; *Atlas Classique*, 1812.

LAURIE, Robert: 67, *68*, 72, 142

In partnership with James Whittle as Laurie and Whittle, publishers and engravers; many atlases from 1794 to 1814.

LAVOISNE, C. V.
American cartographer; *American Atlas*, 1823, published by Carey and Lea, folio; *Complete Genealogical, Historical, Chronological and Geographical Atlas*, 1829, maps and guides, folio.

LEA, Philip: 43, *43*
British cartographer and publisher; published an edition of Saxton's maps *c.* 1690.

LEIGH, Samuel
New Atlas of England and Wales, 1820, 56 maps, 12mo, several editions to 1842, engraved by S. Hall.

LEWIS, Samuel
British cartographer and publisher; *Topographical Dictionary of England*, 1831, 43 maps, 4to, editions to 1849; *Topographical Dictionary of Wales*, 1833, 12 maps, editions to 1829.

LHUYD, Humphrey: 22, *33*
British cartographer; map of Wales, published by Ortelius, 1573 and subsequent editions; also map of England and Wales, until the Vrints' map superseded it.

LINSCHOTEN, Jan Hugo: 93, 127, 140, *140*, 147
Dutch cartographer; *Navigatio ac Itinerarium*, folding charts and plates, 1596.

LOON, Johann van: 122
Dutch engraver; Cellarius' charts of the heavens, 1660.

LOON, Jan van
Dutch cartographer and publisher; compiled sea atlases from 1661 to 1668.

LOPEZ, Thomas
Portuguese cartographer; mainly atlases and maps of Spain and Portugal from 1778 to 1830.

LOTTER, Tobias Conrad: 88, *88*
German cartographer and publisher; son-in-law of M. Seutter; took over the business and published Seutter's work in his own name from 1756.

LUFFMAN, John
British engraver and publisher; *New Pocket Atlas & Geography of England and Wales*, 1803, 8vo, with unusual circular maps.

MARTIN, R. Montgomery
British publisher; an edition which included Tallis maps of the world, *c.* 1850.

MARTINI, Martin: 140, *141*
Italian cartographer and Jesuit missionary; maps of China, published by Blaeu, 1655.

MARTYN, Thomas: 104
British surveyor; map of Cornwall, 1748, 9 sheets, 1 inch to 1 mile.

MATHEWS and LEIGH
British publishers; *Scripture Atlas*, 1812, 20 maps, 4to.

MAYO, William

British cartographer; *Barbadoes Surveyed*, 1774, improved by Jefferys.

MERCATOR, Gerard: 12, 21, 24, *24*, 29, 31, *32*, 53, 54, 56, 96, 126, 130, 141, *141*, 146
Dutch cartographer; atlases from 1595; firm continued by H. Hondius and then Jansson.

MERIAN, Matthaus: *85*, 87
German engraver and publisher; many maps and atlases from 1642, continued by his son of the same name, until 1680; maps based on Blaeu.

MEURSE, Jacob: *127*
Dutch cartographer; maps for Ogilby's *Africa* and for Dapper's *Africa*, 1670.

MITCHELL, John: 138
British cartographer; map of the British and French dominions in North America, 1755, engraved by Thomas Kitchin.

MITCHELL, Samuel Augustus
American cartographer; maps of North America from 1839 to about 1850.

MOLL, Herman: 64, *64*, 65, *65*, 67, 79, 108, 131, *138*
Dutch, settled in England, cartographer and publisher; *A New and Compleat Atlas*, 1720, folio; *New Descriptions of England and Wales*, 1724, 50 maps, 4to, with antiquities; 1728 to 1753 without antiquities.

MORANT, P.: 107, *107*
British historian and cartographer; *History of Essex*, 1768, 33 plates with maps, folio.

MORDEN, Robert: 9, *51*, 52, 60, 120
British cartographer and publisher; *Pocket Atlas of all the Counties*, 1680, 52 maps, 8vo; *Geography Rectified*, 1680, 8vo; county maps as pack of cards, 1676 and 1750; Camden's *Britannia*, 50 maps by Morden, 1695, folio; editions of 1722, 1753 and 1772 contain 51 maps.

MORGAN, William: 59
British surveyor; large scale maps of London, 1681, and Essex, 1678, both with Ogilby.

MORRIS, Lewis: 94
British cartographer; plans of harbours, bars, bays and roads in St Georges Channel, 1748, 4to.

MORTIER, Corneille: 38, *85*, 137
Dutch publisher, with Jean Covens; printed and published maps by many cartographers, 1714–1761.

MORTIER, Pierre: *2*, 84, 93, 114, *133*, *134*, 149
Dutch publisher; *Neptune Francois*, 1700, varying maps, folio.

MORTON, John: 107
British historian; *The Natural History of Northamptonshire*, 1712, folding map and 14 plates, folio.

MOULE, Thomas: *76*, 78, 118
British cartographer and publisher; *English Counties Delineated*, 1836, 58 maps, 4to; *Barclay's Dictionary with some maps*, several editions, 1842–1852.

MOUNT, Richard: *92*, 94

British publisher; founder of firm publishing many charts, from 1702; firm had several titles–Mount and Page, Mount and Davidson, Thornton and Mount; flourished into the 19th century.

MUDGE, William: *193*
British cartographer; Ordnance Survey maps.

MUNSTER, Sebastian: 20, *20*, 21, *22*, 86, 126, 130, 140
German, settled in Basle; cartographer; edition of Ptolemy's *Geographia*, 1544, enlarged editions to 1552, folio.

MURRAY, T. L.
British cartographer; *Atlas of the English Counties*, 1830, 44 maps, folio.

MYERS, Thomas
British cartographer; *Modern Geography*, 1822, 49 maps, 60 plates.

NEELE, Samuel John and George: 82
British engravers; engraved many maps from *c.* 1795 to *c.* 1830; *Minor Atlas*, 1813, 42 county maps, 4to.

NICHOLLS, Sutton: *51*, 52, *92*
British engraver; some of Morden's county maps, 1695; Wells' *A New Sett of Maps*, 1700; *Plantations of the English in North America*; Bowles' *Sea Ports of Europe*.

NIGHTINGALE, Joseph
British cartographer; *English Topography*, 1816, 56 maps, 4to.

NOLIN, Jean Baptiste
Father and son of the same name; French, cartographers and publishers; many maps and atlases from about 1700 to 1762.

NORDEN, John: 44, *49*, 53, 56
British topographer and surveyor; some maps in Camden's *Britannia*, 1607, 1610 and 1637; his earliest maps, *c.* 1580, are extreme rarities; some re-issues by P. Stent, *c.* 1650, and Overton, *c.* 1690.

NORIE, John William: 128
British hydrographer; *East India Pilot*, many editions from 1816.

OGILBY, John: 12, 43, 52, 57ff, *58*, 60, 72, 127, 147, *149*
British dancing master, theatre manager, surveyor, printer and bookseller; *Britannia*, 100 road maps, 1675, two issues, and 1698; *Description of Africa*, maps and views, 1670; *Description of America*, maps and views, 1670.

ORDNANCE SURVEY: 75, 96, *103*

ORTELIUS, Abraham: 21–29, *30*, 45, 48, 96, 126, 130, 141, 142, *142*, 146, 148
Dutch cartographer and publisher; *Theatrum Orbis Terrarum*, many editions from 1570 to 1612, folio; maps by many other cartographers.

OTTENS, Reiner, Jaochim and Joshua: 38
Dutch cartographers and publishers; *Atlas Major*, 1740, 8 vols; maps by many makers.

OWEN, George

Welsh cartographer; map of Pembrokeshire published in Camden's *Britannia*, 1607, 1610 and 1637.

OWEN, John: 72
British cartographer; with Emanuel Bowen, *Britannia Depicta*, road maps and county maps, 8vo, 1720, several editions to 1764.

OVERTON, Henry: 44, 56
British publisher; editions of Speed, 1713 and 1743; Bowen's *English Atlas*, 1764.

OVERTON, John
British cartographer; worked with Philip Lea, c. 1690.

OVERTON, Philip
British cartographer; some English county maps, 1715–1740.

PACKE, Christopher
British surveyor, map of East Kent, 1743, 4 sheets, 1½ inches to 1 mile.

PAGE, Thomas: *92*, 94
British publisher; worked with Mount as Mount and Page.

PALAIRET, Jean
French cartographer; *Atlas Mèthodique*, 53 maps, 1755, folio.

PALMER, Richard: 82
British publisher, cartographer and engraver.

PARKER, Samuel: *98*, 107
British engraver; map for Harris' *History of Kent*, 1719.

PARIS, Matthew: 40
British monk, historian and cartographer; manuscript map of England.

PARR, Richard: 115
British engraver; Rocque's London plan; Dickinson's map of south Yorkshire, 1750.

PATTERSON, Capt. Daniel
British cartographer; *British Itinerary*, 1785, road maps, 8vo; map of 24 miles round London, 1791.

PETTY, Sir William: *80*
British physician and statistician; *Hibernatio Delineatio*, 1683, 36 folding maps, folio, re-issued in 1690; *A Geographical Description of the Kingdom of Ireland*, 1689, a reduced version of *Hibernatio Delineatio*, engraved by Lamb.

PIGOT, James; *72*, 78
British topographer and engraver; *British Atlas of the Counties of England*, 1829–1844, 41 maps, folio; also regional directories in wrappers with the same maps.

PINE, John: 115
British engraver; Rocque's plan of London, 1747; *The Tapestry Hangings in the House of Lords* (now burnt), 16 plates of the Spanish Armada, including some charts, 1739.

PINKERTON, John: 67
British cartographer; *Modern Geography*, 1804; *A Modern Atlas*, 1815 and 1818.

PITT, Moses: 66, *66*
British publisher and printer; *English Atlas*, 173 maps based on Dutch carto-

graphers, 1680–1683, folio; published J. Moore's map of The Fens, 1684, 16 sheets, 2 inches to 1 mile.

PLANCIUS, Peter
Flemish cartographer; world map for Linschoten's *Itinerario*, 1596.

PLANTIN, Christopher: 22, 23, 90
Dutch printer and bookseller; printed some editions of Ortelius and Wagenhaer.

PLOT, Robert: *100*, 107
British historian; *The Natural History of Staffordshire*, 1686, map engraved by Joseph Browne; *The Natural History of Oxfordshire*, 1677, map engraved by M. Burghers.

PONT, Timothy: 37
Scottish minister and surveyor; maps of the Scottish counties, improved by Gordon, published by Blaeu, 1654, folio.

POPPLE, Henry: 82, 137
British cartographer; *A Map of the British Empire in America*, 1732, 20 sheets, published by Stephen Austen; reduced edition, six sheets, published by Covens and Mortier.

PORCACCHI, Tomaso: 21, *29*
Italian cartographer; *L'Isole Piu Famose del Mondo*, 1572 to about 1620.

PORRO, Girolamo
Italian engraver and publisher; Porcacchi's *Isole Piu Famose del Mondo*, 1572, with S. Galignani; Mercator's *Atlas Minor*, 1596; edition of Ptolemy's *Geographia*, 1596.

PROBST, Johann Balthasar: 88
German engraver and publisher; worked for Lotter, c. 1730–1750.

PTOLEMY, Claudius: 8, 12, 20, *23*, 24, 126, 140
Egyptian geographer and astronomer; *Cosmographia*, editions from 1477.

PURCHAS, Samuel: 146
British author; *Purchas his Pilgrims*, 1625, map by R. Elstracke.

QUAD, Matthias: 86
German cartographer and engraver; *Europae Totius Orbis Terrarum*, 1592; *Fasciculus Geographicus*, 1608.

RAMBLE, Reuben: 123
British topographer; *Travels through the Counties of England*, 1845, 40 maps, 8vo, intended for children.

RAMUSIO, Giovanni Baptista
Italian cartographer; maps *c*. 1588.

RAPKIN, John
British cartographer and engraver; Tallis maps of the world, about 1850.

RAYNAL, Guillaume
French cartographer; *Atlas Portatif*, 1773, folio.

REA, Roger (father and son): 56
British publishers and booksellers; editions of Speed, 1650 and 1662.

RENARD, Louis: 93
French cartographer and publisher; *Atlas de la Navigation*, 1715, later published by Ottens, 1739 and 1745.

RENNELL, Major James: 142
British cartographer; *A Bengal Atlas*, 1779.

REYNOLDS, Nicholas: 42
British engraver; maps for Saxton's atlas, published 1579, folio.

ROBERT DE VAUGONDY, Gilles: 86, *86*, 129
French cartographer; several atlases from 1748.

ROCHETTE, Louis de la: 129
French cartographer; mainly charts published from 1780.

ROCQUE, John: *102*, 104, 115, *116*
French, settled in London; engraver, surveyor and publisher; important large scale maps of Paris, London and some English counties; *English Traveller*, 1746; *The Small British Atlas*, 1753; Rocque died in 1762, but his wife Mary Ann continued to publish his maps.

ROGERS, J.: *143*, 147
British engraver and illustrator; engraved some of the vignettes on Tallis' maps, c. 1840.

ROLLO, G.
British engraver, publisher and printseller; *English County Atlas*, c. 1760.

ROPER, John: *117*, 118
British engraver; co-operated with G. Cole on *British Atlas*, 1810, 79 maps, 4to, published by Vernor and Hood.

ROUX, Joseph
French cartographer; *Recueil des Principaux Plans des Ports de la Mer Mediterranée* c. 1780, 170 charts and plans, oblong 4to.

RUSSELL, John
British cartographer and engraver; Russell's *General Atlas*, 1795; maps for Gutherie's *System of Geography*, from 1795, 29 maps.

RUSSELL, P.
British topographer; *England Displayed*, 1769, county maps by Kitchin and Rocque.

RYTHER, Augustine: 42
British engraver; engraved some maps for Saxton's atlas, published in 1579.

SANSON, Nicolas: 64, 65, 84, 127
French cartographer; many maps and atlases from *c*. 1650; business continued by his sons, Nicolas, Gillaume and Adrien, finally bought by Jaillot.

SAXTON, Christopher: 9, 12, 13, 15, *25*, *26*, 29, 40ff, *40*, *41*, *42*, *43*, 49ff, *59*, 56, 96, 148
British surveyor and cartographer; first set of county maps of England and Wales, 1579; re-issue by Webb, 1646; re-issue by Philip Lea, c. 1690; another issue by Willdey, 1720; some maps in Camden's *Britannia*, 1607–1637.

SAYER, Robert: 67, 72, 77, 94, 129, 138
British publisher; many atlases from 1757 mostly in conjunction with John Bennett, as Sayer and Bennett.

SCALÉ, Bernard
Irish surveyor and topographer; *Hiberian Atlas*, 1798.

SCATTER, Francis: 42

British engraver; two maps in Saxton's atlas, published in 1579.

SCHENK, Peter: 38
Dutch publisher and engraver, with Gerard Valck; bought many of Jansson's plates and published several atlases from 1695; Schenk's son, also Peter, continued the business until about 1750.

SEALE, Richard William: 67, 82
British engraver and cartographer, mainly English maps, from 1740 to 1770.

SECCO, Fernando Alvarez: 22, *34*
Portuguese cartographer; published map of Portugal, later copied by de Jode and Ortelius.

SECKFORD, Thomas: 9, 40, 41
British; Christopher Saxton's sponsor.

SEILE, Henry
French publisher; Heylin's *Cosmographie*, 1657–1677; continued by Anna Seile.

SELLER, John: *81*, 94, 129
British cartographer and publisher, mainly sea-charts, some county maps; *Atlas Maritimus*, 1670; *English Pilot*, 1671; *Antiquities of Great Britain*, 1777–1787, 52 maps, 4to, reprints of Seller's maps, by Francis Grose.

SENEX, John: *61*, 62, 65, 67, *115*, 129, 137
British cartographer, engraver and publisher; *Modern Geography*, 1725, large folio maps of all parts of the world; *Actual Survey of all the Principal Roads of England and Wales*, 1719, 100 road maps taken from Ogilby, 8vo.

SEUTTER, Georg Mattheus: 87, 88, 129
German cartographer and publisher; apprenticed to Homann, set up on his own in 1707; many maps and atlases included maps by Lotter, Probst, and Seutter's sons, Georg Mattheus and Albrecht Carl.

SHARMAN, J.
British cartographer; *General Atlas*, c. 1830, 4to, 29 maps.

SIMONS, Matthew
British cartographer and publisher; *A Direction for the British Traveller*, 1636, 39 maps, 8vo; re-issues by Thomas Jenner, 1643, 1650 and 1657, and John Garrett, 1645, 1662 and 1668, unusual maps with triangular distance tables.

SIMPSON, Samuel
British geographer; *Agreeable Historian, or Compleat English Traveller*, 1746, 41 maps after Moll, 8vo.

SKINNER, Andrew: 82
British surveyor; with George Taylor, road maps of Scotland and Ireland, 1777 and 1783.

SLATER, Isaac
British publisher; *New British Atlas*, after Pigot, 41 maps, from 1846 to 1859.

SMITH, Charles: 78
British engraver and publisher; *New English Atlas*, 1804, editions to 1864, 42 maps, folio; *New English Atlas*, 1822, 44 maps, 4to.

SMITH, Capt. John
British cartographer; maps of Virginia

and New England: these maps are rare but were used as a basis for the maps of Blaeu, Jansson and Speed.

SMITH, William: 78
British cartographer; *A Delineation of the Strata of England and Wales with Parts of Scotland*, based on Cary's map, published 1815, the first geological map of the country, oblong folio.

SOCIETY FOR THE DIFFUSION OF USEFUL KNOWLEDGE: 144
Maps of the Society, 1844, maps and plans, published by Chapman and Hall; *A series of Maps, Modern and Ancient*, published by Cradock and Baldwin, 1835.

SPEED, John: 6, *6*, 9, 15, 31, 37, 52ff, *53*, *54, 55, 57, 111,* 114, 127, 131, *137*, 146, *146*, 147
British cartographer; *The Theatre of the Empire of Great Britain*, various editions from 1611; *The Prospect of the Most Famous Parts of the World*, combined with the county maps from 1627 to 1770, folio, various publishers; the miniature atlas with maps by Peter Keere is known as 'Miniature Speed'.

STACKHOUSE, Thomas
British cartographer and publisher; *New Universal Atlas*, 39 maps, 1783.

STENT, Peter: 44
British publisher; edition of the Anonymous maps, c. 1650, folio.

STEPHENSON, John
British cartographer; with George Burn, *Channel Pilot*, 26 maps, published by Laurie and Whittle, 1795, large folio.

STOCKDALE, John: 82
British publisher; *New British Atlas*, 1805, 44 maps of the counties and six general maps, folio.

STOW, John
British historian; *Survey of London*, 1720, folio, plans of City wards.

STRYPE, John: *116*
British cartographer; plan of London, 1720.

STURT, John: 52
British engraver; some of Morden's maps in Camden's *Britannia*, 1695.

SUDBURY, John: 54, 55
British publisher; with George Humble published the early editions of Speed whose maps bear their imprint up to 1627.

SWALE, Abel: 52
British publisher; Camden's *Britannia*, 1695 and 1722, folio, with Awnsham and John Churchill; Ogilby's *Britannia*, 1698 edition, folio, road maps.

SUECO, Andrew Bureo
Swedish cartographer; Scandinavian maps published by Blaeu.

SYMONSON, Philip
British surveyor and cartographer; map of Kent, 2 sheets, 1 inch to 1 mile, 1596, very rare, later editions, 1650, published by Peter Stent, and 1770.

TALLIS, John: 67, 118, *118*, 129, *129, 143*, 144
British publisher.

TAYLOR, George: 82
British cartographer; with Andrew Skinner, road maps of Ireland and Scotland.

TAYLOR, Isaac: 96
British surveyor and engraver; 1 inch to 1 mile county maps of Dorset, 6 sheets, 1765 and 1795; Gloucestershire, 6 sheets, 1777, 1786 and 1800; Hampshire, 6 sheets, 1759; Worcestershire, 4 sheets, 1772 and 1800.

TAYLOR, Thomas: 57
British publisher; Blome's *England Exactly Described*, 1715, 42 maps, 8vo.

TAYLOR, Thomas: 97
British surveyor; *Environs of the City of Bath*, 1742.

TAYLOR, William
British publisher; Camden's *Britannia*, 1722.

TEESDALE, Henry: 67, 82
British publisher; *New British Atlas*, 1829, 45 maps, folio; re-issues to 1848; *New Travelling Atlas*, 1830, 45 maps, 4to.

TERWOORT, Nicholas: *26, 40, 41*, 42
Flemish engraver; engraved some maps in Saxton's Atlas, published in 1579.

THOMPSON, John: *70*, 144
British cartographer; *A New General Atlas*, 1814, folio.

THOMSON, John: 67, 72
British publisher; *A New General Atlas*, 1817, folio; *Atlas of Scotland*, 1831, folio.

THORNTON, John: 94, 129
British hydrographer; Thornton and Mount, *Atlas Maritimus*, c. 1700, folio.

TINDAL, Nicolas
British historian; maps and plans of Tindal's Continuation of Rapin's *History of England*, published by Harrison, some maps by R. W. Seale, 1789, folio.

TINNEY, John
British engraver and publisher; published some of Emanuel Bowen's maps; engraved some of Rocque's maps.

TIRION, Isaac
Dutch cartographer and publisher; *Nieuwe Hand Atlas*, 1744; *Atlas of Zeeland*, 1760.

TOMBLESON, W. G.: 108
British publisher; map of the River Thames, c. 1840.

TOFINO DE SAN MIGUEL, Vicente
Spanish cartographer; *Atlas Maritimo de Espana*, 1787 and 1789, folio.

TOMS, W. H.: 82
British engraver; he engraved Henry Popple's *Map of the British Empire in America*, 1732; *Chorographia Britannia*, 1742, 46 maps, 8vo, published by Badeslade.

VALCK, or VALK, Gerard
Dutch cartographer and publisher, with Peter Schenk; re-issued some of Blaeu's and Jansson's maps with their own imprints, from about 1700.

VALGRISI, Vincenzo: 21
Italian cartographer and publisher.

VAUGHAN, Robert

British cartographer and engraver; maps in Dugdale's Warwickshire, 1656, folio.

VAUGONDY, *see* ROBERT

VERNOR AND HOOD: *117*, 118
British publishers; *British Atlas*, 1810, 58 maps, and 21 plans, by Cole and Roper, 4to.

VERTUE, George
British engraver; engraved maps for Herman Moll.

VIRTUE, George
British publisher; Moule's maps from 1834.

VISSCHER, Nicolas Jansz: *36*, 38, 66, 127, 131
Dutch engraver and publisher; many maps and atlases from 1651; the business was continued by the son and grandson of the same name, into the 18th century.

VRINTS, Johannes Baptista: 22, *30*, *48*
Dutch publisher; some editions of Ortelius from 1603.

WAGHENAER, Luke Jansen: 33, 90
Dutch cartographer; *De Spieghel der Zeevaerdt*, the first sea atlas, 1584, folio; *Mariners Mirrour*, English edition, 1588, published by Sir Anthony Ashley.

WALKER, John and Charles: 78
British cartographers; *British Atlas*, 1837, 47 maps, folio; many editions to about 1880; maps used for Hobson's *Fox Hunting Atlas*, 42 maps, 1850.

WARREN, H.
British engraver; Tallis' maps, about 1850.

WEBB, William: 43, *43*
British publisher; edition of Saxton's atlas, 1645.

WEIGEL, Christoph
German publisher and engraver; published a number of atlases from 1712 to *c.* 1760.

WELLS, Edward: 66, 107
British cartographer; *A New Sett of Maps*, 1700 and 1701, folio maps of all the world, published in Oxford, maps engraved by Burghers, Sutton Nicholls and Robert Spofforth.

WHITTAKER, G. and W. B.
British publishers; *Travellers' Pocket Atlas*, 43 county maps, 1823 (dated 1821) 8vo.

WHITE, John
British cartographer; map of East America, engraved by de Bry, 1590.

WHITTLE, James: 67, *68*, 72, 142
British publisher and engraver, in partnership with Robert Laurie.

WILD, James: 142
British publisher and cartographer; *General Atlas*, *c.* 1840, folio.

WILD, Joseph
British publisher; *Camden's Britannia abridg'd*, 1701, 8vo.

WILKINSON, Robert
British publisher; succeeded John Bowles in about 1780; *A General Atlas*, 1794, folio.

WILLDEY, George: 43, 67, 72
British publisher and map-seller; atlas of the world, about 1720, tall folio; edition of Saxton's atlas, 1720.

WINTERBOTTOM, William

American cartographer; *The American Atlas*, 1796.

WIT, Frederick de: *37*, 131
Dutch publisher and cartographer; several general atlases were published from 1670, mainly folio; business was continued by Covens and Mortier from 1706.

WOLFE, John
British printer; English edition of Linschoten's maps, 1598.

WRIGHT, Benjamin
British engraver.

WYLD, James (father and son of the same name)
British publishers; *General Atlas*, 1819, folio; *A New General Atlas*, 1840, folio.

WYTFLIET, Cornelius: 130, *132*
British cartographer; *Descriptionis Ptolemaicae Aagmentum*, 1597, 4to, the first printed atlas devoted to America.

YATES, William
British surveyor; map of Lancashire, 1786, 1 inch to 1 mile, 8 sheets engraved by T. Billings; map of Staffordshire, 1775, 1 inch to 1 mile, 6 sheets; map of Liverpool and district, 1774, 2 inches to 1 mile, with P. Perry.

YEAKELL, Thomas: 96
British surveyor; with W. Gardener, map of Sussex, 1778, 4 sheets, 2 inches to 1 mile.

ZATTA, Antonio
Italian cartographer and publisher; *Atlante Novissimo*, 1779, 4 vols, folio; *Nuovo Atlante*, 1799, folio.